WHAT DID YOU SAY?

A Guide to the Communication Skills

Second Edition

STANLEY B. FELBER

ARTHUR KOCH

Milwaukee Area Technical College

PRENTICE-HALL, INC. Englewood Cliffs, New Jersey 07632

Library of Congress Cataloging in Publication Data

Felber, Stanley B., 1932–
  What did you say?

  Includes index.
  1. Communication. I. Koch, Arthur, 1931–
joint author. II. Title.
P90.F4   1978   808   77–26035
ISBN 0–13–951996–3

Cover illustration by Jaf. Reprinted by permission of The
Village Voice. Copyright © 1973 The Village Voice, Inc.

Printed in the United States of America

10   9   8

PRENTICE-HALL INTERNATIONAL, INC., *London*
PRENTICE-HALL OF AUSTRALIA PTY. LIMITED, *Sydney*
PRENTICE-HALL OF CANADA, LTD., *Toronto*
PRENTICE-HALL OF INDIA PRIVATE LIMITED, *New Delhi*
PRENTICE-HALL OF JAPAN, INC., *Tokyo*
PRENTICE-HALL OF SOUTHEAST ASIA PTE. LTD., *Singapore*
WHITEHALL BOOKS LIMITED, *Wellington, New Zealand*

CONTENTS

Chapter 4   READING AND LISTENING   49

Chapter 5   AUDIENCE ANALYSIS   69

Chapter 6   ATTENTION   91

Chapter 7   SUPPORTING YOUR IDEAS   107

Chapter 18 **MASS COMMUNICATION**   345

PREFACE

With the multitude of textbooks available to freshman English classes, any one must justify its existence by offering something special. The distinctive feature of this second edition of *What Did You Say?* like its predecessor, is that it combines both oral and written communication within an integrated framework. An ever-increasing number of career-oriented educational programs in our community colleges, vocational and technical institutes, and universities has occasioned the rapid growth of communication courses. These courses seek to provide occupationally-minded students with the language skills that will enable them to function with efficiency and perception in society. It is to this market that our book is aimed.

Chapter 1 introduces the four basic skills of reading, writing, speaking, and listening and defines a communicative act, laying the foundation for the units that follow. Because the communication skills have much in common, most of the chapters in this book fully integrate all of them. However, in view of differences among the various skills, the separate chapters in speaking and writing have been supplemented with a new one, "Reading and Listening." In response to suggestions from many of our colleagues, specialized chapters in "The Business Letter," "The Technical Report," and "Mass Communication" are new to this edition.

We begin each chapter with a listing of learning objectives in the belief that students learn better when they know exactly what is expected of them. While all but one of the chapters in our first edition appear in this revision, many have been revised extensively.

To Chapter 7, "Supporting Your Ideas," a new section on using the library, taking notes, and writing footnotes and bibliography entries has been added.

In Chapter 8, "Effective Sentence Structure," new sections include agreement, parallel structure, sentence economy, and misplaced modifiers.

In Chapter 9, "Effective Paragraphs," the section on organization has been expanded to include three additional developmental patterns. New sections treat unity and coherence.

Chapter 12, "Speech Content," has been expanded to include a new section on gathering supporting material and organizing the speech. A new speech evaluation form has been added.

Chapter 13, "Speech Delivery," contains new sections on controlling stage fright and practicing the speech.

In Chapter 14, "Persuasion," new suggestions are included for utilizing personal proofs more effectively.

In Chapter 15, "Logical Proof," new syllogistic forms and fallacies have been added.

Chapter 16, "Psychological Proof," has a new section on propaganda devices.

In Chapter 17, "Group Communication," five forms of discussion, including role playing, are new to this edition.

In addition, readers familiar with the previous edition will recognize in this one revised examples and exercises and new illustrations.

With the second edition of *What Did You Say?* our debt to our colleagues at the Milwaukee Area Technical College has increased. We are grateful to John Lewinski, Mary Jane Irwin, and Laurance Riley for authoring new chapters in their fields of specialization; to the MATC English Department Book Committee for permitting us to incorporate material from *The Bear in a Phonebooth* into Chapters 8 and 9; and to the members of the Departments of English and Speech for their many constructive suggestions.

We are also indebted to Deborah Israel (South Oklahoma City Junior College), Sara E. Sanders (Mountain View College, Dallas), and James W. Woolsey (North Central Technical Institute), for evaluating the entire manuscript and making us more aware of student needs outside of MATC. Finally, to our wives—Estelle and Betty—and to our children—Mike, Rachel, Kai, Christian, Carl, Debbe, and Jeff— we publicly proclaim our gratitude for their inspiration, their understanding, and their love.

Stanley B. Felber
Arthur Koch

PROLOGUE

The role of the broadcaster, the communicator, the advertising copy writer, the public relations man, the public speaker, the guy who writes the business letter, the guy who writes the love letter, the guy who writes the letter home—is to get ideas and information across simply, in an easy to understand and attractive way. Elizabeth Barrett Browning, in one of her Sonnets from the Portuguese, "How Do I Love Thee," said more in a very few lines about love than many of us could say in our broken prose if we filled up as many pages as are in a Sears Roebuck catalog.

What it all boils down to is this: Anybody who has anything to say in words or in pictures to be transmitted from one mind to another—regardless of all the modern electronic paraphernalia and hard work you go through to reach that reader, viewer or listener—has to ask himself the question "What did you say?" before he begins to transmit. The only way we can be sure that our ideas achieve their objective is to be clear about what we want to say and who we are trying to reach. That means understanding the guy on the other end. . . .

William A. Nail, "What Did You Say?"
Vital Speeches, 38, no. 23 (September 15, 1971), 726.

CHAPTER 1

An Overview

OBJECTIVES

After studying this chapter, you should be able to:
1. Answer the question, "Why study communication?"
2. Explain the philosophy of communication that governs this text.
3. Define and briefly describe the expressive communication skills.
4. Define and briefly describe the receptive communication skills.
5. Define a communicative act, indicating its essential components.
6. Explain how communication breakdowns occur.
7. Analyze communication situations, identifying essential components or indicating where breakdowns occur.

WHY STUDY COMMUNICATION?

If you are like most high school graduates, the prospect of another year or two of English far from excites you. You have formally studied our complex, at times illogical language since elementary school, and you have engaged in the process of communication all your lives. Now college. And more English!

English teachers often pride themselves on the importance of their discipline. "We are the largest department on campus and rightly so. All students, regardless of future educational and vocational objectives, need to learn to communicate more effectively. A good command of language skills can lead to a challenging, creative future. Inadequate mastery of the techniques of communication can only lessen the possibilities available to you."

In recent years, English teachers have found a powerful ally in industry. Employees are frequently sent to college at company expense in an effort to improve their communication skills. The following excerpt from an industrial publication addressed to technical students is typical of industry's concern with language skills:

To understand and be understood. A good education provides the tools for understanding. The first and most important of these tools is language for communication. It may surprise you that we've begun by putting the need to study English first rather than stressing science or mathematics. After all, our business is primarily concerned with science and the useful application of technological developments. Nevertheless, stimulating as a course in your area of specialization, but we don't want you to think of your communication study as just another English course.

The pages that follow will involve you in the practical aspects of written and oral communication. You will discover that in the performance of one of life's most important functions — communicating effectively with your fellow human beings — language can be one of the most exciting and demanding of studies.

A PHILOSOPHY OF COMMUNICATION

Traditionally, language study has been fragmented and compartmentalized, involving separate courses in grammar, composition, and literature. Reading and listening have recently emerged as highly specialized fields within the study of language. Most high schools and colleges offer reading workshops, reading and study skills programs, and courses in speed reading. The last named has become a lucrative enterprise for private educational concerns that capitalize on our inability to assimilate ever-increasing amounts of printed material with speed and comprehension. According to the *Harvard Business Review*, "The busy executive spends 80% of his time ... listening to people ... and still doesn't hear half of what is said." *Nation's Business* reports that most of us "really absorb only a scant 30%" of what we hear. Our increasing awareness of the importance of effective listening has resulted in some highly specialized listening courses, most of them programmed. The subject matter of this book — language and communication — has been subdivided into numerous highly specialized fields which are usually studied separately. For practical and philosophical reasons, we propose to treat the study of language as a single subject.

Our treatment of communication is primarily intended for you, the college student. Because most of your course work is directly related to your chosen field of specialization, the amount of time set aside for general education courses in your curriculum is necessarily limited. It is usually impractical to schedule separate courses in speech, composition, literature, grammar, reading, and listening. Although the study of literature is beyond the scope of this book, we include a discussion of all of the remaining communication skills. Despite their distinctive aspects, these skills have much in common. We propose to indicate both their similarities and differences throughout our study. Furthermore, we believe our integrated approach to the study of communication to be philosophically sound.

we are convinced that no matter what your career, a command of the English language is the most important skill you can acquire. Learning rules of grammar and acquiring the abilities to write effectively and to read accurately are vital. This background provides the skill to express yourself in speaking and writing and to extract maximum meaning from the spoken and written words of others.

This process is called communications. In today's world, and even more so in tomorrow's, the person who cannot communicate clearly labors under a tremendous handicap.

The young engineer, for example, might have his most brilliant idea rejected if he is unable to explain its significance to others. In addition, he will be unable to keep up with advances in his own field if he cannot get the facts from the flood of technical information available to him.

Think of any career you like: teacher, naval engineer, actor, salesman, auditor, lawyer, physician, news reporter. Is there one in which you won't have to communicate effectively with others in order to perform successfully?

A time to prepare. The best foundation for whatever career you eventually choose is a broad-based education that increases your understanding and appreciation of everything in life.

It is essential that you start "building in" this kind of background now, for there is no way that you can predict the exact requirements of life or what your interests will be in the future. In short, now is the time to prepare for an education rather than a job.

Obviously, most successful careers today call for special training—often long and intensive. Does this mean that you must commit yourself now to a specific plan of action? Not necessarily. How can you plan for a career that may not even exist today?

The answer is stay flexible. Don't cut yourself off from the future. Keep to the march of knowledge in general. Top careers will more and more demand people with specialized skills in combination with diversified backgrounds.

If there is one rule you can apply that will keep the door open to almost any future career, it is this: when you have a choice of courses, pick those which will help broaden your background—mathematics, language, physical sciences, literature, the social studies.

There's always the chance you'll want to switch your field of study in midstream. Why not? That's one and only one of the advantages of starting with a sound basic education and staying flexible.

Reprinted with the permission of General Electric Company.

You probably agree that the arguments of education and industry have validity, but somehow a continuance of the day-to-day struggle with "nouns and verbs and stupid things like that," as one student put it, leaves you a bit cold. Perhaps you feel that English cannot be a

THE SKILLS OF COMMUNICATION

Expressive Skills

Speaking and writing are generally referred to as expressive skills; they provide the means whereby we express ourselves to others. Both skills are usually discussed under the same heading, because effective speaking and writing involve many similar problems, such as selecting a subject, communicating purposefully, relating material to a single, dominant idea, and organizing logically.

Obviously, there are also important differences. Writing is a relatively private affair between you and your reader, allowing ample time for revision and correction. When you are speaking publicly, however, all eyes are focused on you. A mistake cannot be readily erased. Speaking and writing employ different means to achieve emphasis and variety, but the primary purpose of both skills is the same: to get the message to your audience in an interesting way.

Receptive Skills

When we listen or read, we receive information through the spoken word or printed page. However, frequently we *hear,* but do not really *listen.* An entry in the *American College Dictionary* clarifies the distinction between these two terms:

> Hear, Listen apply to the perception of sound. To hear is to have such perception by means of the auditory sense: *to hear distant bells.* To listen is to give attention in order to hear and understand the meaning of a sound or sounds: *to listen to what is being said, to listen for a well-known footstep.*

Similarly, sometimes we read words without understanding their meaning. Have you ever spent an hour or so reading an assigned chapter without having more than a vague notion of its contents? Perhaps you were distracted by interruptions or your own thoughts. Concentration is essential to both listening and reading, with the basic difference that if you cannot concentrate on what you are reading, you can always return to it at another time. You cannot, however, expect your instructor to repeat his lecture after class because your thoughts drifted during his presentation. Both skills involve breaking down a communication into main ideas and supporting details. Listening to your instructor's lecture is more demanding than listening to a friend relate a personal experience; reading Spenser's *The Fairie Queene* requires more concentration than reading a popular novel like *The God-father*. However, all effective reading and listening share a common purpose: to receive messages clearly.

THE COMMUNICATIVE ACT

Communication results when a response occurs to a stimulus. For example:

Stimulus	Response
1. Strong winds and heavy rain	Baby cries
2. Strong winds and heavy rain	Man closes window

Our stimuli for the above examples, strong winds and heavy rain, produce varied responses from different people. The baby is frightened by the stimuli, and his response is an automatic one based on fear. In the second example, the man's response is motivated by other considerations, perhaps his desire to block out outside noise, or to protect his family and his belongings. Because he must decide among alternatives, the man's response involves reasoning. Thus, we see that a response to a stimulus may or may not be automatic.

Let us consider another stimulus-response situation:

Stimulus	Response
3. Dog barks	Baby cries
4. Dog barks	Man feeds dog

The baby's response to the stimulus is again an automatic one based on fear. The man's response is a nonautomatic one—feeding—to the same stimulus. Thus far we have seen how stimuli can produce automatic and nonautomatic responses.

The stimulus in a communicative act includes a sender and a message. Study the following analyses of stimuli previously referred to:

Stimulus	=	Sender	+	Message
1. Strong winds and heavy rain				Depending upon your philosophical and theological convictions, you may conclude that "nature" or a supreme being is the *sender;* the *message,* strong winds and heavy rain, is then transmitted to a receiver.
2. Barking dog				The dog is the *sender;* his bark is the *message.*

Before one can respond to a stimulus (sender and message), he must first receive the message. Therefore, the response in an act of communication implies a receiver. Initially we defined communication as a response to a stimulus, but our modified definition now includes a sender, a message, a receiver, and a response.

Sender	Message	Receiver	Response
1. "Nature"	Strong winds and heavy rain	Baby	Crying
2. "Nature"	Strong winds and heavy rain	Man	Closing window
3. Dog	Bark	Baby	Crying
4. Dog	Bark	Man	Feeding dog

In our subsequent discussion of mass media, we will distinguish between interpersonal communication and mass communication in detail. (See Chapter 18.) In the meantime, the following distinction will suffice: Interpersonal communication involves face-to-face communication between two (or more) people; in mass communication, either print or electronic, the message is channeled through a *medium*. When we read an editorial or view our favorite show, the newspaper or television set represents the *medium* through which messages are sent and received.

The *medium* represents our final modification of our definition of communication, which can now be summarized as follows:

1. The sender perceives something in his environment.
2. The sender *encodes* the message — that is, he puts the message into code.
3. The sender transmits the message through a particular medium.
4. The message is received . . .
5. and *decoded.*
6. The message is understood by the receiver in the same way it was meant by the sender.
7. The receiver responds (provides feedback) to the sender.

A communication "loop" has been formed. Communication is now complete. In everyday situations, communicative acts are not isolated. Instead, they flow one into the other and become part of a process. Understanding the steps involved in a single communicative act will provide you with a better understanding of that process. The chart on page 8 illustrates these steps.

How Communication Works

THE FAMILY CIRCUS, by Bil Keane. Reprinted courtesy of the Register and Tribune Syndicate, Inc.

"Albert! You've gone and blown another fuse!"

Drawing by Chas. Addams; © 1971 The New Yorker Magazine, Inc.

II. From your own experience, cite two examples of communications breakdowns, one involving speech, one involving writing.

1. Identify the causes of the breakdowns.

2. State what could have been done to improve the communication.

III. Study the following photographs and respond to the questions asked.

Reprinted by permission of the photographer, Robert B. Tai.

1. Suggest an appropriate caption.
2. Should teachers (and other public employees) have the right to strike?
3. What conclusions, if any, do you draw from the facial expressions of the striking teachers?

Reprinted with permission of the photographer, Samuel Gansheroff.

1. Does the boy in the photograph have the same opportunities you had when you were his age? Discuss.
2. Suggest an appropriate caption.
3. Can we provide equality of opportunity for minority groups without infringing on the rights of the majority? Discuss.

Reprinted by permission of the photographer, Samuel Gansheroff.

1. How has our society handled the problems of its aged citizens? Discuss.
2. How have the chess players in the photograph adjusted to old age?
3. Suggest an appropriate caption.

Reprinted with permission of United Press International.

1. What is your reaction to this photograph? Shock? Dismay? Indifference? Gladness? Explain.
2. Is such a marriage legal in your state? Should it be?
3. Discuss your feelings about the individuals involved: the two bridegrooms, their families, and the minister who officiated.

With permission of the photographer, David Bernacchi.

1. Suggest an appropriate caption.
2. What message do you receive from the player's facial expression—Pain?
   Defeat? Disgrace? Frustration? Disappointment?
3. Suggest the events that may have occurred before the picture was taken.

SPEECHES AND COMPOSITIONS

I. Develop a presentation, written (200–400 words) or oral (2–4 minutes), in which you: (1) introduce yourself to the audience; (2) explain an area of interest, e.g., a sport, hobby, or pastime.

II. Experience any two of the following sensitivity modules. Prepare a written report of one of the two experiences. Be prepared to relate the other to the class orally.

Sensitivity Modules

1. Wear old clothes and sit in the waiting room of the Welfare Office. Listen, observe, read the announcements on the bulletin board, and talk to some of the other people there.
2. Attend a church or temple service for those of a religious faith different from your own.
3. Go to a magistrate's court and keep a list of the kinds of cases brought before the magistrate. Who are the "customers" being tried? How are they dealt with?
4. Sit in the waiting room of a maternity ward of a city hospital whose patients are mostly charity cases. Strike up a conversation with any other person in the waiting room.
5. Live for three days on the amount of money received by a typical welfare recipient.
6. Read at least two issues, cover to cover, of a newspaper primarily aimed at a racial or ethnic group different from your own.
7. Go to the community health center and take a place in line. Watch the attitude of the personnel who work there. Talk to some of the patients coming for help.
8. Turn off the heat in your own house some night in January or February and spend the night in a cold house.
9. Attend a meeting of a civic group, such as the Human Relations Committee, the Welfare Rights Organization, or the Neighborhood Association.
10. Talk to someone whose landlord has not given him heat or has not attended to a needed repair. Offer suggestions to remedy the problem.

CHAPTER
2

Purposeful Communication

OBJECTIVES

After studying this chapter, you should be able to:

1. Classify the primary purpose of a communicative act under one of five major headings: to inform, to entertain, to convince, to actuate, or to reinforce.
2. List and briefly explain five considerations for selecting a subject.
3. Determine, after examining a list of subjects, which ones are sufficiently restricted for a composition or speech of a specified length.
4. Formulate a statement of specific intent for a subject you have selected and adequately restricted.
5. Explain how a statement of intent differs from a main idea statement.
6. Revise unsatisfactory main idea statements.
7. Plan and execute a written and/or oral communication for which you have determined the primary purpose, selected and restricted an appropriate topic, and formulated a specific intent statement and/or main idea.

CLASSIFYING THE PURPOSE

The purpose of this course is not to teach you how to communicate, but rather to help you communicate more effectively. This distinction is not merely one of semantics, since we have all engaged in the process of communication with varying degrees of success from the day we were born.

When we were hungry, we cried, and our message was answered. When we experienced pain or discomfort we made our feelings known long before we learned to talk, and our parents responded. We sent and received messages of sorrow, despair, frustration, joy, and ecstasy. As we learned our native language, our messages and responses became more sophisticated, and consequently our communication grew more complex. As we matured, we learned how to manipulate symbols, starting with pictures, progressing to letters, and finally to words, word groups, and sentences. Because the process of communication parallels the life cycle, we have experienced and will continue to experience hundreds of thousands of communicative acts. Our purpose, therefore, is not to learn new skills, but to refine and polish those we already possess.

Have you ever listened to a speaker ramble on without a sense of direction? Have you ever, merely to get the job over with, written a paper about a subject of no particular interest to you? When we try to communicate about a subject without sufficient organization, without relating each point to a controlling dominant idea, our speech or paper will lack a *sense of purpose.*

The effective speaker or writer has his purpose in mind during the planning stages of his communication. The overall purposes of a communicative act may be divided into the following categories:

1. *To inform,* to add to the knowledge of the reader or listener. News stories, weather reports, wedding invitations, stock market closings, traffic reports, baseball scores, and simple descriptions are examples of informative communication.

2. *To entertain,* to provide pleasant diversion, to amuse, to hold a passive audience's attention. All forms of comedy, television, games and quiz shows, music, sports events, and escape literature have entertainment as their primary purpose. Humor, while frequently employed, is not necessarily a prerequisite of entertainment.

3. *To persuade,* to convince, to actuate, or to reinforce. Because persuasion is more complex than information or entertainment, we shall deal with the three types of persuasion separately.

   a. *To convince,* to change a reader or listener's mind, or to commit him to our point of view on a subject upon which he is still undecided. A politician addressing an audience previously committed to another candidate or as yet uncommitted to any candidate must first convince them that he is the best man for the job. For example, Republicans have seldom received strong labor support in recent national elections. While a Republican may realistically write off the support of the organized labor movement, he will, nevertheless, attempt to *convince* working men to support his candidacy. In urban areas, Republican candidates must *convince* growing numbers of traditionally Democratic voters to support them if they are to win elections, while the converse is frequently the situation in rural areas. The politician must analyze his constituency in order to decide whom he must convince and how best to accomplish that task.

   b. *To actuate,* to put into action. In our previous example, the politician's task was to convince his constituents to vote for him. Having accomplished this purpose to the best of his ability and resources, convincing large blocks of voters—blacks, Jews, businessmen, white collar workers, blue collar workers, professionals—his purpose then shifts to one of *actuation.* If voters committed to his candidacy do not actually get to the polls in sufficient numbers, he will not be elected. Many a politician has lost an election because prospective voters committed to him never exercised their ballots. A change in the weather may keep the farmer on his farm and lose the election for his candidate. In 1948 pollsters and political analysts agreed that Thomas E. Dewey would easily defeat Harry Truman for the Presidency, yet the ballots returned President Truman to office in the major political upset of our century. The postelection analysis was that Dewey supporters suffered from complacency, staying away from the polls in the conviction that their candidate could not lose. The Republicans failed to actuate sufficient qualified voters committed to the Dewey candidacy. Jimmy Carter's unprecedented, meteoric rise in popularity in the months preceding the 1976 Democratic Party convention is a more recent example of a politician's ability to convince, then actuate his constituency.

c. *To reinforce,* to strengthen and invigorate those previously committed to the point of view of the communicator. Note the basic distinction between persuasion to convince and persuasion to reinforce. In the former, the sender attempts to change his receiver's point of view; in the latter, the sender and receiver are already in agreement.

Why would a communicator attempt to persuade a receiver with whom he is already in agreement? Consider a coach who talks to his team before an important game. He need not convince them of the importance of winning. But he does want to prepare them psychologically and emotionally for the big game. The late coach Vince Lombardi was a master at persuasion to reinforce.

In another example of reinforcement, it has become customary for both major political parties to designate a keynote speaker to address their national conventions. His fellow party members are generally committed to the same candidates and political philosophy, so his primary purpose is to emphasize party unity and deemphasize minor differences, thus enabling the party to emerge from the convention on a positive, unified note.

The football coach and political keynoter in our two previous examples are both addressing members of their respective teams. Because they seek to strengthen those previously committed to their points of view, their primary purpose is to reinforce.

EXERCISES

What is the primary purpose in each of the following situations – (a) to inform, (b) to entertain, (c) to convince, (d) to actuate, or (e) to reinforce? Be prepared to explain and defend your answer in class discussion.

1. A defense lawyer's pleading for the acquittal of his client during his final summation to the jury
2. Cheerleaders "doing their thing" as their team drives down field toward the goal line
3. A short speech entitled, "How to Peel a Grape"
4. A meeting agenda
5. A course in beginner's bridge
6. An instruction booklet for your own camera
7. An episode of your favorite situation comedy show
8. A door-to-door salesperson who would like to demonstrate his company's latest vacuum cleaner for you
9. A solicitation for a contribution to charity
10. A carnival barker in action

SELECTING AND RESTRICTING A SUBJECT

Once you understand clearly the purpose of a speaking or writing assignment, you are ready to think about a specific choice of subject. Your decision should be based on a number of considerations:

1. Is my subject in keeping with the general purpose of the assignment?
2. Is my subject interesting to me?
3. Is my subject one about which I am sufficiently knowledgeable?
4. Will my subject be of interest to my audience or reader?
5. Is my subject sufficiently restricted?

Let us consider each of these questions in some detail.

1. *Is my subject in keeping with the general purpose of the assignment?*

Assume that you are asked to prepare a composition or speech whose primary purpose is to inform. If you select as your tentative subject, "Why I Believe Air Bags Should Be Required in All New Cars," your communication will be primarily persuasive, not informative. However, air bags could be a proper subject for an informative or even an entertaining communication. If you concentrate on *how* the air bag works, your communication will be in keeping with the informational purpose of the assignment. When the writer of a television skit has the air bag misfire at a drive-in movie, his primary purpose is to entertain.

2. *Is my subject interesting to me?*

Students rightfully complain when they are assigned such chestnuts as "How I Spent My Summer Vacation." When you have the opportunity of selecting your own subject, choose one in which you are genuinely interested. Your communication will thus be easier to prepare, because interest leads to enthusiasm, and enthusiasm is contagious.

3. *Is my subject one about which I am sufficiently knowledgeable?*

Interest and knowledge are not necessarily synonymous. You may be interested in finding out about a given subject, but if your interest is relatively recent, you may not have had sufficient time to acquire enough information to prepare a well-developed communication. When selecting a subject for an impromptu, adequate knowledge is especially important; the wrong choice will invariably result in superficial communication.

Even when you have the time to plan and prepare at a more leisurely pace, it is usually a good idea to select a subject with which you are already familiar. An introductory course in communication skills is not primarily a course in research. Your instructor is interested in purposeful, well-organized, and well-developed communication. Selecting subjects close to your own experiences will help you to achieve positive results.

4. *Will my subject be of interest to my audience or reader?*

At this point our emphasis shifts from the communicator and his message to the receiver and his response. Let us assume that your assignment is to prepare a demonstration speech for classroom presentation. You tentatively decide to explain how to score a bowling match and to accompany your explanation with an enlarged score sheet. This subject is in keeping with the purpose of the assignment, and you are interested in and knowledgeable about it. Is it, however, a subject which will engender the response you desire from your audience? For

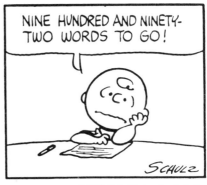

those who bowl regularly, your explanation would be repetitious, while those who do not bowl may have no reason for learning how.

Perhaps your part-time job involves skills that are particularly interesting and valuable to you, but ask yourself whether a speech about them would be of interest and value to your audience. You must adapt your communication to your audience. Of course, it is impossible to interest different individuals with varying backgrounds in everything you say or write about. The point is simply to consider your receiver and prepare your communications accordingly.

5. *Is my subject sufficiently restricted?*

The secret of a well-developed communication is to begin with a subject which is sufficiently restricted and then to develop that restricted subject in detail.

A former student recently told us about his experience in an undergraduate course in modern poetry. His assignment was to select an appropriate subject, restrict it, submit it to his instructor for approval, and then write a term paper. Remembering what he had learned about the importance of beginning with a properly restricted subject, he decided to write about a single poem, T. S. Eliot's *The Waste Land.* He further restricted his discussion to the symbolism in the poem and submitted to his instructor the following tentative subject: "An Interpretation of the Symbolism in T. S. Eliot's *The Waste Land.*"

After the student received his instructor's approval and began his research, he decided to write a line-by-line, symbol-by-symbol interpretation of the lengthy, four-part poem. However, he found that his discussion of Part One alone occupied about twenty pages of manuscript. Continuing with his original plan would have resulted in a manuscript of approximately 80 pages, well beyond the scope of the assignment. Should he change his subject to one less ambitious and involved? But what about all the time and effort already expended on research? He resolved the problem satisfactorily by changing his title to "An Interpretation of the Symbolism in Part One of T. S. Eliot's *The Waste Land.*"

When we are involved in research, we cannot always know beforehand whether a tentative subject is sufficiently restricted. The problem of adequate restriction is not as difficult when we prepare a communication based on our own experiences, because the subject is thoroughly familiar to us before we begin.

Sometimes a subject which appears to be sufficiently restricted at first glance really isn't. A recent trip may provide you with a good subject for a speech or composition, but any trip, even a short one, is a combination of many experiences. Listing some of these should help you to further restrict your tentative subject.

My Trip to Washington, D.C.

I. The Plane Ride to Washington
II. Visiting John Kennedy's Grave at Arlington
III. A Visit with Senator Nelson
IV. The Lincoln Memorial at Night
V. Our Nation's Capitol
VI. The Smithsonian Institution—A Magnificent Complex

If you attempt to deal with all of these experiences, your communication will read like a shopping list. A "first we did this, then that" approach, with a sentence or two devoted to each experience, would result in an uninteresting and superficial communication. Let us continue to analyze our tentative choice of subject, a trip to Washington, D.C.

Restricted Subject	Analysis
I. The Plane Ride to Washington	The airline hostess spilled some coffee on my suit when the plane hit an air pocket. Perhaps I should describe this experience in detail?
II. Visiting John Kennedy's Grave at Arlington	I was deeply moved. Could I recreate in words the feelings I experienced as I watched the eternal flame?
III. A Visit with Senator Nelson	Meeting the Senator gave me the opportunity to chat with him about his proposal to recycle glass, metal, and paper products. I could share these thoughts with the class.
IV. The Lincoln Memorial at Night	The photographs I took would help me to recall the specific details of this scene and to recreate them for the class.
V. Our Nation's Capitol	Much too broad. Perhaps I could restrict this subject to my visit to the Senate Gallery.
VI. The Smithsonian Institution— A Magnificent Complex	Again, much too broad. There are nine different Smithsonian buildings, each containing a multitude of exhibits.

EXERCISES

Determine which of the following subjects are sufficiently restricted for a three-minute speech or a 400-word composition. Further restrict those subjects that are too broad to be developed adequately.

1. Photography
2. My Most Unusual New Year's Eve Celebration
3. How to Bathe a Poodle
4. Grocery Shopping on a Shoestring
5. The Drug Problem
6. The Aftermath of Watergate
7. Is There Really Love at First Sight?
8. How to Study
9. My Visit to a Bohemian Night Club
10. The Equal Rights Amendment
11. Is Religion Relevant?
12. Is There a Pollution Solution?
13. Hitchhiking to Mexico
14. Political Protest
15. Recycle Your Scrap!
16. Stamp Out VD!
17. The Women's Movement
18. How to Build a Good Hi-Fi Speaker for $15.00
19. The Gas Guzzler—And What to Do About it
20. Registration—A Twentieth Century Horror

STATING THE INTENT

Once the purpose of an assignment is clear to you and your subject is carefully selected and sufficiently restricted, you are ready to formulate a statement of specific intent. We have classified purposeful communication under three main headings: to inform, to entertain, or to persuade. Our next task is to relate this purpose to the specific content of our communication. Note the following examples:

1. **To Inform**
   a. to explain how to take pictures with a Polaroid camera
   b. to describe the view from my bedroom window

c. to define "love"

d. to summarize the Mayor's five-point approach for eliminating substandard housing from our town

e. to relate the difficulties I encountered when registering for classes

2. To Entertain

a. to poke fun at television comedies

b. to prepare a program of folk music for our talent show

c. to tell my favorite mother-in-law story to a recently married friend

3. To Persuade

a. to convince you to support my candidacy for the presidency of the student body

b. to explain why the President's wage and price freeze is unfair to labor

c. to convince members of the Council to support a new sports arena for our town

All of these statements of specific intent are infinitive phrases beginning with the infinitive form of the verb: to explain, to describe, to define, and so on. When the intent of your communication is to develop a main idea, and this is generally true of persuasion, stating that main idea in a complete sentence will help you plan your communication.

Statement of Specific Intent: to convince you to support my candidacy for the presidency of the student body

Main Idea: My election to the presidency of the student body will insure organized student resistance to a raise in tuition.

Statement of Specific Intent: to explain why the President's wage and price freeze is unfair to labor

Main Idea: The President's wage and price freeze is unfair to labor because profits, insurance rates, and dividends are not included.

Statement of Specific Intent: to convince members of the Council to support a new sports arena for our town

Main Idea: Building a new sports arena will attract professional hockey to our town.

The main idea statement should fulfill four specific characteristics:

1. It should state a point of view, not a fact.
2. It should be restricted to that which can adequately be developed in a subsequent communication.
3. It should deal either with a single idea or two closely related ideas.
4. It should contain specific language.

Main Idea: The unemployment rate in our community is 6.2 percent.
Analysis: Since this is a statement of fact, not a point of view, it requires no further development.
Revision: The unemployment rate in our community will continue to increase unless new jobs are created more rapidly.

Main Idea: There are many reasons why the Yankees will again be American League Champions.
Analysis: "Many reasons" is too broad. It is better to restrict your main idea to one or two specific reasons and develop them in detail.
Revision: The Yankees will again be American League Champions because their pitching depth and long-ball hitting are superior to those of the other contenders.

Main Idea: Raising tropical fish and collecting stamps are interesting hobbies.
Analysis: This main idea statement contains two flaws:
    1. Raising tropical fish and collecting stamps are two entirely unrelated activities.
    2. The word "interesting" is vague.
Revision: Stamp collecting is a painless way to learn world geography.

EXERCISES

Analyze the following main idea statements. Revise any that are not satisfactory.

1. The Milwaukee Bucks are the most interesting team in professional basketball.
2. My sewing machine enables me to keep up with the latest fashions and still stay within my budget.

3. Employer commitments to affirmative action have successfully combated the adverse effects of discrimination against minorities and women.
4. Speeders lose their licenses in New Jersey.
5. The Women's Movement has irreparably harmed American family life.
6. Stock car racing is an exciting sport.
7. Jogging is a great way to stay physically fit, and physical fitness is necessary for a full life.
8. Gays are people, too.
9. Prostitution should be legalized.
10. Our welfare system is obsolete.

PERSUASION TO ACTUATE

Write a 200–400 word appeal or deliver a 2–4 minute speech to persuade your audience to do something specific as a result of your communication. Make clear to your audience exactly what action you wish them to take. Your purpose is to get a physical response. You are asking your audience to act: to buy, to join, to vote, to help, to donate, to march, to sign, or to participate.

Suggestions

1. *Be realistic.*Make sure you know exactly what action you wish your audience to take, and be certain that it is reasonable. You can't expect an audience to do something which they are incapable of doing; e.g., most students could not afford to sponsor a child for $15 a month. Nor could you expect an audience to do something to which they are opposed to doing, i.e., you could not expect your fellow students to join the Communist Party.
2. *Insure understanding.* Make clear to your audience exactly *what* they must do. You must point out such things as when they should act, what the exact cost will be, and whom they should contact.
3. *Be sincere.* Before you can get others to act, you must be sold on the suggested course of action. Be sure you believe that what you propose is in the best interest of your audience.
4. *Be accurate.* Make sure that what you are saying is absolutely true. Use only information that you have checked thoroughly.

Sample Main Ideas

1. Join the crusade to cure sickle cell anemia.
2. Install a smoke and fire detector in your home.
3. Work for the candidate of your choice in the forthcoming election.
4. Donate a life-saving pint of blood.

Assignment

Plan and execute a composition, a speech, or both (as your instructor indicates), according to the following procedure:

1. Indicate the primary purpose of your communication:
   a. to inform,
   b. to entertain,
   c. to convince,
   d. to actuate,
   e. to reinforce.
2. Does your subject fulfill the following criteria?
   a. Is it in keeping with the primary purpose indicated above?
   b. Is it interesting to you?
   c. Is it one about which you have sufficient knowledge?
   d. Will it be of interest to your audience or reader?
   e. Is it sufficiently restricted?
3. Formulate a statement of specific intent and deliver a main idea statement, if needed.
4. Write your composition and/or deliver your speech.

CHAPTER
3

The Forms of
Discourse

Once the purpose of your communication has been clearly established, you are ready to begin developing your subject. Which form of discourse will be best to help you accomplish your purpose? Should you tell a story? Explain a process? Describe a person, place, or event? One of these forms of discourse should suffice for brief communications, while longer communications may require combinations of the different forms.

NARRATION

Can you imagine one of your ancestors attempting to relate a personal experience to a friend? Perhaps he was stung by a bee as he walked through the forest seeking food or shelter. Later, when the pain subsided, he recreated this experience for his companion by imitating the buzzing of the bee, gesturing to depict its flight, and uttering a sound that articulated the pain he suffered when he was stung. A baby's early attempts to communicate follow a similar pattern. The baby frequently imitates the sound associated with a particular animal or object, and this sound becomes a word in his limited vocabulary. The cat is a "meow," the dog a "bow-wow," and the train a "choo-choo." An exclamation of joy—"Ah!"—or pain—"Ow!"—accompanied by an occasional gesture help him to tell his story. Narration or storytelling is our oldest form of communicating experiences.

Classifying Narration According to Purpose

We have stressed purposeful communication as one of the primary objectives of the planning stage. A narrative may be employed in a communication whose purpose is to inform, to entertain, or to persuade.

If you simply relate to a friend the events that occupied your day, the purpose of your narrative is to inform. You might, however, attempt to communicate a humorous experience. Perhaps when you opened the front door to get your morning newspaper one cold, January morning, the wind blew the door shut, leaving you stranded outside in your T-shirt and jockey shorts. You ultimately saw the humor of the situation, although it may not have been evident to you when the door first blew shut. In relating this experience, you would want to provide your friend with an understanding of the events themselves, but your primary purpose would be to entertain.

Frequently an experience is incidental to its message. Anecdotes, fables, parables, and some personal experiences are examples of narration whose primary purpose is to persuade. Consider the following example of persuasive narration:

> I am forty-four years old now and have a wife and two small children. By 1963 I had reached a comfortable salary level with an insurance firm and the future seemed bright for us all. In May of that year I developed a slight difficulty in swallowing. Our family physician said that if it persisted for another week he would arrange an appointment for me with a throat specialist. It did persist. The specialist diagnosed it simply as "a case of nerves," a diagnosis he was to reaffirm in October of 1963. Finally, in January of 1964, convinced that it was more than a case of nerves, I entered a hospital, where I learned that I had cancer of the throat.

The writer goes on to describe in detail the horrors he experienced in the cancer ward of a well-known hospital. He employs a narrative technique to accomplish the primarily persuasive purpose of his article. This purpose is clearly indicated in the two concluding paragraphs:

> If anyone tells me it hasn't been proven that smoking causes cancer, I won't argue with him. The chances are his mind is made up anyway.
> If, on the other hand, what I've written here can save even one man, woman or child from the horrors I've known, I'll be content.

EXPOSITION

Do you want to build a shortwave receiver? Bake a cake? Design your own dune buggy? Add some electrical outlets to your home? Operate a sewing machine? Tile your basement floor? Make a fortune in the stock market? Ferment your own wine? Tune your car's engine? Just go to your library or local book store, borrow or buy the appropriate do-it-yourself book, and follow the "simplified, illustrated instructions."

We define exposition as communication which explains a concept, idea, belief, or process. In the examples above we act as receivers of expository prose. The writer is the sender; his book, pamphlet, or instruction sheet contains the message to which we respond. Some manufacturers take pains to enclose a clear set of instructions with their product. They have learned that clear expository communication is in their own best interest. Other manufacturers, however, have yet to learn this lesson. On Christmas day, for example, thousands of fathers sit on living room floors attempting to assemble their children's newly acquired toys. After an hour or so of frustrating trial and error, Dad may utter some angry words, return the parts to their original container, and decide to replace the item with something easier to assemble. The child is disappointed, the parents frustrated, and the manufacturer has lost a sale because of unclear exposition. One manufacturer, obviously blessed with a sense of humor, began his instruction sheet as follows: Step one — mix yourself a good, stiff drink.

The accompanying assembly instructions for a utility bin cabinet are typical of expository material which accompanies products that must be assembled by the consumer. Notice how the various steps in the assembly process are clearly and concisely described. Key words are underlined, and repeated references are made to the accompanying drawings.

EXERCISES

I. Describe to the class an experience you had in attempting to assemble a product for which the instructions were not clear.

II. Bring an instruction sheet (similar to the example) to class, and comment on its effectiveness as exposition.

III. In a paragraph, explain as clearly and concisely as you can an everyday process with which you are thoroughly familiar. Assume the reader has never performed this process himself.

ASSEMBLY INSTRUCTIONS

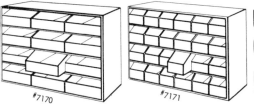

UTILITY BIN CABINET

MODEL NUMBERS
7170 & 7171

#7170   #7171

PARTS DESCRIPTION

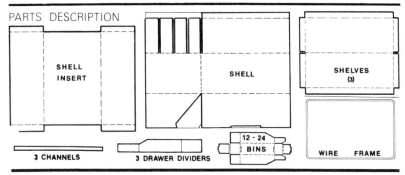

SHELL INSERT	SHELL	SHELVES (3)

3 CHANNELS   3 DRAWER DIVIDERS   12 - 24 BINS   WIRE FRAME

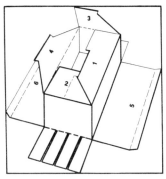

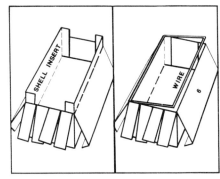

FIG.1
Square up shell and fold in rear Flaps 1, 2, 3, 4 in order as shown. Press down to engage flaps. Flip shell upright.

FIG.2
Slide shell insert into position as shown. Position wire frame on top of shell insert.

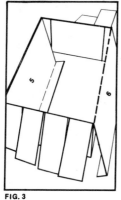

FIG. 3
Fold flaps 5 & 6 up and over wire and tuck down inside shell.

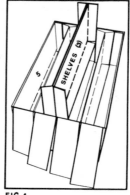

FIG. 4
Fold shelves with white side out, insert into shell, seeing to it that the narrow flaps of the shelves butt up against other shelf flaps and rest beneath wire frame as shown.

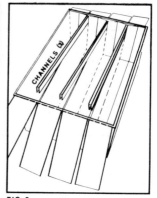

FIG. 5
Firmly press shelf channels over shelf.

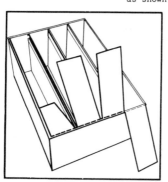

FIG. 6
Fold in remaining flaps and tuck securely against inner wall.

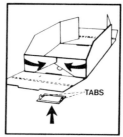

FIG. I BINS
Insert card holder tabs into the slots provided. Fold tabs over. Fold sides up, fold attached end flaps (front & back) over as shown.

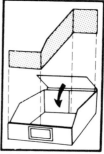

FIG. 2
Fold end panels up and over at double crease. Engage tab in slots on bottom. Repeat operation opposite end. Add drawer divider as shown above.

Fidelity Products Company *A Division of Fidelity File Box, Inc*
705 PENNSYLVANIA AVENUE SOUTH, MINNEAPOLIS, MINN. 55426 • TELEPHONE (612) 544-6644

Suggestions

1. How to lace your shoes
2. How to make a cream cheese and jelly sandwich
3. How to brush your teeth
4. How to fry an egg

Classifying Exposition
According to Purpose

Exposition is sometimes referred to as utilitarian prose because its effectiveness is measured by its usefulness and clarity. By definition, pure exposition is informational; however, it may also be employed in persuasive and entertaining communication.

Tom decides to convince his friend Bill to meet him at the stadium for a big football weekend. Sensing Bill's reluctance, Tom decides on a positive, enthusiastic approach:

Tom: I've got a couple of great seats for the State game. After the game Joe's throwing a big beer bash, and we're invited. Meet me at the Stadium Saturday at two, and we'll have a gas of a weekend.

Bill: Thanks for asking, Tom. But you know my sense of direction; I'd never find the place. Besides, I've got some studying to do for Monday's history exam.

Tom: Nothing to it, Bill. Take I-93 to the Iroquois Road Exit, about fifty miles North. When you exit, drive due East for four miles, and you'll run right into the stadium. We'll all be leaving Sunday, right after breakfast, so you'll get home in plenty of time to study.

Bill's tentative refusal is based on two reasons: He doubts his ability to find the stadium, and he needs time to study for Monday's examination. While Tom's primary purpose is persuasive (to convince), he utilizes exposition to answer Bill's first argument. Second, by arranging for an early Sunday departure so that Bill has ample time to study, Tom's chances of convincing Bill to join him have been enhanced.

Surely you have seen performers who employ varying degrees of audience participation in their acts. The singer who asks his audience to join him in the refrain or the MC explaining the rules of a TV game to contestants is involved with exposition. Explanations should be clear and brief when the purpose of a communication is primarily persuasive or entertaining. Exposition is merely a means to an end.

Definition: A Special Type of Exposition Involving Denotative and Connotative Meaning

Look around you. Regardless of where you may be at the moment, you see numerous objects whose names are familiar to you. The names we assign to objects like *door, window, book, desk, floor, ceiling, grass, tree,* and *shrub* are concrete words, relatively easy to define specifically. The literal definition of a word is its *denotative* meaning. If we tentatively define a desk as a piece of furniture, our definition is too general, because there are many pieces of furniture that are not desks. The *American Heritage Dictionary* definition—"a piece of furniture typically having a flat top for writing and accessory drawers or compartments"—is more specific, and consequently more satisfactory. Notice that this definition is still sufficiently flexible to include unusual desks. The dictionary's use of the word "typically" indicates that some desks may be atypical, thereby deviating from the usual pattern.

The words indicated all refer to objects, which are easy for us to visualize. Sometimes, however, words refer to concepts, ideas, or emotions, and mean different things to different people; consequently, they are more difficult to define satisfactorily. Words like *communism, hate, love, sorrow,* and *idealism* are abstract words referring to no specific objects. They are *connotative* in that different people have favorable or unfavorable attitudes about them, depending upon individual associations and experiences. The dedicated Communist's definition of his political ideology would be very different from that of a Wall Street banker. Defining an abstract word is a more demanding task than defining a concrete word, because the communicator must go beyond the literal meaning.

If you are asked to define an abstract word, a good starting point would be a reliable, up-to-date dictionary. The more information you discover about your word, the more complete your definition. Therefore, you might wish to consult an unabridged dictionary.

You should also pay particular attention to synonyms for the word you select. (Synonyms are words that have meanings similar to other words in the language.) However, since no two words have exactly the same meaning, distinguishing differences among similar abstract words will help you to make your definition clear and complete, and aid you in selecting precisely the right word for each situation. How, for example, does communism differ from socialism? How does hate differ from loathing, animosity, or dislike? How does love differ from affection, fondness, or infatuation? If your general language dictionary does not contain lists of synonyms, consult a specialized dictionary of synonyms and antonyms, or a thesaurus.

Our main concern thus far has been with the literal or denotative meaning of a given word. Once you have established a working definition with the help of a good dictionary, you continue the process of definition through reference to your own attitudes, values, and experiences. Your definition of "love" is probably different from your neighbor's. One of your primary objectives in defining an abstract word is to make your connotative meaning clear to your reader or listener. You might view love between the sexes as primarily a physical attraction, while another might see it as a meeting of the minds on such issues as raising children, and sharing similar moral and religious convictions. Someone else might think of love as synonymous with companionship. Each of you has an obligation to supply specific examples that will enable the receiver to understand your connotative definition.

The process of definition of abstract words can be summarized as follows:

1. Consult a good dictionary, preferably unabridged, to establish a complete denotative definition.

2. Distinguish the denotative meaning of your word from that of similar abstract words with the help of a good dictionary, a specialized dictionary of synonyms and antonyms, or both.

3. Supply your own connotative definition, supporting your judgments with specific examples.

EXERCISES

Define an abstract word in an extemporaneous speech or short composition, as your instructor directs. Follow the three-step process summarized above.

Sample Words

1. love
2. sorrow
3. idealism
4. faith
5. success
6. despair
7. solitude

8. individualism

9. tenacity

10. hope

Indicate whether the italic terms in the following sentences are denotative or connotative. If the term is connotative, determine whether the connotation is favorable or unfavorable.

1. I think John is *thrifty;* Mary thinks he is a *tightwad.*

2. Jim always addresses the *policeman* on the beat as *"officer"* but calls him a *pig* behind his back.

3. Sally, the *hairdresser* at Antoine's, refers to herself as a *beautician* or *cosmetologist.*

4. My *boss* is a *slave driver* if there ever was one.

5. Sam Farber is a *real American,* but all the *do-gooders* will vote for his *egghead* opponent.

6. I waited more than two hours for the *doctor* to see me; boy, those *pill pushers* don't care how long a *patient* is inconvenienced.

7. Fred thinks he is *honest* and *straightforward,* but he is really rather *simple.*

8. Two members of the history faculty *collaborated* on a book about Nazi *collaboration* during World War II.

9. For a *lawyer* who has been out of school for only a year, he certainly has been a busy *ambulance chaser.*

10. How's a *brother* going to make it if *Whitey* runs the establishment?

DESCRIPTION

Simple descriptions of people, places, and events are part of our everyday communication. A friend requests a description of your date's roommate before agreeing to a blind date. A classmate stops you at registration to ask whether you know the teacher of the history section he plans to enroll in. You make a mental note to write home to the folks, describing your new college campus. You tentatively select your senior high school trip as the subject of your next composition.

Your response to each of the above messages is primarily descriptive. Description, like exposition, is basically informational. Our primary purpose with both forms of discourse is to add to the knowledge of our audience. Expository communication, at its best, is generally simple, clear, direct, and detached. Description is more personal, more subjective. Its effectiveness depends upon how specific our details are.

Sensory Appeals

One method for achieving specific detail in description is to employ effective combinations of sensory appeals (the five senses being sight, hearing, taste, touch, and smell). Although it isn't necessary to employ all five in a single description, appeals to different senses will enable you to communicate a more complete description. Which combination is most effective will depend, of course, on your choice of subject.

Let us assume that your assignment is to describe a place on campus. The overall purpose of the assignment is to inform, but the specific choice of subject is left to you. After considering your English classroom, the library, the testing center, and the automotive shop as possibilities, you tentatively decide on the student center, a place with which you are thoroughly familiar. Checking your tentative choice against the criteria detailed in Chapter 2, you conclude that your subject is in keeping with the general purpose of the assignment (to inform), is interesting to both you and your prospective audience, and is one that you are sufficiently knowledgeable about. But can it be further restricted?

Perhaps the most obvious way of restricting your subject is to describe only one part of the student center, such as the snack bar. It might also be helpful to further restrict your subject to a place in time. The snack bar during the hectic rush of lunch hour is very different from its relatively deserted atmosphere of late afternoon. Eventually you decide on "The Snack Bar at Noon" as the revised subject of your descriptive communication.

Regardless of how familiar you think you are with the snack bar, it would be a mistake to attempt to prepare your communication from memory. Go there again, notebook in hand, to find specific details that will eventually be incorporated into your finished work. Recording these details as separate sensory appeals will provide you with the raw materials needed for successful description.

Sight: long lines of students patiently awaiting their hamburgers and fries, long-haired, jeans-clad students rapidly munching their food at crowded tables, the blue and white tiled floor covered with litter carelessly dropped by students oblivious of the perils of pollution, one unhurried couple, holding hands, having eyes only for each other in the ever-changing crowd.

Hearing: endless clanging of plastic trays making contact with the steel food rails, the din of happy, carefree voices, the raucous sound of rock music blaring

over the intercom, the voice of the order-taker bark-
ing out the jargon of his trade—"BLT down"—to the
busy short order man.

Taste and Smell: Spicy chili, frothy malts and shakes, freshly baked
cakes and pies, the aroma of freshly brewed coffee,
the smell of stale tobacco throughout the eating
area.

Touch: bodies brushing against one another as students enter and leave the crowded area, the constant blast of
warm air from the powerful, wall-mounted heater,
the intermittent blast of cold air as entering students
bring the winter chill with them.

The Snack Bar at Noon

The relative calm of coffee break time at the snack bar changes to
chaos as the noon hour approaches. At exactly 11:50 a.m. the bell tolls;
fifth hour class has ended, and hundreds of students converge on the
northwest side of the student center, where the snack bar is housed.

Bodies brush against one another as students hurriedly enter the
crowded area, bringing a bit of winter's chill with them. The freshly
scrubbed blue and white tile floor is soon covered by litter carelessly
dropped by those oblivious to the perils of pollution. Jeans-clad students noisily await their hamburgers and fries. The constant clanging of
plastic trays making contact with the steel food railings competes with
the raucous sound of rock music blaring over the intercom. Smells of
spicy chili, freshly baked cakes and pies, and richly brewed coffee fill
the air.

The voice of the order-taker barks out the jargon of his trade—"BLT
down," "One burger, with"—to the busy short order man. The customers dig down into their pockets for change, pay for their selections, and
scramble for the few vacant butcher block tables.

Students rapidly munch their food amidst the din of happy, carefree
voices. One unhurried couple holds hands, having eyes only for each
other in the ever-changing crowd.

Gradually the food line begins to subside. Students empty their trays
into the huge, gray rubbish containers, then bundle themselves for departure. When the bell signals the end of the lunch hour, bodies converge on the exits, some leaving their debris behind on the tables. Soon
the maintenance crew will tackle the seemingly endless job of preparing for the next stampede.

You may have noticed that not all of the sensory appeals in the
notes were incorporated into the composition, and a few appeals that
were in the composition are not found in the notes. Since effective

communication involves repeated modification and revision, it is not necessary for you to follow your record of sensory appeals to the letter. Remember, you have merely made a random listing of initial impressions; additions, deletions, and modifications are expected and desirable.

The composition that you have just read represents one student's attempt to write an informative description. How successful is it? Is it sufficiently specific? Is it well organized? Purposeful? Interesting? Perhaps you can make suggestions for improvement.

Specific Language

A closely related technique for making details vivid is to use specific language. Try walking into your local market and asking the clerk for three pounds of fruit. He knows the meaning of the word "fruit" as well as you do, but he cannot fill your order without more specific information. What *kind* of fruit do you want? "Three pounds of apples, please," is better, but still not specific enough. As the clerk visualizes his stock of Delicious, Winesap, and Macintosh apples, he might become impatient with your lack of specificity. A critical reader or listener becomes equally disenchanted with vague description.

EXERCISES

Write a descriptive sentence about each of the following, employing appropriate sensory appeals and specific details. A sample sentence is provided for the first phrase.

1. A pair of shoes—My two-tone, black and rust sueded ties with wing-tip styling are perfect back-to-school shoes.
2. Something good to eat
3. A rock singer or group
4. Your room
5. A teacher
6. A musical instrument
7. A soft drink
8. A game-winning touchdown
9. A treasured possession
10. An article of clothing

Classifying Description
According to Purpose

The primary purpose of most simple descriptions of people, places, and events is to inform. But sometimes the information is subordinate to another purpose: to entertain or to persuade. Notice how the effective use of sensory detail and specific language enables the reader to experience vicariously the scene described in the following example of entertaining, descriptive poetry:

The Once-Over

The tanned blonde
          in the green print sack
in the center of the subway car
          standing
        though there are seats
        has had it from
1 teen-age hood
1 lesbian
1 envious housewife
4 men over fifty
(& myself), in short
the contents of this half of the car

Our notations are:
long legs, long waist, high breasts (no bra), long
neck, the model slump
       the handbag drape and how the skirt
cuts in under a very handsome
         set of cheeks
'stirring dull roots with spring rain' sayeth the preacher

        Only a stolid young man
        with a blue business suit and the New York
         Times
        does not know he is being assaulted

So.
She has us and we her
all the way to downtown Brooklyn
Over the tunnel and through the bridge
       to Dekalb Avenue we go

all very chummy

She stares at the number over the door

and gives no sign
> yet the sign is on her

Paul Blackburn From *The New American Poetry,* edited by Donald M. Allen ©
Grove Press, New York, 1960.

Has your mouth ever watered over an advertising brochure's description of a new summer outfit, a stereo receiver, or a vacation in some far-off exotic place? In advertising description, the information given is subordinate to the persuasive purpose of selling the product or service. After studying the following example of persuasive description, answer the questions provided:

Fly away to Nassau's most fabulous world of complete resort activities . . . Nassau Beach Hotel. Just steps from your room are 660 yards of sunny, soft sandy beach washed by waters as clear, blue and warm as the breeze-swept Bahamian sky. Start your day with a suntan a la chaise, punctuated by periodic plunges into our ocean or sparkling pool. Explore the underwater world off-shore with snorkel, mask and fins. Skim the waves on water skis or sail a salty catamaran. Charter a sporty cruiser for deep-sea fishing. Go scuba diving around a coral reef. Dry off with a spot of volleyball, a shot of shuffleboard, a set of tennis. Cool off with a Tropical Temptation from our beachside bar. Then, head off on a jaunty golf cart for an afternoon round of 18 challenging championship holes at the Nassau Country Club right next door. If you prefer spectator sports, don't miss the crab or goat races down by the beach . . . with the added excitement of parimutuel betting! Go sightseeing in Old Nassau town by scooter, bike, . . . or hire a clip-clop carriage to squire you around (your horse may be wearing a straw hat). See the Old World pomp of Rawson Square. Climb the Queen's Staircase for a panoramic view of Nassau. Visit the native Straw Market. Buy free-port booty along bustling Bay Street. But don't linger too long downtown . . . Nassau's most exciting nightlife begins right here at the Nassau Beach Hotel. Stop in at the Out Island Bar or the romantic Rum Keg for an exotic cocktail (and try the hot conch fritters appetizers). Then there's the gleaming candlelight atmosphere and gourmet dining on native and continental cuisine in the elegant Lamplighter Room. Spend a lively hour or two in the colorful Rum Keg dancing to native rhythms, disco, steel band or Calypso. And come to the glittering sophistication of the Colony Room for the greatest nightclub shows. Wrap up your evening with a walk through our tropical garden under the stars and watch the moon turn the waves to silver along our beautiful beach. You'll understand the magic that makes one resort the most successful vacation spot on the Island . . . Nassau Beach Hotel.

EXERCISES

ANALYSIS OF NASSAU BEACH HOTEL DESCRIPTION

1. Formulate a statement of specific intent for the foregoing advertising copy.
2. Which of the five sensory appeals (sight, hearing, taste, touch, smell) are represented? Give examples.
3. Which of the five sensory appeals predominates? Why?
4. Which sensory appeals are particularly effective? Are any of them trite, or otherwise ineffective?
5. Briefly comment on the effectiveness of this advertising copy as persuasive description.

USING NARRATION TO PERSUADE

Deliver a 2–4 minute speech or write a short essay of 200–400 words in which you tell a story to persuade. Describe the material in enough detail to create a mental picture for the reader or listener. Develop your material informally, with emphasis on details of action. An interesting story is an excellent means of reinforcing or clarifying your ideas.

Delivery: If you present this assignment orally, it should be delivered extemporaneously. An audience will expect you to have almost total eye contact when talking about your own experience. The more spontaneous and relaxed you are, the more your audience will enjoy your presentation.

Sample Main Ideas

1. Seat belts save lives.
2. Drinking and driving don't mix.
3. It pays to be courteous.
4. Never buy anything sight unseen.
5. Never judge a person on the basis of your first meeting.
6. Keep dangerous products out of the reach of small children.

CHAPTER
4

Reading
and
Listening

OBJECTIVES

After studying this chapter, you should be able to:
1. Identify "key" parts of a chapter before reading it in its entirety.
2. Formulate the kinds of questions that will increase your understanding of the material being read.
3. Retain the information you have learned for a longer time.
4. Identify similarities between reading and listening skills.
5. Discuss the procedure to follow in preparing to listen.

WHAT DID THE AUTHOR SAY?

How do you study your daily assignments? Does your instructor assign a particular number of pages to be read? Does the instructor give you questions to be answered? Does the instructor ask for an outline or summary of the material?

When only a designated number of pages are assigned, most students begin at the beginning and read straight through the lesson. Most students know "how to read" the words. When they have finished reading every word of the lesson, they may say to themselves, "I have completed my assignment, which should give me a good grade in this class." Wrong! Just reading the words in an assignment will never guarantee understanding what the author said. *And* you must not only understand what the author said, but you must also be able to remember and apply it.

Sometimes highly intelligent students have trouble in school. They may read well, but they do not realize that reading is only a part of studying. On the other hand, less intelligent students frequently earn good grades because they have learned how to study. Just reading an assignment will not guarantee a good grade on a quiz or in the course.

In order to *study* a lesson, you must first consider what your purpose is in reading it. The purpose in reading assigned material in a textbook is usually to master it. In order to *study* the written words of any assignment, you must (1) prepare to read, (2) read to answer questions, (3) reflect on what you have read.

This chapter was written by Mary Jane Irwin.

"Don't worry about passing reading.
Take a remedial course when you get to college."

Preparing to Read

The first step in preparing to study a lesson is to determine the specific purpose for which the material is being studied. Is it necessary to master the material by understanding the main ideas and show the relationship of the details to the main ideas? Or is it just necessary to hit the high spots? Mastery is not always required.

When you have determined how much you are going to have to "know" about the lesson, it is necessary to know what the author is writing "about." A student's first reaction is, "How do I know what he is writing about until I have read it?" Of course, you won't know what he *says* until you have read it, but you can find out the subject of the lesson by reading the title carefully and *thinking* about what it says. (Some students don't bother with the title at all because they are anxious to "get into the chapter" and get the studying finished as quickly as possible.) When you have determined the subject, ask yourself what you already know about this subject. No one ever read anything with any degree of understanding when he knew absolutely *nothing* about the subject.

For example, if the title of a lesson were "Atomic Energy," your first impulse might be to say, "I don't know anything about this subject." This is because you think it is necessary to know the scientific aspects of the splitting of the atom. Detailed scientific knowledge is not necessary in order to prepare to read about atomic energy, but you must set your mind in motion in the proper direction so that you can build on your present knowledge. Your present knowledge may be limited to the fact that energy from the atom is extremely powerful — so powerful that it can power submarines and electric power plants as well as cause devastating destruction. Now your mind is ready to receive further information about atomic energy.

After you have understood the subject of the lesson and have recalled what you already know about the subject, read the first and last paragraphs, putting into your own words what the author has said. Most writers tell you at the beginning what they are planning to write about, and at the end they sum up what they have said. *Do not read the entire lesson yet.* It is all right to skip from the first to the last paragraph in a textbook assignment because your textbook is not like a novel that has a plot, and the textbook material will never build up to a climax or contain a surprise ending. Your textbook author is trying to help you understand subject matter.

Next read the main and subordinate headings, which will allow you to understand exactly what aspects of this subject the author has emphasized. One of the most difficult tasks for students is to determine what is important in a lesson. These preparatory steps to reading an assignment will tell you exactly what the author thinks is important.

If there are maps, charts, graphs, or pictures in the lesson, be sure to read the captions and try to understand the reason the author included them.

Using this preparatory process, it should take you no more than five minutes to find out what 30 pages are "about" in a textbook assignment.

Let's review *how* you find out what a textbook lesson is "about" *before you read it.* Study the:

1. Title
2. First and last paragraphs
3. Main and subheadings
4. Pictures, charts, maps, and graphs

Below is an example of how you would go about *preparing* to study a 30-page chapter in a psychology textbook. *Before* you read the chap-

ter in its entirety, you would read only these parts. Follow along carefully, and you will see how much information you can get just by
reading certain parts that reveal what the author has decided is important.

Title   MEASUREMENT AND INDIVIDUAL DIFFERENCES

First   "In whatever way we look at individuals we find differ-
paragraph   ences: in size, health, strength, ability, and emotional
                     stability. Each differs in one way or another from every-
                     one else. This is no recent discovery—for some time you
                     have been aware that there are others who possess
                     more intellectual ability than you have, and some who
                     possess less. Even the ancients recognized such differ-
                     ences and took account of them in training their youth.
                     Why the psychological emphasis today in this area?"

Headings   *Measuring Units*
                     Mental Age/Chronological Age
                     Intelligence

Chart

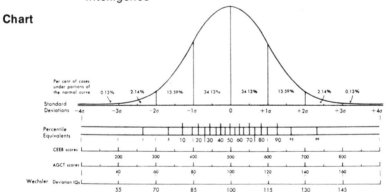

Distribution of IQ's (From Madigan, *Psychology*, 5th Ed.)

Heading   *Innate and Acquired Differences*

Chart

The individual is a product of heredity and environment (From Madigan, *Psychology*, 5th Ed.)

Headings   *Causes of Individual Differences*
DEVELOPMENTAL FACTORS
RACIAL FACTORS
FAMILY FACTORS
SEX FACTORS
AGE FACTORS

Temperamental Differences
ENVIRONMENTAL INFLUENCES
HUMAN DRIVES OR MOTIVES
ATTITUDES AND EMOTIONS

Physiological Differences
SENSE ORGANS
GLANDULAR CONDITIONS
PHYSICAL CAPACITY
STRENGTH
SENSITIVITY TO PAIN
REACTION TO FOOD AND DRUGS

Recognition of Individual Differences

Last   "The causes of individual differences are designated as
paragraph   heredity and environment. Heredity sets the limit to the
pattern of potential growth, but environment maximizes
or minimizes this development."

Textbook extracts from *Psychology, Principles and Applications*, 5th ed., by
Marion East Madigan. St. Louis: C.V. Mosby Company, 1970.

Now that you have "hit the high spots" in this chapter by reading
only certain parts of it, you have discovered what the author is talking
"about." If this were an actual assignment in your textbook and you
had called to mind what you already know about heredity and environment, you would have a good idea about the author's main ideas.
Then when you actually read the chapter, it would be easier for you
to sift and sort the details that support these main ideas.

The Importance of Questioning and Curiosity If you have been
thinking as you read these particular parts of the assignment, your curiosity would probably help you formulate questions that the author
will be likely to answer. There are different kinds of questions you
might formulate. Some would be "surface" questions in which all you
do is turn a heading into a question. Others might be called "in-
depth" questions, which enable you to delve further into why the author has included something in order to make a point.

Using the above material from an actual textbook, you might formulate some surface questions as follows:

Heading	*Innate and Acquired Differences*
Surface question	What are innate and acquired differences?
Heading	*Measuring Units*
Surface question	What are measuring units?
Heading	*Mental Age/Chronological Age*
Surface questions	What is mental age?
	What is chronological age?
Heading	*Causes of Individual Differences*
Surface question	What are the causes of individual differences?

Since reading is a *thinking* process, it is not enough to resort to surface questions alone. You must think more deeply and come up with some in-depth questions. These are questions that show a relationship between a heading and the title of the chapter, or perhaps they will show the relationship between a subheading and its heading. Here are some examples:

Title	MEASUREMENT AND INDIVIDUAL DIFFERENCES
Heading	*Measuring Units*
Surface question	What are measuring units?
In-depth question	How are these measuring units used to determine individual differences?
Heading	*Causes of Individual Differences*
Subheading	DEVELOPMENTAL FACTORS
Surface question	What are developmental factors?
In-depth questions	How do these developmental factors cause individual differences?
	What are the individual differences caused by these developmental factors?

All in-depth questions must be formulated within the area of the title. As you formulate these questions, you are beginning to think. You may even guess what answers the author is likely to give to these questions. When you have speculated on the answers, you will be delighted as you read the chapter to find out that the author's ideas agree with yours. If you find that your answers do not agree with the author's, your curiosity will be aroused and you may develop further questions. In either case you will be reading *actively,* and you will become involved in what is written just the same as you become involved in watching a good television program. You always enjoy a movie when you anticipate what is to come next. Asking questions *before* you read can make a dull and uninteresting subject come alive.

It is absolutely necessary for anyone to know *before he reads* what questions the author is likely to answer. Everyone knows it is absolutely necessary for you to know what you lost before you begin to look for it; otherwise, how would you know when you had found it? And yet, students begin reading an assignment without the slightest idea of what they are looking for; thus, they are very unlikely to find it.

Although it has taken a long time to explain *how to prepare to read* an assignment, to actually apply this to a textbook assignment takes very little time. Just knowing how to prepare to read is not enough. You must be able to apply these techniques on your own lessons, and this takes practice.

EXERCISE

Fill in the blanks at the end of these instructions *as* you accomplish each task. The blanks and tasks have corresponding numbers. Use a lesson which has been assigned for another class and one *which you have not read.* (Any textbook will be all right. Perhaps psychology or sociology may be easier for your first practice lesson, but the technique works equally well with a math or science lesson.)

1. Write the name of the *course* in which this lesson has been assigned.
2. Write the complete title of the textbook lesson.
3. What do you already know about this subject? Write some specific facts. Do not tell when or where you studied this subject, but give some specific facts you learned about it.
4. Read the first paragraph. *Restate* the main idea *in your own words.*
5. Read the last paragraph. *Restate* the main idea *in your own words.*
6. List the main and subheadings. (If you are reading an essay or a textbook without headings, read *only* the first sentence of every third or fourth paragraph and write *in your own words* what the author said in each of these sentences.)
7. Were there any pictures, charts, maps, graphs in the lesson? If so, study them and write the main idea expressed in the heading under each one.
8. For each of the headings in this assignment, write (1) a surface question and (2) an in-depth question.

(When you have become adept at using this technique for preparing to read, you will not have to write out all of this information. Writing it is time-consuming, but it is necessary until you perfect the technique.)

Fill in the Blanks:

1. Name of the course for which you are reading this assignment.

_____

2. Give the title of the lesson to be studied.

_____

3. What do you already know about this subject?

_____

_____

_____

_____

4. RESTATE the main idea in the first paragraph. USE YOUR OWN WORDS.

_____

_____

_____

_____

5. RESTATE the main idea in the last paragraph. USE YOUR OWN WORDS.

_____

_____

_____

_____

6. LIST the main and subheadings.

_____

_____

_____

_____

_____

7. LIST pictures, maps, graphs, charts, etc.

KIND of pictorial aid   Write the caption under each of these aids

_____   _____

_____   _____

_____   _____

_____   _____

8. Formulate a SURFACE QUESTION for each heading and subheading. Write it under A. Formulate an IN-DEPTH QUESTION for each heading and subheading. Write it under B.

A. (surface)   _____

B. (in-depth) _____

A.   _____

B.   _____

A   _____

B.   _____

A.   _____

B.   _____

A.   _____

B.   _____

Reading to Answer Questions

The questions you have raised about your assignment and your review of what you already know about the subject should increase your interest and curiosity. When you have become interested in and curious about what you are going to read, it is much easier to find out what the author "says."

You already know how to read words, or you would not have reached this point in the textbook. You already know what important questions the author is likely to answer. Now the problem is to find out how the author answers these questions.

How to Read Sentences In order to understand what a sentence "says," it is necessary to understand sentence structure. More detailed information regarding sentence structure is found in chapter 8 of this book.

In reading to answer questions, you must know that each sentence tells about someone or something, and it tells what is said or done about that someone or something. If you were to read directions, your purpose for reading them would be to find out what you were supposed to do. Here is a good example of how you could do the wrong thing if you were not able to read sentences properly. Here are the directions: "A synonym or an antonym for the word in Column I can be found in Column II." Some students find this to mean that the sentence is talking about the "word in Column I." This is *not* what the sentence means. It is talking about the "synonym or antonym in Column II." The next sentence in the directions states, "The word should be written on your paper. Indicate whether this word is a synonym or an antonym." This time "word" refers to the synonym or antonym in Column II, the very thing the author was talking about in the first sentence. When the student writes the "word" from Column I rather than the choice from Column II, his answer will be wrong because he has not read the sentences properly.

HOW TO READ PARAGRAPHS

Paragraphs do not make much sense if you cannot read a sentence.

For many years before a student reaches college, his instructors have been asking him to pick out the most important idea in a paragraph or to underline the topic sentence. Seldom is the student told *how* to do this.

When the author writes a paragraph, he has one main idea to convey to the reader. It will be about one topic or one subject. By reading rapidly you can identify the topic or subject by noticing that each sentence of the paragraph will refer to one thing or idea. Each sentence will say something different about this subject, but each sentence will be about the same topic. When you have discovered what this thing or idea is that the author is writing about, you must decide what is so important about it that he found it necessary to devote an entire paragraph to it. Many ideas may be expressed in a paragraph, but the author will write only one main idea, with all of the other ideas supporting this main idea. Sometimes an author will give examples or an explanation of a point he is trying to make. These are given to help you understand the main idea and are relatively unimportant if you understand the author's idea itself. Some students are able to remember the examples or explanations, but they can't remember what the point was the author was making. The author uses many methods to make a main idea clear to you. You must understand what material is supportive to the main idea and this requires *thinking*. Reading is a *thinking process*.

In a way, reading a paragraph is similar to reading an entire lesson. First, you find out what the author is talking "about," and then you find what he "says" by recognizing the difference between his main idea and the supportive details.

Authors develop the main idea of a paragraph by using a variety of methods:

1. Use of a definition to give the main idea
2. Use of examples and illustrations to explain main ideas
3. Use of comparison and contrast to show similarities and differences
4. Use of explanations or descriptions to expand a main idea and clarify the meaning of the paragraph
5. Use of a combination of some of the above

EXERCISE

In each of the following paragraphs, the author has used one of the above methods to develop his main idea. Indicate by using the proper number which method he has used for each of them.

_____ At the turn of the century, small towns were isolated because means of communication were very limited. With the revolutionary developments of radio, television, and even radar, the world became smaller, and the population of isolated areas is now as well informed as those who live in large cities. The horse and buggy has given way to fast automobiles, trains, and planes to further improve communications in our country.

_____ Many people consider the Teton Mountains the most majestic in North America. They are made up of ten peaks, the highest of which is the Grand Teton. It rises 13,766 feet above sea level. These high peaks are snow-covered most of the year.

_____ There is an abundance of game in Arizona. Animals you are likely to see are mule deer, antelope, mountain sheep, and black bears. Some Mexican jaguars live in the southern mountains. Smaller animals, valuable for their fur or as food, include the fox, beaver, bobcat, raccoon, squirrel, and weasel. Arizona's game birds include grouse, quail, wild turkey, and various waterfowl.

_____ Menominee is the name of a tribe of North American Indians living in central Wisconsin. Their tribe is one of the Algonquin tribe, and they formerly spoke the Algonquian language. The word "menominee" means "wild rice people." They received this name because they ate wild rice that grew in the area where they lived. They were brave warriors and swifter runners than any other tribe of Indians. The story is told that no other tribe was ever able to capture one of them alive. They lived peacefully with the white man.

_____ Myopia is a visual defect in which images are focused in front of instead of on the retina. Objects are seen clearly only when close to the eyes. Myopia is also called nearsightedness.

The following paragraph, from Dr. Madigan's *Psychology, Principles and Practices,* may help you to understand how to read a paragraph.

MEANINGFULNESS (This is a subheading)

Significant material is more slowly forgotten than nonsense syllables. Nonsense material barely learned is almost forgotten in four months, but poetry barely learned has been known to be retained for twenty years. Material in which the elements are related as parts of a whole is more readily learned than nonsense material. This is due to interrelationships which in turn depend on past experience. The reader would probably have no background to utilize in committing to memory a sentence written in Greek.

As a student reads this paragraph quickly, he can see that the underlined words in each sentence are making comparisons of material that may be either meaningful or meaningless. Anything that relates to one's experience or shows relationships between parts of a whole must be meaningful. The subheading has already told him that the paragraph has to do with "meaningfulness."

The heading under which this subheading comes is entitled "Retention and Forgetting." Now it is easy to see that the writer is trying to convey to the reader that meaningful material is more readily remembered than nonsense material.

If the student were to use the question technique, he would find:

Heading   RETENTION AND FORGETTING

Subheading   *Meaningfulness*

Question   What does meaningfulness have to do with remembering or forgettng?

If you go back and read the paragraph, it is easy to come up with the same answer this time: Meaningful material is more readily remembered than nonsense material. This, of course, is the idea the author is trying to emphasize.

Any of these techniques will help you come up with the main idea of a paragraph. As you sift and sort when you read, you will select those points the author considers important, and you will find the answers to your questions.

Each time you find an answer to a question you should stop, look away from your textbook, think about it, and recite the answer in your own words. This means that you will *learn as you read*. As you think about these new ideas, you will relate them to what you already know about the subject. In this way you place these ideas in your mind in an organized fashion, keeping in mind the relationship of the supporting details to the main ideas. Organization always aids memory of material. No one's mind soaks up knowledge the way a sponge soaks up water; rather it is more like a sieve through which ideas and words are likely to leak. It takes much *thinking* to *learn from reading*.

If at first you are unable to find answers to your questions, do not become discouraged. It takes much practice to be able to turn headings into surface and in-depth questions. If you have done a good job of speculating on what you are looking for, you are quite likely to find it. And when you find the answer to a question, you will know that the idea is an important one. If, however, you did not develop the proper questions, you will be sufficiently interested at this point to be impressed with the information that you do find. Formulating good questions comes with practice.

It is not necessary for you to study the entire chapter all at once. You can take only a few pages at a time if you wish. The amount of material you learn at one time may depend upon how profound or detailed the lesson turns out to be. It may also depend upon what your purpose is for studying it. Must you master it? Or do you need only the main ideas?

Thinking About What You Have Learned

It is not enough to prepare to read by finding out what the lesson is about, formulating questions, and then learn while reading. True, at this point you have *learned*, but now it is necessary for you to *remember* what you have learned. Most forgetting takes place soon after something has been learned; therefore, a review soon after something has been learned is necessary as well as at frequent intervals thereafter. As you review, you will find there are some things you must go back and *relearn*. This doesn't mean that you have a poor memory, because it happens to everyone. However, if you can recite what you have learned perfectly some time after you have learned it, it means that you have *overlearned* — something that is necessary in obtaining good grades in college.

How should you review? First, if you have written in your notebook the questions you have formulated and have found the answers to them, you may record these answers below the questions. This will give you good notes for review. Of course, you will not have written the answers in your notebook until you have turned away from the textbook and recited them in your own words. To review these notes, cover the answer, read the question, and recite the answer aloud. It is easy to uncover the answer and check to see whether or not you were correct.

There are other ways to *think* about what you have learned. When the entire lesson has been studied and you have given some thought to the answers to your questions, you might find someone who would be willing to listen to what you have just learned. The listener will not learn much, but you will have fixed many ideas and concepts more securely in your mind as you told him what you learned from the assignment. If you can't find anyone who is willing to listen to you, you can always go into a room, close the door and repeat to yourself aloud what you have learned. In either case you will have *tested* yourself to see exactly what you have learned. Don't forget that *learning* takes place *while* you read. Everyone is capable of *forgetting;* thus, *review* is necessary for *relearning* and *remembering.*

EXERCISE

1. **Choose a reading assignment made for another class in which you are enrolled.**
2. **Prepare to read the lesson by reading the title, first and last paragraphs, headings, and subheadings, and look at the charts, maps, and graphs.**
3. **Recall what you knew about the subject before you looked at the chapter.**
4. **Turn the headings and subheadings into surface and in-depth questions.**
5. **Write these questions on a sheet of paper, leaving room for answers.**
6. **Read several pages until you have found the answers to eight or nine questions.**
7. **Write the answers to these questions in the space left on your paper for this purpose. Use your own words.**

8. **Continue reading several pages and writing answers to the questions until the entire lesson has been completed.**

9. **Review: Cover your answers, read the questions, and recite answers to test your learning. Check immediately to see if you were correct. If you were not correct, this is the time to relearn.**

10. **Reviewing should be done soon after the lesson has been studied and periodically until the final examination. Daily preparation of this kind will rule out the necessity for cramming before examinations.**

WHAT DID THE LECTURER SAY?

Words are heard with one's ears, but it is necessary to listen to ideas with the mind in order to understand what has been said.

Although many students will say they learn more in a lecture class than they do from studying their textbooks, listening to a lecture can be a difficult task. Listening is an active process requiring full attention and concentration. Students may "miss" a large part of a professor's lecture because they have never learned to *listen*.

Preparing to Listen

The same techniques are involved in listening well that are involved in reading well. You must prepare to listen. The question is: How can you do this when you can't look at the lecturer's headings and subheadings beforehand to find out what the lecture is to be "about"?

You must prepare to listen by knowing something about the subject beforehand so that you can think ahead of and along with the speaker and thus listen actively rather than passively. In addition, if you know something about the subject beforehand, you will have something with which you can associate the new material and thus be better able to understand and remember it.

First of all, the instructor usually gives some kind of title to his lecture. In this case it is necessary for you to *think* about the subject and recall what you already know about this subject. It is not enough to say to yourself, "I learned all about that in high school." You must try to remember *what* you learned about the subject in high school. This will help you to become involved and interested in what the speaker has to say. *Thinking* is an extremely important process in good listening, just as it is in reading.

When you know beforehand the subject of the professor's lecture, it is easy for you to enter the lecture room with information about the subject. If you have no information stored away in your brain, you should go to the library *before* the lecture and obtain information that will help you to understand what the speaker has to say. When you are well enough acquainted with the professor's mode of operation, you can anticipate whether or not the lecture will be on the same material you studied from the textbook. You can always study the lesson beforehand for this kind of lecture class and be informed about the subject before you enter the classroom.

The good student is usually a questioning one. When he has some information on a subject, it is easy for him to raise further questions that the speaker is likely to answer. It is difficult enough to concentrate on a familiar subject, but much more difficult if the subject is an entirely new one. Everyone will agree that students are likely to be more interested in subjects with which they are familiar—and when you are interested, your listening task is much less difficult.

LISTENING TO LEARN

You learn by listening every day in all kinds of situations. On the other hand, you can "turn off" your listening if what you hear is something in which you are not interested or something you do not agree with or understand. That is why it is necessary to listen when you have some knowledge about the subject.

Assuming that you have prepared yourself for the listening experience, one of the most important things you must do is to identify the main ideas of what the lecturer is saying. The first clue will be in the title or the subject of his lecture. Then it takes concentration and clear thinking to sift and sort out main ideas from the details, explanations, and examples.

The good speaker will plan his lecture around several main ideas. As you listen, you must recognize each new idea as well as the technique the speaker is using to make a particular point. Is the speaker supporting each new idea with explanations or examples? More than likely the speaker will come back frequently to his main ideas, and you must be aware of this repetition.

If the instructor has prepared his lecture well, he will begin by introducing the subject, possibly take a stand on the subject, and even give his purpose for choosing this particular subject. Listening to his introduction is like reading the first paragraph of an assigned textbook lesson. Then he will give a point-by-point presentation of the steps in his discussion of the subject. In order to follow the speaker's reasoning as this information is presented, you must listen carefully for words that will show the direction of his thinking. Is the speaker using such words as "furthermore" or "consequently" to show that his thinking is moving forward, or is he using "on the other hand" or "however" to show that he is reversing his thinking? There are many of these transitional words the speaker will use to help to direct your thinking. Everyone would agree that when a driver returns to his parked car and finds a policeman writing out an overtime parking ticket, the driver quickly reverses his thinking when the policeman says, "I was going to give you a ticket, *but* now that you are here, I'll tear it up." The small word "but" made the driver reverse his thinking.

The conclusion of the lecture, of course, pulls all of the speaker's ideas together, and his words are similar to those in the final paragraph of a reading assignment. However, when you listen to a lecture, you cannot hear the summary or conclusion until the end of the lecture, whereas in reading you can read the final paragraph before you study the lesson.

When a professor begins a lecture with, "Today we shall talk about the five good reasons why . . . ," you must "pick out" and remember these five reasons. You must think about them and translate them into your own words and relate them to what you already know about the subject. In other words, you must become so actively involved in the lecture that you will be *learning* as you are *listening*.

When a speaker suggests that an idea is important, you should take his word for it and make special mental note of what is being said. When he gives an example or tells an anecdote to clarify a point, you must listen carefully to the example; however, the example or anecdote is not important in itself. What is important is the idea or concept the speaker is trying to explain. Unfortunately, some students remember the funny story but are unable to remember what point the speaker was trying to make. Here again, it is a good idea for the student to think of this point in his own words and to relate it to what he already knows. Remember, the professor is not likely to include the anecdote or example on his examination.

It is easy for you to "turn off" what you are hearing if it is not what you want to hear. Often a lecturer presents ideas that are diametrically opposed to yours. In such situations it is even more important for you to listen in order to be informed on all sides of a controversial question. As you listen, you must try to understand the lecturer's point of view in order to remember how he feels about the topic, because his ideas will be reflected in the way he scores any examination that is given on the material. If the class discusses the issue at a later date, it is necessary for you to understand the ideas you are going to have to refute if you wish to give your side of the argument.

It is necessary for you to understand every point the professor makes in a lecture. You must understand the organizational pattern of what is said so that you can distinguish between the main ideas and the supporting details. However, it is not enough to understand the organizational pattern and every point that is made. You must also learn to evaluate the information in the light of what you already know about the subject.

Why do students take tape recorders to class? Probably the only reason is to be able to replay the lecture. What a waste of time! You can learn *as* you are listening the first time just as well as when you replay a tape. When you tape a lecture, all you are doing is postponing your learning and wasting your time in class. You are admitting to yourself that you have not yet learned how to listen. The one advantage of a tape is that it can be replayed again and again if the lecture was on a particularly difficult subject. However, few students replay the tapes, and because they have the information on tape they seem to feel they have it in their heads. When you learn to listen, a tape recording of a lecture is usually not necessary.

Remember, a professor is able to present fewer ideas in an hour than a good reader can get from reading a book for the same length of time. Learn to listen actively to what he has to say, and learn *while* you listen.

To be a good listener you must:

1. Prepare to listen by knowing something about the subject.
2. Identify main ideas.
3. Understand relationships of supporting details to the main ideas.
4. Think along with the speaker, anticipating what he will say next.
5. Translate the speaker's ideas into your own words.
6. Evaluate what he has said.

EXERCISE

1. **Prepare to listen to the lecture in one of your other classes by recalling what you already know about the subject.**

2. Raise questions in your mind that you think the speaker might answer in his lecture.

3. Translate the speaker's main ideas into your own words and jot them down in your notebook. Then include the important details that support his main ideas. (Most students should *think more* and *write less* while listening to a lecture.)

4. As you listen, think along with the speaker and anticipate what he will say next.

5. Write a summary of what has been said as soon as possible after the lecture is finished.

CHAPTER
5

Audience
Analysis

George Johnson is a marketing student at a large Midwestern junior college. One Monday his speech assignment in his communication skills course was to tell a story that makes a point. Even before he finished reading the assignment sheet, he remembered a story he had heard a few weeks earlier at a party for members of the school orchestra. It was a funny story at which the audience had been hysterical with laughter, and it made a clear point. He practiced it a few times to get the timing down pat.

On the day the speeches were due, George was the first to volunteer. He walked confidently to the speaker's platform, smiled at his audience, and began. In his introduction he reminded his audience that people often waste time because they become enthusiastic about something and follow through with action before carefully considering the situation. "Let me tell you a story that I think demonstrates the danger of this," he said.

A man who lived in Chicago noticed in the paper that Jascha Heifetz was appearing the next night in Minneapolis. That evening he packed a few things, and the next day gathered his family in the car and headed north. After traveling a few hours, he ran into a violent snowstorm. The further north he traveled, the worse it got. Finally, he hit a slick spot, lost control of his car, and skidded into a ditch. An ambulance came and rushed his injured children and wife to the hospital, but he was determined to go on. He rented a dogsled and continued his journey. About 25 miles out of Minneapolis he lost his sled, but still he staggered on. Finally, he reached the concert hall. Looking at his watch, he saw that in five minutes the concert would begin. He quickly bought a ticket, rushed into the hall, and collapsed exhausted into his seat. As he looked around, he noticed that, except for three other people, the hall was empty. Just then, Mr. Heifetz strode out onto the stage, and announced that since the four people in his audience had shown so much courage in coming out on such a horrible night, he wanted them to be his guests at dinner in his hotel across the street. The other three responded enthusiastically, but the fellow from Chicago said, "Mr. Heifetz, I started out from Chicago this morning with my wife and three children to hear your concert. Halfway here I ran into a ditch and my family was taken to the hospital. But I didn't give up. I hired a dogsled and pushed on. About 25 miles out of town my lead dog took a wrong turn and the sled and dogs plunged over a cliff. I managed to jump clear and came the rest of the way on foot. I haven't eaten a thing since yesterday, and I'd love to be your guest for dinner. But before we go, could you please sing just *one* song?"

George paused for laughter, but only a few in the audience responded. Obviously shaken, he hastily concluded his speech by restating his central idea that a lot of people waste time by not channeling their energies in the right direction, and returned to his seat.

Why did George's speech fail to arouse as much laughter as he anticipated? At the Christmas party it broke everybody up, but when he told it in class it was a flop. Was it his timing? His personality? What went wrong?

The answer is simple. George was the victim of a lack of audience consciousness. Many of those in George's communication skills class didn't know something vital to the humor of the story, that Jascha Heifetz is a world renowned *violinist*, not a singer. The musicians knew who Heifetz was and laughed; many of George's audience did not know and were confused.

One crucial step in the preparation of both writing and speech is audience consciousness, an aspect too often neglected by writers and speakers. Audience consciousness means that you prepare your message and manner of presentation with your audience in mind. George didn't think of his audience when he chose his story. Chapter 1 states that the audience is a necessary part of communication. If there is no audience, or if the audience fails to understand the message, communication does not take place. To prepare an audience-centered communication, ask yourself the following questions.

WHY HAVE I CHOSEN THIS SUBJECT?

You should choose a subject that you find interesting, because the more interested *you* are in a topic, the better are your chances of maintaining the attention of your audience, and the more knowledge you are likely to have of your subject. Knowledge of your subject is imperative; a good job on a paper or speech requires that you know what you are talking about.

Choosing the right subject can make the rest of your preparation much easier. A good technique for identifying topics related to your own interests and knowledge is called *brainstorming*. List on a piece of paper as many potential subjects as you can. In searching for topics ask yourself: "What work experience do I have? What are my skills? My hobbies? What are my favorite pastimes? What do I like to read about? What do I talk about with my friends?" Write down the answers, and after you have filled the page, place a check next to the topics you find particularly interesting, about which you are knowledgeable, or which might inspire you to do research. Choose the one which interests you most.

WHAT ARE MY QUALIFICATIONS
FOR CHOOSING THIS SUBJECT?

It is important that you examine your qualifications for dealing with a particular subject. Are you qualified because of background or skill? Do you speak from personal experience? Can you offer your audience any credentials to show that what you have to say is reliable? A speech by a member of the school hockey team on buying the best ice skates for your money will probably be well received by his classmates. Similarly, an essay on the perils of combat by a decorated former serviceman carries the weight of experience. If you write or speak as a nonexpert, you will have to prove the reliability of your information. If you have special knowledge or experience, indicate this to your audience.

WHAT IS THE SPECIFIC PURPOSE
OF MY COMMUNICATION?

After you have decided on your subject, you must develop a statement of specific purpose. Write your purpose as an infinitive phrase. Your statement should clearly identify your general purpose as being to inform, to entertain, to convince, to actuate, or to reinforce.

Formulate your purpose statement by considering exactly what you wish to accomplish. You must know your goal before you can plan the best way to achieve it. Most subjects can be developed in different ways in accord with various general purposes. For example, suppose that, because of both interest and knowledge, you choose pollution as your topic. You could write a statement of specific intent for each of the following:

To inform: To explain to my audience the different types of pollution.

To entertain: To entertain my audience by playing and singing Tom Lehrer's song "Pollution."

To convince: To convince my audience that this nation must reorder its priorities to deal with pollution.

To actuate: To persuade my audience to begin collecting their cans and bottles for our local recycling project.

To reinforce: To make my audience more vividly aware of the spectre of a world killed by pollution.

WHAT RESPONSE CAN I REASONABLY EXPECT FROM MY AUDIENCE?

The success or failure of any communication must be measured in terms of audience response. The TV series that fails to entertain is soon cancelled, the unsuccessful salesman will be out of a job, the textbook that is difficult to understand is seldom reordered, and the uninspiring preacher speaks to an empty church. You will communicate more effectively if you plan your message with a specific, realistic audience response in mind.

Some responses are particularly difficult to achieve. A lack of time might prevent you from teaching your audience a complicated technique, such as giving a permanent or using the slide rule. Your audience might not have the background or experience that will enable you to teach them how to replace the bearings in an alternator or sew a collar on a dress. In addition, the attitude of your audience might be so opposed to your subject that they become impossible to approach; an example would be trying to promote George Wallace for President at a black student rally. In such cases the communicator must choose another, more realistic purpose.

The case of Ralph Smith provides an example of how consideration of audience response can help a communicator determine purpose. Ralph, assigned a demonstration speech in his communications class, chose to demonstrate how to fillet a fish, something he enjoyed doing and did well. He jotted down his specific purpose: To teach my audience how to fillet a fish. Then he considered the specific response of his audience to this purpose. In order for his speech to succeed, his audience would have to know how to fillet a fish when he was through. Ralph had learned to fillet fish from his Uncle George, who had first shown him how to do it and then guided him step by step through the procedure. If he wanted to use the same approach with his audience, he would have to give them each a fish and a filleting knife, which seemed impractical. He decided instead to show his audience how to prepare fish for frying, with an emphasis on how filleting the fish made them much more pleasant to both cook and eat. The result, he decided, would be to stimulate his audience's interest in learning how to fillet fish. Ralph rewrote his specific purpose and continued preparing his speech.

WHO EXACTLY IS MY AUDIENCE?

A surprising number of communications fail because the author is not entirely clear as to the exact composition of his audience. Take Fred Johnson, for many years personnel director of a small manufacturing plant. Fred came home one night greatly disappointed because he had been passed over for promotion, and not for the first time. He called his brother-in-law, a golf partner of the company president, and asked him to find out why.

As part of his job, Fred sent out directives to plant employees. Since these were going to ordinary workmen, he was not overly concerned with style or correctness. What Fred failed to realize was that every directive sent to the workers also went to the plant manager, who read it and put it in the files. Whenever an opportunity for advancement occurred that involved Fred, those directives would be examined, followed by the comment, "How can we promote someone who communicates so poorly?" Fred paid a high price for not knowing his audience.

Before you begin to prepare your communication, consider who is included in your audience. Your classmates? Your teacher? Yourself? In this course, you will probably be speaking primarily to your classmates, so you should learn all you can about them. Listen to them carefully, make note of their interests, consider their attitudes, wants, and needs, and then develop your message accordingly.

Most students, unless specifically instructed otherwise, direct their classroom writing assignments to the instructor who gives them their grade. As long as you are not prevented from writing about subjects which you find stimulating and which are within your experience, writing to your instructor offers two distinct advantages. First, you are writing to a trained reader who can evaluate your work critically and accurately. Second, you can develop a clear picture of this reader. Your instructor will give you specific guidelines as to the standards he expects in style and grammar. Furthermore, his lectures and comments will reveal which characteristics of writing he feels are particularly important.

Regardless of whether you are writing or speaking to your classmates, your instructor, or others, strive for a correct and appropriate style. You insult both your audience and yourself when you attempt to communicate material that has not been carefully prepared.

WILL MY AUDIENCE FIND THIS SUBJECT INTERESTING?

All too often communication fails because it has not been developed to interest the reader or listener to whom it is directed. You know how hard it is to pay attention to a speech on a subject of no particular interest to you, or to an essay that you find dull or boring. The harder you have to work to pay attention, the less chance you have of getting something out of the material. Your job as a writer or speaker is to develop your material so that your audience will find it interesting. You do this naturally when communicating with someone you know quite well.

Suppose that the college you are attending is out of town and you want to write a letter home telling what you have been doing for the last few months. What you write will vary considerably, depending on your reader. You might write about the difference between college and high school or about the pains and pleasures of being on your own to a brother or sister who will soon be entering college. The letter you send to an ex-classmate might deal exclusively with your love life or other extracurricular activities. Your parents might get a letter telling about your health, your grades, and your finances. In each case, you wrote what you felt your reader, a person you knew well, would find interesting. But how can you tell what would be of interest to strangers?

If you are familiar with the subject you have chosen, you should be able to make an educated guess. Suppose that you choose to write or speak about one of your two hobbies, coin collecting or antique cars. Your experience tells you which of these topics would be most interesting to a general audience. The majority of your friends have shown more interest in your antique cars than they have in your coins. Some of them have even changed the subject when you asked if they had seen your coin collection. Obviously, a general audience would have greater initial interest in your cars.

This does not mean that you couldn't choose to speak about coin collecting. But if you do, you must build your audience's interest to gain and maintain their attention. You might begin by telling of the time you put a quarter in a coke machine and received as change a dime worth eight hundred dollars. The thought that your knowledge as a coin collector brought you that much profit from a dime that had probably been handled by hundreds of others would be quite an attention-getter.

HOW MUCH DOES THE AUDIENCE ALREADY KNOW ABOUT MY SUBJECT?

Too technical an approach could leave your audience thoroughly confused; merely repeating what they already know will bore them. If you know that your audience has some knowledge in the subject area you have chosen, you must plan your communication accordingly. Perhaps you will deal in depth with a specific area of the subject, or you might select interesting details that are not generally known.

If your audience has little or no knowledge of your subject, you must explain unfamiliar concepts and terminology. When you are uncertain of the extent of their knowledge, treat your audience as intelligent readers or listeners with the same information as the general public has of your subject.

Mary Evans had been assigned a three-to-five-minute visual aid speech for her communications class. Because she was an enthusiastic and skillful bowler, Mary decided to give a speech on bowling. She considered teaching her audience how to keep score, but rejected this idea after estimating that approximately one fourth of a typical audience would already know how to keep score. Even if the percentage were less, she reasoned, those who did know would find her speech dull and uninteresting. She decided instead to deliver a speech on the benefits of bowling, involving details designed to interest both the bowlers and nonbowlers in her audience.

WHAT CHARACTERISTICS OF THE AUDIENCE
SHOULD I CONSIDER IN PREPARING MY SUBJECT?

Education

The educational level of your audience should determine your word choice. The word "communication" comes from the Latin *communicare*, meaning to share what is common. When you communicate to others, you share ideas with them through a common vocabulary. You must write or speak to an audience in familiar words that they can understand. For example, you probably wouldn't explain the process of circulation to your ten-year-old brother with the same words that you

"LIKE YOUR KIDNEY WANTS TO SPLIT THE SCENE, AND YOUR LIVER WON'T DO ITS THING"

Courtesy of Medical World News.

would use with your zoology instructor, because of the limitations of the former's vocabulary.

Consider the vocabulary of your reader or listener when developing your material. Omit words or phrases which might be unfamiliar. If you have the choice of two words with the same meaning, choose the more common one. Your purpose is to communicate, not to impress.

No matter what the composition of your audience, stick to your own vocabulary. Do not inject idiomatic expressions that you would not ordinarily use into your speech or paper to gain effect. Your audience might interpret this as condescension or insincerity, and react unfavorably.

Always treat your classmates as intelligent people with good vocabularies. Unless you are dealing with an unfamiliar subject, present information to them on the level you would want them to present it to you.

Age

Knowledge of the age of your audience can often help you in determining how to handle your subject. As a rule (although not exclusively), young people tend to be more liberal than older people, more willing to try change or to take a chance. They are also usually more physically active, inclined toward being participators rather than spectators. Your approach to selling people on the idea of investing in the stock market would take these factors into consideration. You would probably be wise to appeal to older people with a list of dependable blue chip stocks which offer little risk, while for a younger audience you might choose the more glamorous speculative stocks which could double or triple overnight. Similarly, when talking about a particular sport, you might treat it as a participation sport for the younger, more active audience, and as a spectator sport for an older group. When the age of your audience is varied, you must deal with the topic in more general terms.

Special Interests

Members of an audience frequently have a common interest. They might belong to the same organization or club, be in a similar business or profession, or have gathered together out of mutual concern for a particular problem. You should attempt to determine what these interests are and relate your ideas and supporting material to them.

Consider the common interests of your communications class. As college students, everyone in the class is probably interested in such social problems as poverty, pollution, drugs, and the arms race. In preparing your communication you must be sensitive to the attitudes and needs of your audience regarding these problems; you must want to communicate your ideas about finding solutions.

As a college student yourself, you are aware of other interests shared by your classmates. Perhaps the basketball team is enjoying a winning season, or an important social event is coming up. Keep these interests in mind as you prepare your communication.

IS MY AUDIENCE'S ATTITUDE TOWARD MY SUBJECT FAVORABLE, INDIFFERENT, OR OPPOSED?

An Audience That Is Favorable

People tend to be less critical when they agree with the position of the communicator. Consequently, a favorable audience is likely to be more tolerant of weaknesses in your writing or speech and be willing to accept your evidence. After all, you don't have to prove anything to someone who agrees with you.

This does not mean that writing or speaking to a favorable audience does not offer challenge. The chief goal of communicating to a favorable audience is to reinforce their positive attitudes. If they enjoy guitar playing, the more effectively you entertain them with your guitar, the more successful you will be. If they are looking forward to receiving information from you, their satisfaction will be measured by how clearly you can write out your explanation or directions. The more effectively you can stimulate and intensify their positive attitudes, the more likely you will be to move them to action. One of the world's foremost satirists, Art Buchwald, writes a syndicated column for over 250 American newspapers. He writes out of Washington, D.C., and although his subjects range from space to college graduation, much of his humor is focused on American politics. His readers would be considered a favorable audience whose positive attitudes are reinforced by their responses to the column. A typical Buchwald column lampoons the image-concept in politics:

Jimmy Carter's Walk Wasn't the First

Everyone in Washington is still talking about President and Mrs. Carter's walk from the Capitol to the White House, and Carter watchers are still asking, "Why did he do it?" The obvious answer is, "Because it was there."

The president made the walk in 35 minutes and 10 seconds—a new world record for a head of state. He would have probably even broken that if Amy hadn't had to stop and tie her bootlaces along the way.

This, incidentally, was not the first attempt by anyone to walk from the Capitol to the White House. In 1957, Mr. and Mrs. Henry Gerard of Tampa, Fla., started out from the door of the Senate building and were making excellent time until they were mugged at 7th St. and Pennsylvania Ave.

In 1961, Ezra Beatleman of Racine, Wis., decided to see if he could make it. Following almost exactly the route the Carters took along Pennsylvania Ave. in the middle of the street, Beatleman was almost halfway there when he was hit by a Washington Express Bus and thrown through a window of the Post Office Building. He spent three months at George Washington Hospital and upon his release was given 30 days in jail for jaywalking.

This discouraged people for a little while from walking along Pennsylvania Ave. until 1967 when four Vietnam protesters decided to try it. They were making good time until they passed the FBI building. J. Edgar Hoover happened to be looking out his window. He flew into a rage and 200 FBI men surrounded the protesters and charged them with walking by the FBI building without a permit.

In 1970, Gerald Timmons of Chevy Chase, Md., had a few drinks, and when he couldn't find a taxi he decided to walk the famous route taken by the Carters. Unfortunately, he chose to do it during rush hour and it took an hour to get across 14th St. and Pennsylvania. This discouraged him, and though he was within a few blocks of his goal, he said the hell with it, and stopped into Bassin's bar where he spent the rest of the evening.

Five Cubans hired by the Committee to Re-elect the President were the next people to try the walk. They made it to the White House without incident where they received orders to continue walking on to the Watergate headquarters of the Democratic Party where they were captured.

Had they not stopped at the White House to rest, their walk would have never been traced to President Richard Nixon's staff and Nixon might have been the man last Thursday to turn over the keys of 1600 Pennsylvania Ave. to the Carters.

The most interesting attempt to walk from the Capitol was made by Rep. Wilbur Mills and his party who decided to do it in October, 1974. Mills got off to a good start, but he took a wrong turn at 8th St. and wound up at the Tidal Basin instead. Since it was 2 o'clock in the morning and a dark night, he mistakenly thought he was at the White House.

He suggested to one of his party that she take a swim in the White House swimming pool. Much to his chagrin, he discovered they weren't at the White House, and everyone knows what this simple mistake cost the Arkansas congressman.

When President Carter decided to take the walk, his aides and the Secret Service tried to talk him out of it. But he was adamant and told them, "I have to show the country I can walk and chew gum at the same time."

With permission of the writer, Art Buchwald

Most persuasion to actuate is directed at audiences favorable to the course of action proposed. The clergyman who urges his congregation to demonstrate a positive witness in their actions during the week, the football coach who fires up his team during the half, and the letter asking for a donation to a destitute Indian village are all addressing audiences likely to be predisposed to act in the manner requested. The persuaders don't need to use logical proof to support their appeals because the favorable audience has already intellectually agreed to the desirability of the course of action. This audience is likely to respond to appeals to those motives and attitudes which relate to the motives of approval. Note how the letter on page 82 directs itself at this motive, even promising to put the donor's name on an "Honor Roll" if he contributes.

An Audience That Is Indifferent

If you believe that your audience is indifferent to your subject, your job is to stimulate their interest. You may do this either by getting and holding their attention with a fresh imaginative approach, or by demonstrating the importance of the subject to them, or by a combination of both. This action should be taken immediately, in your introduction. Use the various attention-getting devices (explained in Chapter 6); explain how your audience is affected by your subject, or if they have something to gain by paying attention to it. As you can see, attention is of prime concern with an indifferent audience.

Brian Murphy, a staff writer for *Diablo Valley College Enquirer,* writes about what he feels is a significant issue, the fact that parents in the community are concerned about the drug problem, but no one does anything worthwhile about one of the causes—the lack of activities for young people. In order to awaken his readers (both the young people and their parents) to the seriousness of this inaction, he paints a shocking word picture of the variety of things young people can do at a "party."

Drug Culture Alive, but Sick

What's it like trying to grow in a society that takes Excedrin for headaches, Geritol for tired blood, Doan's Pills for those nagging backaches, Alka Selzer for indigestion, Sleep-Eze for insomnia, and Haley's M.O. for occasional irregularity, then you are arrested for smoking grass instead of drinking Hamm's beer, for dropping bennies and sniffing co-

224 *Illini Union · Urbana, Illinois*

UNIVERSITY OF ILLINOIS FOUNDATION

November 1970

Who cares?

You might think that with over 150,000 alumni of the University of Illinois we wouldn't care that you aren't among the supporters of the Foundation's Annual Fund for 1970.

But we do!

We wonder why you have felt your help isn't needed. And I guess the fault lies with us. Somewhere along the line we haven't emphasized enough just how important your gift can be. No matter what the size.

Take, for example, $1. If you, and every other alumnus, would slip a single dollar bill into the enclosed reply envelope the result would be overwhelming. Over 20 important University projects that directly benefit students and faculty would progress at the rate of $150,000! A small fortune by any standard.

So, you see, it's not always the size of your gift that matters. It's your decision to do something now that counts. Your positive action, combined with a similar action by other alumni, will make possible scholarships and research. Student loans. Library collections. Rehabilitation of physically handicapped students. And many other alumni supported activities.

A dime a day. For just ten days. Please care that much.

Mark the University project you personally want to see accomplished and mail your contribution in the same envelope. Today, if you can.

Sincerely yours,

Joseph W. Skehen
Executive Director

JWS:llv

P. S. We'll show others that you want to help make a great university even greater by publishing your name in the 1970 "Honor Roll" of contributors to the University of Illinois Foundation. You'll receive your copy early next year.

Used with the permission of the University of Illinois Foundation caine instead of taking No Doz or Vivarin, for dropping reds instead of taking Sleep-Eze or Sominex, and for escaping reality for dropping acid, and mescaline instead of drinking too many cocktails.

Parents complain about the terrible drug problem in the community, but nobody wonders why the problem exists.

Let's face it, just what exciting and interesting things are there for young people to do in the community?

Well there are about 18 different movie theatres in the area. Going to the movies every Friday and Saturday night gets to be a drag and expensive. Concord has a teen center, but that's only open till 10 p.m. Pleasant Hill, Lafayette, and Walnut Creek have virtually nothing for young people to do on weekends.

Danville has finally started a teen center. You can listen to folk music on Friday and Saturday nights till midnight. YOU CAN ALSO PLAY POOL AND PING PONG.

I have discussed things that you can do, and things that some people do. The following is what a large number of people do on Friday and Saturday nights because of nonexistent alternatives.

"Parties" have the most variety of things that young people can do. You can go to a "party" and:

A) Drink beer, wine, or hard liquor.
B) Smoke grass, or hash.
C) Drink beer, wine, and drop "Reds."
D) Drop "Bennies," or sniff cocaine.
E) Drop "acid" or mescaline.
F) All mentioned above (and it happens).

Parties these days sure seem to have a great deal to offer providing that you're NOT WILLING to suffer the consequences, not interested in rational thinking, and not interested in using your imagination. So if none of this appeals to you, there you are sitting at home watching TV.

From all of this you can guess how CONCERNED the community is about its young people. Apparently parents and the community at large don't care about people under 21. By doing virtually nothing, they are advocating and promoting the use of alcohol, and drugs. (What else is there to do?)

WHAT WOULD HAPPEN IF

What would happen if a community decided that it's not really a good thing to promote the use of drugs by their young people because of nothing better to do on weekends? And then decided to find out what young people would like to do? And then decided that those things were better to do than to use drugs?

But all that takes a great deal of time, energy, and money. I'm sure that the community has better things to do. They must, otherwise they would have done something about it a long time ago.

The community and law enforcement agencies are very reluctant to set up drug rehabilitation centers. Could you imagine the opposition to setting up programs that would serve as alternatives to drug abuse?

With permission of Brian Murphy and the *Diablo Valley College Enquirer.*

In this article the writer is appealing to two separate audiences: (1) the establishment which doesn't address itself to the prevention and treatment of drug abuse, and (2) the students who unwisely choose drugs as an alternative to boredom.

An Audience That Is Opposed

In most cases, the hardest audience to deal with is one that disagrees with your point of view or dislikes your subject. Who hasn't spent hours arguing about politics or religion only to find himself even more convinced that he was right and the other fellow wrong?

It is difficult to convince a person to change a point of view or an attitude that may have taken him years to form. Studies indicate that there is little change in viewpoint among those who listen to or read things with which they strongly disagree. By the time a person reaches adulthood, many of his attitudes are pretty well fixed.

Fortunately, occasions are rare when a speaker or writer must address an entire audience opposed to his viewpoint or subject. It is difficult, for example, to picture George Wallace addressing a group of militant blacks on what America has to offer them, or to imagine an article in the *Catholic Herald Citizen* on the newest techniques in abortion. Perhaps the best example of successfully changing the viewpoint of a hostile audience is found in *Julius Caesar*, by William Shakespeare. Mark Anthony faces an audience which has been convinced by Brutus that Caesar was an ambitious tyrant who was justifiably killed for the good of Rome. He takes on the seemingly impossible job of persuading the Roman citizens that Brutus, whom they hold in high regard, is actually a despicable assassin.

Anthony begins by establishing a common ground with his audience. They are his "friends," his "fellow Romans," his "countrymen." He has not come to praise Caesar, whom the crowd hates, but to bury him as any friend would do. (His audience can understand this kind of friendship.) He shows respect for the audience's friendship toward Brutus by speaking of the "noble" Brutus. At this point, Anthony raises the first question he wishes his audience to consider. "Brutus hath told you that Caesar was ambitious. If it were so, it was a grievous fault. And grievously hath Caesar answered it."

Anthony: *Friends, Romans, Countrymen, lend me your ears; I come to bury Caesar, not to praise him. The evil that men do lives after them; The good is oft interred with their bones. So let it be with Caesar. The noble Brutus hath told you Caesar was ambitious. If it were so, it was a grievous fault, And grievously hath Caesar answered it. Here under leave of Brutus and the rest (for Brutus is an honor-*

The issue is, *was* Caesar ambitious? At this point, the crowd is convinced he was.

Anthony acknowledges that Brutus permitted him to speak. He calls Brutus an "honorable" man. All those who were involved in the assassination were "honorable" men. Anthony's tone of voice when he says "honorable" should suggest that he might mean just the opposite. Have you ever said one thing and meant another? Have you ever asked someone for a favor and received the response, "I don't mind," when you could tell by the tone of voice that the person really did mind? The *way* you say something can communicate a great deal to others.

Anthony begins questioning whether Caesar actually was ambitious. Brutus said he was, but what are the facts? If Caesar filled the treasury with money, where is the personal gain? If Caesar refused a kingly crown, where is the ambition? Note the reference to the personal experience of the listeners in the words, "You all did see. . . ." "*Brutus* tells you that Caesar was ambitious," says Anthony, "but you all have seen that he wasn't."

Notice that Anthony is still careful not to say anything against Brutus. Even though the audience can see the weakness in Brutus' argument, Anthony still avoids attacking him. After all, Brutus was held in high regard by the crowd for his patriotism and self-sacrifice, and there still may be respect in the minds of some.

The response of the audience onstage should indicate that Anthony has changed their point of view. Although Brutus convinced them that Caesar was murdered to protect them from his ambition to become a dictator and make them his slaves, the fact that Caesar never profited from his position and three times refused the crown proves that he wasn't ambitious. Anthony clearly establishes his image as a faithful friend by what he says and by what he does. He even weeps for Caesar. The crowd responds,

able man; So are they all, all honorable men), Come I to speak in Caesar's funeral.

He was my friend, faithful and just to me; but Brutus says he was ambitious, and Brutus is an honorable man. He hath brought many captives home to Rome, whose ransoms did the general coffers fill. Did this in Caesar seem ambitious? When that the poor have cried, Caesar hath wept; Ambition should be made of sterner stuff. Yet Brutus says he was ambitious; and Brutus is an honorable man. You all did see that on the Lupercal I thrice presented him a kingly crown, which he did thrice refuse. Was this ambition? Yet Brutus says he was ambitious and sure he is an honorable man. I speak not to disprove what Brutus spoke, but here I am to speak what I know. You all did love him once, not without cause. What cause withholds you then to mourn for him? O judgment, thou art fled to brutish beasts, and men have lost their reason! Bear with me. My heart is in the coffin there with Caesar,

"There's not a nobler man in Rome than Anthony." From this point on, Mark Anthony is speaking to friendly citizens who have been won over to his point of view.

and I must pause till it come back to me.

This speech exemplifies two useful suggestions for dealing with audiences opposed to your subject or viewpoint: (1) establish a common ground with the audience, and (2) clear up any lack of understanding or misinformation your audience may have about your point of view or subject.

Mary Smith, a junior college freshman, used a common ground approach in preparing a speech to inform on one of her favorite subjects, opera. She had found that most of her classmates were apathetic or even hostile about her subject. One fellow named Ron intended to cut class on the day of her speech because opera, especially Wagnerian opera, Mary's favorite, really "turned him off."

On the day she delivered her speech Mary identified with many in her audience by beginning:

> You know, like many of you I was really turned off by opera until two years ago, when I found out an interesting fact. I didn't like opera because I didn't know anything about it. Well, ever since then the more I got to know about it, the more I got to like it. I'm sure when you get to know enough about it, you'll like it too.

Mary realized that she needed a fresh, imaginative approach to hold the attention of her audience. She prepared carefully and thoughtfully, and delivered to the class a humorous plot summary of Wagner's opera, *Tannhauser*, which ended to even Ron's delight with the heroine getting stabbed right between the two big trees.

Mary took what many in her audience thought was a dull, boring topic and made it exciting and interesting. She used humor, novelty, conflict, and suspense to hold their attention, and the result was a successful speech.

The second suggestion for dealing with an adverse audience is to clear up any lack of understanding or misinformation they may have about your subject or viewpoint. When using this approach, the first thing you must consider is why your audience is opposed to your subject. Sometimes people form incorrect attitudes or stereotypes on the basis of inaccurate or insufficient evidence. In such cases, your job is to do what the reader or listener has not done for himself—give him the facts.

The letter to the editor below was written in response to a newspaper editorial criticizing a student protest-march against the building of a nuclear power plant in the writer's home town. The student-writer points up some facts about student protests of the past in order to giver her readers the "real picture."

To the *Times:*

To characterize the recent protest by students against building a nuclear power plant in our town as an example of "students getting rid of their excess energy by bucking the establishment" is both inaccurate and unfair.

The present protest movement was begun as a joint effort on the part of area residents and students who were concerned about the dangers that a nuclear power plant would present to our community. The fact that students have become more militant is due to the feeling of helplessness expressed by the area residents with whom they were aligned.

Traditionally youth-student movements have been characterized by selflessness and idealism. This is particularly true of the protests that students have made on campuses around the world. During its infancy, when the civil rights movement got little support from their elders, college students responded with sit-ins and marches. While a majority of older Americans remained silent about the war in Vietnam, students protested—some at the cost of their lives.

It was the student who led the fight for freedom in Hungary, Chile, the Sudan, South Africa, and Uganda. And, it will be the student of the future who strikes out against injustice, fights for an ideal, and struggles to improve the lot of his fellowman.

The point is this. Whatever you think about an issue, don't attack student involvement with it as being frivolous. The evidence is clear. The facts are that the protests of youth—especially college students— have played a significant part in social changes throughout history.

With permission of the writer, Betty White

In order to communicate successfully, it is necessary that you understand your audience. The car salesman who can size up a husband and wife who have come to buy a new car, and determine which of them makes the decisions in that family, knows which sales pitch to use; the politician who can tell the voter what he wants to hear and still maintains his credibility will stand the best chance of getting elected; the charitable organization that can prick the conscience of the person to whom its appeal is made will get the best response.

Remember, before you begin writing or speaking, consider your audience. Put yourself in their shoes. Try to understand them. If you don't, you are liable to wind up writing or talking to yourself.

The accompanying samples of the audience analysis form and au-

---

AUDIENCE ANALYSIS FORM

Name_____   Date_____

Title of Speech or Essay_____

(Answer each question completely)

THE COMMUNICATOR   THE AUDIENCE

1. Why have I chosen this subject?   5. Who is my audience?

                                        6. Will my audience find this subject
                                           interesting?

2. What qualifies me to deal with
   this subject?

                                        7. What is the audience's probable
                                           knowledge of my subject?

THE MESSAGE

3. What is my specific purpose?   8. What characteristics of my audience
                                           should I consider in preparing my
                                           subject?

4. What response can I reasonably
   expect?

                                        9. Is my audience's attitude toward
                                           this subject favorable, indifferent,
                                           or opposed?

---

dience analysis evaluation form are designed to help you become more aware of your audience. When preparing your speech or paper, fill out a copy of the audience analysis form. Have your listeners or readers fill out copies of the evaluation form to give you feedback as to how successful you were in judging and adapting to your audience.

AUDIENCE ANALYSIS EVALUATION

Name_____

1. What was the communicator's subject?

2. How interesting was this subject to you?

    |___|___|___|___|___|
    low   high

3. How useful was this subject to you?

    |___|___|___|___|___|
    low   high

4. How effectively did the communicator get attention during introduction?

    |___|___|___|___|___|
    low   high

5. How much preparation was put into this communication?

    |___|___|___|___|___|
    low   high

6. What was the communicator's specific purpose? (One simple, declarative sentence)

7. How effective was the conclusion to the communication?

    |___|___|___|___|___|
    low   high

8. How well did the communicator accomplish his purpose?

    |___|___|___|___|___|
    low   high

COMMENTS:

EXERCISES

1. Prepare a list of specific topics which should be of particular interest to your classmates.

2. Prepare a list of specific topics which should be particularly useful to your audience.

3. Select five different magazines. Analyze these to determine the characteristics of the audience to which they appeal.

4. Analyze a speech or written communication that you have recently heard or read. To what audience was it directed? How carefully were they considered? Was it effective?

5. Prepare an analysis of your class as an audience. In what ways are they similar? In what ways do they differ?

6. Choose a general topic you are qualified to deal with. Write out a specific purpose statement for a communication to inform, entertain, convince, actuate, and reinforce.

7. List five well-known participation sports, then guess how many in your class have engaged in them. Survey the class to check your answer.

8. Pick a highly controversial statement. Estimate how many in your class would agree with the statement, be indifferent to it, or opposed to it. Survey the class to check your answer.

CHAPTER 6

Attention

OBJECTIVES

After studying this chapter you should be able to:
1. Explain how emphasis and variety add interest to communication.
2. Describe the relationship between utility, interest, and attention.
3. List seven factors of attention.
4. Explain how attention factors can be used to make your communications more interesting.
5. Explain the rules for using humor as an effective attention factor.
6. Include effective attention factors in your communications.

An old Arkansas farmer once bought a mule that was supposed to be the fastest in the whole state of Arkansas. When paying for it, he was told that if he wanted the best possible results from the mule, he should treat it with kindness. So he took the animal home, fed it a hearty supper and bedded it down on fresh straw in a clean stall. The next morning he walked the mule to the field and hitched it to a plow. "Let's go, friend," he said in his most pleasant tone. But the mule didn't budge. Well, the farmer was prepared, and he reached into his overalls and pulled out an apple—and some sugar—and a turnip—but the only thing that moved on the mule was its mouth. This so infuriated the farmer that he stalked back to the house to call the "S.O.B." who had swindled him. Before the telephone wires had cooled off, the fellow who had sold him the mule arrived and headed for the field with the farmer at his heels. On the way, he picked up a big stick and when he reached the mule he let him have it right between the ears. Then he whispered, "Come on, pal; let's plow the field," and the mule took off like a race horse. The farmer stood shaking his head in disbelief. "That's gotta be the fastest mule in the world," he said, "but you told me he had to be treated with kindness." "He does," said the other fellow, "but you have to get his attention first."

This anecdote points out a fundamental principle in communication—to communicate effectively you must have the attention of your audience. Without attention, communication does not exist. However, don't be misled by the way in which attention was achieved in the story. People, unlike mules, are usually unenthusiastic in their response when they are forced to pay attention.

Consider your own experience. Have you ever watched an unimaginative, poorly directed educational film because you were told there would be an exam on it? Have you listened to an uninteresting lecture because you knew the contents had an effect on your grade? How much did you learn in that course? How much do you remember? In both cases you were, in effect, forced to pay attention. Did it pay off?

These are some of the questions with which people in education are becoming increasingly concerned. They have come to realize that "hitting the student over the head" results in short-term learning which is soon forgotten. They have found that attention given on the basis of interest, rather than on the basis of reward or punishment, produces more lasting results.

MAKING YOUR MATERIAL INTERESTING

As speakers and writers you can help hold your audience's attention by making your material clear, vivid, and, above all, interesting. Two rhetorical devices which will help you to achieve these goals in your communication are *variety* and *emphasis*. Mass communicators make use of variety and emphasis to sell their products. The increase in volume when a TV commerical comes on, the vivid contrasting colors of billboards and magazine advertising, the searchlights and fluttering pennants heralding the opening of a new service station, and the sound truck blaring out the qualifications of a political candidate are all directed at capturing attention.

Variety

If you want to be a more interesting speaker or writer, use a variety of sentence patterns (simple, compound, complex, compound-complex), rather than an endless string of simple sentences. Unless your communication contains a combination of effective sentence types, it will be monotonous. In Chapter 8 we discuss a number of ways to achieve variety in expressing your ideas. Become familiar with them.

Like any skill, effective communication takes hard work. If you wanted to become a good golfer, you would learn the fundamentals, do a lot of practicing, and take every opportunity to watch professionals in action. The same procedure holds true for writing and speaking. If you become aware of how professional writers and speakers organize their ideas in meaningful, animated, interesting ways, you will be able to apply these standards to improve your own writing and speaking.

A speaker can achieve variety in his delivery as well as in the language he uses. You have had occasion to listen to a great many lectures by instructors of varying quality. Discounting the subject matter, most of us prefer to listen to the instructor who speaks in a pleasant, conversational style, who talks with you rather than to you. The key to conversational style is speaking in a natural manner. In everyday conversation a person speaks with various inflections to express his true feelings. His voice rises when he says "What a doll!" and falls as he says "What a drag." Our vocal patterns vary to suit the exact meaning we intend to convey. We give little thought to the way in which we say something when we talk to our friends, but in a public speaking situation we get uptight. We are suddenly aware that people are forming opinions about what we say and how we say it. We become conscious of our voices, our physical appearance, and of the words we are using. The result is that we take the variety out of our voices. Unless we can maintain the vocal patterns which are natural to our conversation, we convey words (instead of meaning) in a flat and colorless way.

One of the easiest ways to achieve variety in speech is to vary the speed at which you speak. The average public speaker talks at the rate of about 120 words a minute, but you shouldn't maintain a constant rate throughout the speech. Sometimes you might speak 80 words a minute, and at other times 160 words a minute. An important idea might be spoken slowly, an exciting story told with enthusiastic speed. A good rule is to speak more slowly at the beginning of your speech, so that the audience can become accustomed to your style of speaking. Then, as you warm up to the occasion, you can quicken your pace.

Emphasis

Emphasis is achieved in both writing and speaking by stressing important words and ideas. In speech, we emphasize ideas not only with the words we choose, but also with facial expression, tone of voice, and use of pause, volume, intensity, and gesture. Have you ever had a parent or friend tell you that he didn't mind your going somewhere when his facial expression or tone of voice told you otherwise? You can tell when a person is really concerned by the intensity with which he says something, his increase in volume, or the way he gestures. Therefore, if you want to highlight a particular point for your audience, you must emphasize it through voice and gesture.

Remember that a great many things are conveyed by a shrug of the shoulders, a nod of the head, a look of annoyance, or a pleasant smile.

The next time you are engaged in enthusiastic conversation with your friends, make note of their gestures and facial expressions. If you can transfer your animation and physical expression in informal conversation to your public speaking, you will be more interesting and enjoyable to listen to and to watch.

The use of pause is a particularly effective way of gaining emphasis. Used before an important idea, it says to the audience, "Pay close attention to what is coming next." A pause after an important idea gives the audience a chance to reflect on what was said. Its effectiveness as an attention-getting device can be judged from your own experience. Why do some of us interlace our comments with "ah" or "er" when searching for what to say next? Because we feel that an unfilled pause will call attention to our lack of fluency. However, that solution is more troublesome than the original problem, because the "ah" and "er" become part of our speech pattern and inhibit us from using pause at all. Be aware that a pause *does* call attention to itself, and use it to emphasize your important ideas.

Attaining emphasis in writing is more of a problem. The inexperienced writer often attempts to indicate emphasis with frequent use of intensifiers, exclamation points, underlining, and capitalizing. Perhaps you have written or read a letter that attempts to reproduce the accents of speech by the following mechanical means:

Dearest Emma,
    I had a perfectly marvelous time at your party! I *mean* it was *positively* something else. And the groovy, fantastic music was utterly devastating! I *mean* it! I wouldn't have missed that party for *anything!*

While this technique has its place in informal, personal correspondence, it is inappropriate when there is not a close personal relationship between writer and reader.

Although skillful writers use some of these devices to achieve emphasis, they do so sparingly. They most often achieve emphasis by repeating words and phrases intentionally, choosing forceful words, and changing the word order within sentences (both first and last positions in a sentence are more emphatic). Martin Luther King's speech, *I Have a Dream*, demonstrates how emphasis can be achieved by these means:

There are those who are asking the devotees of civil rights, "When will you be satisfied?" We can never be satisfied as long as the Negro is the victim of the unspeakable horrors of police brutality. We can never be satisfied as long as our bodies, heavy with the fatigue of travel, cannot gain lodging in the motels of the highways and the hotels of the cities. We cannot be satisfied as long as the Negro's basic mobility is from a smaller ghetto to a larger one. We can never be satisfied as long as our children are stripped of their selfhood and robbed of their dignity by signs stating "for whites only." We cannot be satisfied as long as a Negro in Mississippi cannot vote and a Negro in New York believes he has nothing for which to vote. No, we are not satisfied, and we will not be satisfied until justice rolls down like waters and righteousness like a mighty stream.

Reprinted from *Rhetoric of Racial Revolt* (Denver, Colorado: Golden Bell Press, 1964), by permission of the publisher.

The phrase "we can never be satisfied" is repeated by Dr. King to emphasize the idea that the Negro will keep working until he attains complete justice and equality. The contrast between what is and what should be is heightened by King's intentional use of repetition. Be warned, however, that overuse of this device will result in monotony, not emphasis.

Dr. King also gains emphasis by his use of forceful words (e.g., "unspeakable horrors of police brutality"), thus stressing the magnitude of the Negro's plight. Finally, he builds a climax by putting the answer to the question "When will you be satisfied?" in the most emphatic position, the end of the paragraph—when "... justice rolls down like waters and righteousness like a mighty stream."

REASONS FOR PAYING ATTENTION

As we indicated earlier, people willingly pay attention to a communication because (1) they will gain something useful from paying attention, or (2) paying attention satisfies a previous interest.

Thus, you would pay attention to the directions for filling out your income tax because you have something to gain or lose. On the other hand, you might sit up and watch the late show because it satisfies your desire to be entertained. You might listen attentively to a dull story told by your boss or prospective father-in-law (utility), or spend all evening listening to a rock group because you really like it (interest). More effort is required to pay attention to what is useful than to what is interesting.

Let's go back to those dull, educational films. You watched them because you had something to gain if you did or lose if you didn't. The purpose of the films was to teach something, to give information that you could use, but many films of this type fail to teach effectively because they don't arouse curiosity or hold interest. Compare this type of film to the educational TV program, *Sesame Street.* It is estimated that *Sesame Street* has a viewing audience of five million. Many of the children who watch it have learned, in a limited way, to count, read, and write before beginning school. The people who write and produce the program handle their material in such an interesting manner that learning is no longer a chore—it is fun. Suggestions for making your material more interesting follow in our discussion of attention factors.

ATTENTION FACTORS

The Startling

A minister once opened his sermon with the statement, "This is a goddamned miserable Sunday!" Needless to say, his audience snapped to attention. After a brief pause to allow them to recover, he explained that he had been just as shocked as they when he overheard the comment on his way to church that morning, and he followed with a blistering attack on profanity. Used sparingly, the startling can be an effective attention-getting device. Consider how this writer uses the startling to hold her readers' attention:

Dear Mother and Dad:
    Since I left for college I have been remiss in writing and I am sorry for my thoughtlessness in not having written before. I will bring you up-to-date now, but before you read on, please sit down. You are not to read any further unless you are sitting down. Okay?
    Well, then, I am getting along pretty well now. The skull fracture and the concussion I got when I jumped out of the window of my dormitory when it caught on fire shortly after my arrival here are pretty well healed now. I only spent two weeks in the hospital and now I can see almost normally and only get those sick headaches once a day. Fortunately, the fire in the dormitory and my jump were witnessed by an attendant at the gas station near the dorm, and he was the one who called the Fire Deparament and the ambulance. He also visited me in the hospital and since I had nowhere to live because of the burnt-out dormitory, he was kind enough to invite me to share his apartment with him. It's really a basement room, but it's kind of cute. He is a very fine boy and we have fallen deeply in love and are planning to get married. We haven't got the exact date yet, but it will be before my pregnancy begins to show.

Yes, Mother and Dad, I am pregnant. I know how much you are looking forward to being grandparents and I know you will welcome the baby and give it the same love and devotion and tender care you gave me when I was a child. The reason for the delay in our marriage is that my boyfriend has a minor infection which prevents us from passing our premarital blood tests and I carelessly caught it from him. I know you will welcome him into our family with open arms. He is kind, and although not well educated he is ambitious. Although he is of a different race and religion than ours, I know your often-expressed tolerance will not permit you to be bothered by that.

Now that I have brought you up-to-date, I want to tell you that there was no dormitory fire, I did not have a concussion or skull fracture, I was not in the hospital, I am not pregnant, I am not engaged, I am not infected, and there is no boyfriend in my life. However, I am getting a D in History and F in Science and I want you to see those marks in their proper perspective.

Your loving daughter,
Susie

Reprinted with permission of *Forbes Magazine*. Writer unknown.

Humor

Humor can be an effective tool for the communicator. However, listeners and readers will not be amused by hackneyed, clumsy, or "unfunny" attempts at humor, so you as a speaker or writer should observe the following rules.

First, make sure your humor is relevant. Audiences are not impressed with stories which are dragged in by the heels. Your humor should be used to develop the theme of the composition. If you select the main points of your composition merely to permit the use of stock anecdotes or jokes, your humor is likely to appear irrelevant.

Second, make sure your humor is appropriate. There are some situations in which humor is in bad taste and therefore out of place. If the humor is too sarcastic or personal the audience will be offended instead of entertained; if it violates standards of good taste the audience may be embarrassed. A composition whose subject is one of dignity or solemnity will not be aided by humor.

Finally, use humor that is brief and pointed. Humor should not take up more time than it is worth, its purpose being to provide relaxation, enjoyment, and entertainment.

If humor is relevant and well handled, it is an impressive attention-getter. One particularly effective form of humor, satire, pokes fun at a subject by reducing it to ridicule. Note how effectively Tom Lehrer satirizes what he feels is an American hypocrisy.

National Brotherhood Week

Oh, the white folks hate the black folks
And the black folks hate the white folks—
To hate all but the right folks
Is an old established rule.

But during National Brotherhood Week,
National Brotherhood Week,
Lena Horne and Sheriff Clark are dancing cheek to cheek.
It's fun to eulogize the people you despise.
As long as you don't let them in your school.

Oh, the poor folks hate the rich folks
And the rich folks hate the poor folks—
All of my folks hate all of your folks,
It's American as apple pie.

But during National Brotherhood Week,
National Brotherhood Week,
New Yorkers love the Puerto Ricans 'cause it's very chic.
Step up and take the hand of someone you can't stand;
You can tolerate him if you try.

Oh, the Protestants hate the Catholics
And the Catholics hate the Protestants
And the Hindus hate the Muslims
And everybody hates the Jews.

But during National Brotherhood Week
National Brotherhood Week,
It's National Smile at Oneanotherhood Week.
Be nice to people who are inferior to you;
It's only for a week, so have no fear—
Be grateful that it doesn't last all year!

Suspense

Everyone knows the value of suspense as an attention factor. We follow avidly the serial on TV or the comic strip of our local newspaper. We eagerly seek out the details of a local or national crime or scandal. We watch a football or baseball game, sweating it out with our favorite team.

When using suspense as an attention factor, remember not to tip your hand too soon. For instance, don't give away the outcome of the story in your title. Titling an essay *The Game We Lost by Inches* would reveal the conclusion before the reader even begins. A composition can be organized so that the reader or listener is uncertain of

The Case of the Shocking Carpet.

"*There was something strange about that house. The thermostat registered normal, but everyone felt chilly. Furniture creaked. House plants drooped. A thin film of dust covered everything, even with daily dusting. Rufus, the family dog, was nervous and whiney. And crackling jolts of static electricity leaped from door knobs and light switches to shock unsuspecting victims.*"

If you've noticed some of these tell-tale signs around your house, the culprit is probably low humidity. Other clues are: family complaints about dried out skin and nasal passages; wooden furniture coming unglued; wall paper cracking and peeling; wood trim pulling away from walls; piano getting out of tune; paintings cracking.

So if your evidence points to low humidity, investigate getting a West Bend portable humidifier for your home. It will keep the humidity level just right throughout an average 8-room house. A West Bend humidifier looks like an at-

tractive cabinet. But inside, West Bend's famous waterwheel action is working quietly, dependably to circulate fresh, moist air.

Want more clues on how to rid your house of low humidity? Send for our FREE 12-page booklet, "The Shocking Facts About Low Humidity." Use the handy coupon below.

Used with the permission of The West Bend Company.

the outcome of events. If you can excite the curiosity of your audience by developing your material in the form of a mystery or problem that they can solve with you, their attention will be aroused by their desire to find out the answer.

Questions also present incomplete situations. Sometimes a question or a series of questions will create suspense, as in the following example from a student theme:

> Now, he opens his mouth to speak. His answer is awaited eagerly. Will he reveal the truth? Will he rat on his friend? The courtroom is hushed. The jury and spectators lean forward on their seats. He begins hesitatingly, almost in a whisper. "The defendant and I. . . ."

The Familiar

Use of the familiar is particularly effective in speaking situations. For years comedians have used the "local" joke, a reference to people, places, or events which are distinctly familiar to the audience. In New York, Johnny Carson uses this technique in his opening monologue on the *Tonight Show*. He makes jokes about Consolidated Edison (the New York electric power company), the Mayor, or the New York streetwalkers, and the audience roars.

You can add local color to your material by using names and places that the audience will recognize. For instance, in describing a night on the town, a reference to a popular hangout would be appropriate to a student audience. Refer to the interests and experiences of your audience whenever practical. It is also effective to refer to something said by a previous speaker. The audience can relate to it easily, so it will help hold their attention. Whenever appropriate, make references to events or instances that are fresh in the listeners' minds. One University of Wisconsin lecturer began with an effective use of the familiar some years ago: "Today we're going to study the giant sequoia redwoods—a tree you'll be seeing when you go to California to see Wisconsin win the Rose Bowl Game!"

The Vital

The vital can be the most forceful attention factor of all, especially when it relates to a strong motive inherent in the audience. People attend to what affects them directly—their health, their security, their survival. Slogans like "Fight Cancer with a Checkup and a Check" are directed at these motives.

The student speaker who began, "Within the next ten years three people in this audience will be dead from the effects of DDT in our environment," had his classmates eager to hear what followed. In his book, *The Population Bomb,* Dr. Paul Ehrlich begins with a prologue designed to secure the interest of his potential readers by combining the startling and the vital.

> The battle to feed all of humanity is over. In the 1970's the world will undergo famines—hundreds of millions of people are going to starve to death in spite of any crash programs embarked upon now. At this late date nothing can prevent a substantial increase in the world death rate, although many lives could be saved through dramatic programs to "stretch" the carrying capacity of the earth by increasing food production. But these programs will only provide a stay of execution unless they are accompanied by determined and successful efforts at population control. Population control is the conscious regulation of the numbers of human beings to meet the needs, not just of individual families, but of society as a whole.
>
> Nothing could be more misleading to our children than our present affluent society. They will inherit a totally different world, a world in which the standards, politics, and economics of the 1960's are dead. As the most powerful nation in the world today, *and its largest consumer,* the United States cannot stand isolated. We are today involved in the events leading to famine; tomorrow we may be destroyed by its consequences.

From Dr. Paul R. Ehrlich, *The Population Bomb.* © 1968 by Paul R. Ehrlich. Reprinted by permission of Ballantine Books, Inc.

The Real

Have you ever been caught up in a story in which the characters and plot were described with such vividness and clarity that you actually became part of the narrative? Writers and speakers able to create this response use the attention-getting technique called the "real"— descriptive language to present a clear and definite picture of what is taking place. The person who describes a scene for his audience is, in effect, placing a mental picture before them. It is his job to select those details that the audience needs to know in order to get a clear picture of the situation. This might involve appropriate modifiers. Note the following two statements: (1) I sat next to a girl eating fruit. (2) I sat next to a voluptuous blond in a short, tight, green skirt who was munching a crisp, red apple. Which statement is more likely to hold attention and establish the picture clearly in the mind?

Sometimes effective description calls for the use of specific rather than general terms. The word "car" offers only a vague picture; the word "Ford" is more clear, and to say Thunderbird, Maverick, or Pinto helps in establishing a precise mental image. Don't say a man "walked" into the room when he "ambled," "edged," "strutted," or "staggered." Use the precise word.

Since using the "real" involves talking about actual people and places, it is wise to give names to the characters you describe, especially if they are important to the story. For example, it is easier to see you sitting next to "Marvin" or "Lolita" than next to your "friend." It is easier to picture "Miss Stonebreaker" than "the math teacher" you had.

Finally, the use of the "real" involves a combination of both abstract and concrete language. The storyteller has the advantage of being able to include his impressions of the things he is describing. In this instance, the old adage that "a picture is worth a thousand words" is not true. For example, a snapshot can show you what kind of clothes a person is wearing or the shape of his head, and from these you might draw some conclusions about his life style or intellectual ability, but it cannot show you that he is a loudmouth, an introvert, or an agnostic. That is up to the storyteller. If the fact that your companion is superstitious has a bearing on your story, make sure that your audience knows this.

The Novel

Most of us are attracted by the unusual. Some people spend hours looking through a hole in the fence of a construction site at workers erecting a building, while others spend hours in line waiting to see the latest innovation on stage or in the movies.

Unusual personal experiences arouse interest on the part of the audience. A deep sea diver or parachutist would undoubtedly have a list of surefire experiences for holding the attention of an audience.

As a speaker or writer, you should constantly be on the lookout for new ways of saying things. Use your imagination; avoid the hackneyed and trite. Which of the following is a more interesting use of description: "The virgin forest," or "the unaxed woods"? While both say the same thing, the latter says it in a newer, more imaginative way.

Finally, consider combining the novel with the familiar. An old story with a new twist is a certain attention-getter. Obviously, not all the problems of communication are solved simply by getting and holding the reader or listener's attention.

A writer or speaker might get attention and yet fail to obtain a desired response. However, you can be sure that the better you control the audience's attention, the better are your chances of accomplishing

The sniff that launched a million sips.

Scratch the tape then sniff the tape for the world's driest martini

Back in 1870, Fleischmann developed the world's first dry gin. And today we still make the driest.

To tempt you to try it, we've even taped the scent of a Fleischmann's martini right on this page. Merely

scratch the piece of tape below and then sniff it.

We hope that once you have taken a whiff of our martini, you won't be satisfied until you have a taste. Then you'll be extremely satisfied.

Fleischmann's. World's driest gin.

DISTILLED FROM AMERICAN GRAIN · 90 PROOF · THE FLEISCHMANN DISTILLING CORP. N.Y.C.

Used with the permission of the Fleischmann Distilling Corp.

your purpose. The ad on page 104 uses a technique called "scratch 'n sniff," to add the extra dimension of scent. The tape is odorless until scratched with the fingernail. Once scratched, the tape actually demonstrates the product by putting its aroma right under the reader's nose.

EXERCISES

A DEMONSTRATION SPEECH

Deliver a 2–5 minute speech in which you demonstrate a technique or procedure. Accompany your delivery with an appropriate visual aid. Pick something that you enjoy doing and do well. Consider whether the audience will see the usefulness of your information. Topics which offer little utility to the audience must be made interesting in order to hold attention.

Delivery: This speech should be delivered extemporaneously. Demonstrating something requires freedom of movement. You might have to use your hands, arms, legs, or body to explain something to your listeners. Therefore, the less dependent on notes you are, the better.

Sample Topics

1. How to take an effective snapshot
2. How to fillet a fish
3. How to set a broken leg
4. How to mix a strawberry daiquiri
5. How to dance the "Big Apple"

1. Select an instructor and analyze his effectiveness in holding the attention of his audience of students. Write a three-to-four-hundred-word report in which you refer specifically to his use or omission of the attention factors above. Do not name the instructor.
2. Select five of your favorite short stories or TV programs. List the attention factors in each.
3. Write an introductory paragraph to an essay or the introduction to a speech using one or more of the attention factors. Write an alternate using different factors. Hand both in to your instructor indicating which is better and why.
4. Analyze an essay or speech by a classmate and indicate how it could have been made more interesting by the use of specific attention factors.
5. Analyze a particular ad or TV commercial that uses one or more attention factors to sell its product. Comment on its effectiveness.
6. Choose a novel by a significant writer. List the number of simple, com-

pound, complex, and compound-complex sentences found on any two pages.

7. Make a list of names and places that your audience will recognize and relate to.
8. Make a list of issues with which your classmates are strongly concerned.

CHAPTER
7

Supporting Your Ideas

OBJECTIVES

After studying this chapter you should be able to:

1. Explain how supporting detail helps make ideas clearer or more persuasive.
2. After selecting a specific topic for a communication, choose appropriate and interesting examples to support your main idea.
3. Determine how much detail to include in an example for a given audience.
4. Explain how statistics can be made more interesting and meaningful.
5. Define testimony as a type of supporting material and explain how to use testimony effectively in a communication.
6. Explain the differences between figurative and literal comparison and contrast.
7. Give an example of each of the following forms of explanation and explain how these forms can be used effectively:
   a. Definition
   b. Analysis
   c. Description
8. Locate relevant sources from the card catalogue, the *Reader's Guide*, the *Guides to Books in Print*, the *Biographical Dictionary*, or the *New York Times Index*.
9. Prepare an accurate bibliography card.
10. Prepare an accurate note card.
11. Write footnotes correctly for a research assignment.
12. Arrange a bibliography for a research assignment.

The fact that you say something in a positive way is seldom enough to insure that your reader or listener will either understand or agree with you. In most cases, you must use supporting detail to make your ideas clear or persuasive to others. For example, in a communication to inform intended to give your audience an understanding of George Washington's performance as a general, you might choose from a variety of supporting techniques. You might relate a few of his experiences on the battlefield (examples). You might describe the hardships he and his men faced or analyze his battlefield strategy (explanation). You might quote significant military experts or historians who have commented on his competency as a general (testimony). You might liken him to other generals (comparison). Finally, you might cite the number of his successes and failures on the battlefield and the odds he faced (statistics).

These same five techniques can also be used in communication to persuade. In persuasion they usually appear as evidence, supporting a positive statement or assertion. Suppose, for example, that a mother wants to convince her young son to stop climbing trees. "Carl," she says, "you shouldn't climb trees." She might use any of the five supporting devices to support her assertion:

Example: "Climbing trees is dangerous, Carl. When I was your age, I had a friend named Timmy who was always climbing trees, even though his parents warned him not to. Then, one day Timmy slipped on a wet branch and fell out of a tree. He fell twenty feet to the ground and broke his neck. Two days later, Timmy died."

Statistics: "You know, Carl, last year in our state over one hundred boys and girls were killed or crippled falling out of trees."

Testimony: "Your Uncle George often climbs trees as part of his job and he says he wouldn't do it if he didn't have to. It's too dangerous."

Comparison: "Falling twenty feet out of a tree is like someone hitting you as hard as they could with a sledgehammer."

Explanation: "Sometimes a branch that looks safe can be rotten inside, eaten up by insects or disease. You might step on it, crack it, and come tumbling to the ground." (This explanation could be made even more impressive if the mother could find such a branch and show Carl how easy it is to break.)

As you have seen, supporting material may be divided into five classes:

1. Examples
2. Statistics
3. Testimony
4. Comparison/Contrast
5. Explanation

EXAMPLES

An example can be thought of as a "specific instance," a sample chosen to show the nature or character of the rest. Examples can be either abbreviated or detailed. One might cite the skateboard as an example of a fad; *Jesus Christ, Superstar* as an example of rock opera; the late Vince Lombardi as an example of the power of positive thinking; or the high unemployment rate as an example of the government's inability to cope with domestic problems.

When preparing for a particular speech or essay, look for appropriate and interesting examples that fit the subject, arouse curiosity or concern, avoid wordiness, and make a point.

The amount of detail included in the example is often dependent upon your audience. If the example you choose is familiar to your readers or listeners, you need only cite it briefly. If it is unfamiliar to your audience, you must develop it in enough detail so that its point is made clear to them.

Sometimes a speaker or writer will keep his examples brief so that he can present them in groups. Note how the frequency of the examples in the article below seems to strengthen the writer's point that many hospital emergency rooms are "overcrowded, incompetently staffed, and inadequately equipped."

Americans Take Big Chance in Hospital Emergency Rooms

The oft-repeated myth by the American Medical Association that while costs are the highest, Americans receive the best health care in the world, took another solid blow to the chin last week as a result of a most revealing article in the Wall St. Journal entitled "Grim Diagnosis." After citing incredible cases of medical bungling, the article says: "This kind of horror story is being told with increasing frequency these days. As the shortage of doctors becomes acute, more and more Americans are turning to hospital emergency rooms for injuries or illnesses of all types. And often, authorities say, the emergency rooms they turn to are overcrowded, incompetently staffed, and inadequately equipped.

STUDIES ARE QUOTED

"Two studies in Baltimore bear out that contention. Research published last year by two specialists at the Johns Hopkins University School of Hygiene and Public Health found that less than one-third of a group of patients showing up at a big-city hospital emergency room with nonemergency complaints were treated adequately.

"Shortly after that, another medical team at the school reported that more than half of a group of auto accident victims who died from abdominal injuries 'should have had a reasonable chance for survival' had not hospital errors in diagnosis and treatment occurred."

Here are some typical examples cited in the article:

George McGraw considered himself a lucky man.

PATIENT SENT HOME

To all appearances, he had emerged from a serious automobile accident near Baltimore recently with only a scraped elbow and a cut on one ear. Or at least, that's what he was told by the hospital emergency room physician who examined him and sent him home.

But for some reason the physician didn't have any X-rays made, and George McGraw walked out of the hospital door with a fractured neck and skull.

On the ride home from the hospital, bone fragments sliced into Mr. McGraw's brain and spinal cord. Today, the 58-year-old construction worker from New Freedom, Pa., is paralyzed for life.

EXAMPLE IS GIVEN

In New York, a 35-year-old unemployed man went to a hospital emergency room and complained of stomach pains. He was given a painkiller and sent home. He died 24 hours later, in another hospital, from massive hemorrhaging of stomach ulcers.

A Dallas nurse is still haunted by memories of an episode in a local hospital one night. An accident victim brought to the hospital was admitted as dead on arrival, on the word of the ambulance attendants. The emergency room was so crowded that night, according to the nurse on duty, that no one bothered to examine the man.

Several hours later, the supposed corpse coughed. The victim survived, but with serious brain damage apparently caused by the delay in treatment.

In a shocking number of cases, blatant incompetence by medical people is indicated. In Tennessee a few years ago, for instance, a teenage boy died of a ruptured liver after interns in a crowded emergency room diagnosed him as drunk and sent him away.

Nurses in Mississippi ignored a man who was bleeding to death. Near Chicago, a college football player broke his leg during a game. The general practitioner on duty at the hospital emergency room put the cast on so tightly that the boy's leg later had to be amputated above the knee.

Hence, it's not surprising that recent studies suggest a significant portion of the 700,000 medical and surgical emergencies that occur in the United States every year are mishandled in some way that often result in preventable death or permanent injury.

AMPUTATION FOLLOWS

In the emergency room of one Chicago private hospital, a 12-year-old boy with an open fracture of the right arm had to wait so long for treatment that gas gangrene developed in the wound and his arm had to be amputated.

The Milwaukee Labor Press, Oct. 21, 1971. Reprinted by permission.

At other times it may be more effective to communicate one example in detail. Detailed examples usually take the form of stories, which are easy to organize, since they are developed in chronological order. These stories may take the form of personal experiences, allegories, anecdotes, parables, or fables. They are excellent devices for clarifying and reinforcing ideas, and can often give the reader or listener a clear mental picture of the characters, setting, and action. For this reason, they are sometimes called word pictures, or *illustrations*. These detailed examples may be real or hypothetical, humorous or serious. They should be completely relevant to the point or moral principle being illustrated. One good example of a story that illustrates a moral principle is the Parable of the Good Samaritan, found in the tenth chapter of Luke in the Holy Bible. In response to the question, "Who is my neighbor?" Jesus replies:

A certain man was going down from Jerusalem to Jericho when robbers attacked him, stripped him and beat him up, leaving him half dead. It so happened that a priest was going down the road; when he saw the man he walked on by, on the other side. In the same way a Levite also came there, went over and looked at the man, and then walked on by, but a certain Samaritan who was traveling that way came upon him, and when he saw the man his heart was filled with pity. He went over to him, poured oil and wine on his wounds and bandaged them; then he put the man on his own animal and took him to an inn where he took care of him. The next day he took out two silver coins and gave them to the inn keeper. "Take care of him," he told the inn keeper, "and when I come back this way I will pay you back whatever you spend on him." And Jesus concluded, which one of these three seems to you to have been a neighbor to the man attacked by the robbers?

From *Today's English Version of the New Testament.* Copyright © American Bible Society, 1966, 1971.

STATISTICS

When used properly, statistics provide an excellent means of clarification or support. However, when handled clumsily, they confuse and discourage understanding. Few readers or listeners would struggle to pay attention to an uninteresting and complicated set of statistics. Therefore, if you want to be effective, make them interesting and meaningful. Here are some suggestions you should consider in using statistics.

You may use charts, tables, graphs, or pictures to help your audience grasp what is being presented. A student used the bar graph

Percentage of Women in the Medical Profession (excluding nursing)

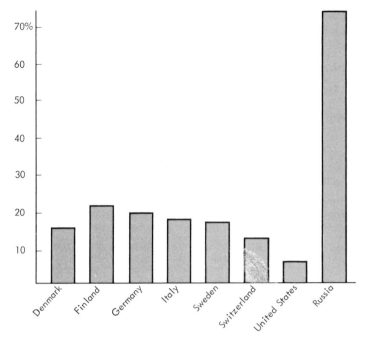

shown above in a research paper to show more clearly the small percentage of women in the medical profession of this country.

If you wanted to make use of this graph in a speech, you would either have to enlarge it so it could be seen easily or make enough copies for each listener. Using a chart too small to be seen by everyone in your audience would be ineffective, and passing one around through the audience would be distracting.

Dramatize Your Statistics

Whenever possible, your statistics should be stated in terms which relate to the interest and experience of your listener or reader. If you can form a mental picture for your audience by presenting your statistics in some dramatic form, they are more likely to be understood and remembered.

In an emotional speech to his classmates, Tom Nawrumba, a junior college student from West Africa, spelled out how the money college students spend for enjoyment could provide life-sustaining food and water to those in desperate need.

... the price of a drive-in movie for you and your date plus a snack afterwards would pay for a month's supply of food for a family of four in Bangladesh. One less night out on the town would buy from fifty to one hundred feet of water pipe, and the cost of an Easter vacation in Florida could provide a complete water system for a drought-stricken village in West Africa.

Tom Nawrumba. Used with permission of the speaker.

Round Off Your Statistics

Whether you are writing or speaking, when dealing with large numbers it is a good idea to round them off. Instead of saying that the 1970 census lists the population of New York City as 7,792,892, round it off to an approximately 7.8 million. The shorter figure is easier for the reader or listener to understand and remember. In the excerpt below the student-speaker rounds off the statistics he uses to support his proposition that the United States should begin a system of population control:

The United States has remained affluent and isolated while much of the rest of the world starves. In this country 218 million people, only 6 percent of the world's population, use over one-half of the world's resources. It is estimated that our nation is responsible for about 60 percent of the world's pollution. Ours is a country of monumental waste. We throw away enough garbage each day to feed a third of the world's starving. But the even more appalling problem is the way we have glutted ourselves on the world's limited resources. A child growing up in this country today uses fifty times as much of the world's raw materials as a comparable child in Africa or India. By the time he reaches 70, he will have consumed 50 tons of food, 20 thousand gallons of gasoline, 10 thousand pounds of meat. . . .

Erik Jackson. Used with permission of the speaker.

Document Your Statistics

Avoid using such vague phrases as "recent studies indicate" or "the last surveys show." Instead, indicate clearly when and by whom the statistics you are quoting were compiled. Chances are that some in your audience have been deceived in the past by statistics. Set their minds at ease by indicating exactly where the statistics came from.

This does not mean that you must document every statistic that you use. To do so would be both uninteresting and overly complicated.

When the statistics you present are consistent with the general knowledge and experience of your audience, there is probably no need to indicate their exact source. Although none of the statistics in the student speech above are documented, few would question them, as they are widely known.

TESTIMONY

It is often wise for a speaker or writer to support his own ideas with the testimony of others. We live in a complex and technical age; ours is increasingly a society of specialists. The statement of an expert on a particular subject carries the weight of his education and experience. Most of us would not quarrel with a doctor who recommended an emergency appendectomy or with a TV repairman who told us that our set needed a new vertical output transformer. Unless we doubted their competency or honesty, we would have little reason to question their judgment. If you want your audience to give credence to the authorities you cite, choose people they will consider well-qualified and objective. If the experts are unknown to your audience, give facts about them to establish their qualifications. William A. Nail, Public Relations Director of the Zenith Radio Corporation, uses this method of introducing Dr. Charles Keller.

> Dr. Charles Keller, retired director of the John Hay Fellows program and retired professor of history at Williams College, goes around the country talking with teachers and young people in high schools. He has devoted the last years of his career in education to listening and sharing experiences with others—try to demonstrate what you learn, when you listen to others.
> Dr. Keller listens continually to young people and their ideas. In a talk that he made to a meeting of librarians last year, he used a poem by a high school student that he had met in Portland, Oregon. I would like to share with you a part of this poem, which illustrates in a way the answer to the question—"What did you say?"

> > I found beer cans floating under dead fish,
> > and a forest converted to a chemical factory—
> > an image on the boob-tube
> > informed me of "100 per cent chance precipitation"
> > and spoiled the surprise.
> > I looked for the moon and found Apollo 8, Telstar,
> > Halley's Comet and a Boeing 707.
> > Beauty is neither electronic nor man-made.
> > Stars are more silver than aluminum, and

wax fruit are blasphemous. Beauty is
that which is natural, original, and unexpected.
I am waiting for the day when computers
program themselves,
and leave us to ourselves, and
I am watching for the day that
the last blade of grass is removed
to make room for a missile factory.
I am waiting for a machine that can
fall in love, and
I am watching for an IBM card for God.

Vital Speeches, XXXVII:23 (September 15, 1971), 726.

The poem above is also a form of testimony. If someone else has said something in poetry or prose that you feel is particularly well related to your subject, quote him. Besides clarifying or reinforcing what you have said, this technique will add interestingness and variety to your writing or speaking.

Testimony is usually less effective as a support when you are dealing with a controversial subject. Experts tend to disagree on controversial issues. While one economist may believe in rigid price controls, another believes in none at all; one group of scientists advocates the use of unmanned rockets to explore space, another group defends our present use of manned rockets. Thus, experts who disagree may, in effect, cancel each other out.

When using the testimony of another, you can either quote him verbatim or paraphrase what he has said. However, in most cases the testimony will be made stronger by direct quotation. When you quote an authority directly, your reader or listener can decide the authority's meaning for himself. He doesn't have to depend on the accuracy of your interpretation.

In this excerpt from a symposium-speech entitled, "The Danger of Nuclear Energy Production," the student-speaker quotes a number of authorities to back up her contention that there should be a five-year moratorium on the construction of nuclear power plants in the United States.

David Lilienthal, the first chairman of the Atomic Energy Commission, put his finger on the heart of the matter—the enormous dangers of nuclear waste—when he stated: "These huge quantities of radioactive wastes must somehow be removed from the reactors, must, without mishap, be put into containers that will never rupture; then these vast quantities of poisonous stuff must be moved either to a burial ground or to reprocessing and concentration plants, handled again, and disposed of, by burial or otherwise, with a risk of human error at every step." But if these storage facilities fail, what then? In a June 22, 1977, speech to the U.S. House of Representatives, New York Congressman Frederick W. Richmond stated, ". . . scientists have estimated that if evenly distributed among the world's population only two pounds of plutonium would be necessary to contaminate each and every one of us with a lethal dosage. . . . By 1985 if the nuclear industry gets its way we will be producing 140 tons of plutonium and by the year 2000 some 1,700 tons of the substance."

It is clear that the possibilities for a catastrophe are there. I'm not proposing that we scrap nuclear energy. What I'm asking for is a five-year moratorium on the construction of nuclear reactors to give us time to observe the deficiencies in the present reactors and to answer the questions posed by nuclear power. Let's not, in an attempt to find ample and cheap power "right now," threaten the health and safety of future generations. Let's not, without considering all the facts, commit this nation to a nuclear energy program which, Ralph Nader has suggested, may well be our "technological Vietnam."

Used with permission of the speaker, Karen Johnson.

Direct quotations can also be used if a person has said something so clearly or succinctly that you could not possibly say it as well, or if you want to project an image of a person by what he has said. Suppose that Professor Smith has a particularly clear explanation of deviant behavior in his sociology textbook. Instead of using your own words you may choose to quote the professor verbatim. There are also times when someone has said something so well that you reinforce your ideas by simple quotation. Here are a few examples of memorable phrasemaking:

The only thing necessary for the triumph of evil is for good men to do nothing.   *Edmund Burke*

Ask not what your country can do for you, but what you can do for your country.   *John F. Kennedy*

This above all,—to thine ownself be true; And it must follow, as the night the day, Thou canst not then be false to any man.
                                                    William Shakespeare

In Chapter 14 we indicate that a person projects his image to others in part by what he says to them. In the speech, *A Tribute to His Brother,* on pp. 286–88, Edward Kennedy devotes almost his entire content to quoting what his brother wrote about their father and what he said in a speech to the young people in South Africa. The intention was to enable the audience to perceive an image of Robert Kennedy through what he had written and spoken.

The question of ethics in testimony arises in advertising, where well-known personalities endorse some product or idea. One wonders about the individual's competency to evaluate the product being endorsed. Does athletic ability give authoritative knowledge about the nutritional value of a breakfast cereal? Does being a movie hero make one an expert on the subject of patriotism?

As a writer or speaker you have an ethical responsibility to choose your supporting material honestly and accurately. When selecting testimony ask yourself these questions: Will the authority be acceptable to my audience? Is he qualified by training and experience? Is the statement I am using an accurate expression of the author's opinion?

COMPARISON AND CONTRAST

You might describe your history teacher as an intellectual Phyllis Diller, your new boy friend as a chubby Richard Harris, or your parents as the Mr. and Mrs. Archie Bunker of Roseville, Ohio. Comparison/contrast can be used in an exacting manner, e.g., a statistical comparison of the infant morality rate in civilized countries, or rather casually, e.g., your description of last night's date as "the battle of Bunker Hill revisited."

You were probably first introduced to comparison/contrast as a child. One of the best ways to teach the new or unknown to someone is to compare it to what is known. In answer to his child's question, "What does a zebra look like?" the parent replies, "Like a horse in striped pajamas." A teacher introducing her class to the concept of food as energy might compare food with the gasoline put in a car to keep it running.

Comparison

You would probably compare Shelley and Keats (both romantic poets of the same period) and contrast farm life with city life. Comparisons may be *literal* or *figurative*. A literal comparison describes similarities between things in the same category. Comparisons between infant mortality in America and infant mortality in Sweden, between unemployment rates in 1975 and 1977, between Republican and Democratic candidates are literal comparisons. When we describe the similarities between things in different categories, we call this figurative comparison.

Examples of figurative comparison would be the comparison of communism to an ant colony, an occupied country to a canary in a cage, or a union-management bargaining session to a game of chess. Like all supporting devices, comparison can be used in communication to inform, entertain, or persuade. In his novel *Victory*, Joseph Conrad uses the technique of comparison to create for his reader a vivid picture of Heyst's tropical island.

An island is but the top of a mountain. Axel Heyst, perched on it immovably, was surrounded, instead of the imponderable stormy and transparent ocean of air merging into infinity, by a tepid, shallow sea; a passionless off-shoot of the great waters which embrace the continents of this globe. His most frequent visitors were shadows, the shadows of clouds, relieving the monotony of the inanimate, brooding sunshine of the tropics. His nearest neighbour—I am speaking now of things showing some sort of animation—was an indolent volcano which smoked faintly all day with its head just above the northern horizon, and at night levelled at him, from amongst the clear stars, a dull red glow, expanding and collapsing spasmodically like the end of a gigantic cigar puffed at intermittently in the dark. Axel Heyst was also a smoker; and when he lounged out on his verandah with his cheroot, the last thing before going to bed, he made in the night the same sort of glow and the same size as that other one so many miles away.

Joseph Conrad, *Victory* (London: J. M. Dent & Sons Ltd., 1915), p. 3.

Comparison is often used as a technique in persuasion. How many times have you heard or used arguments similar to these? "John's parents are letting him go and he's even younger than I am." "Oh, come on and try it. Everyone else is doing it. Why miss out on all the fun?"

It is also frequently used in combination with other supporting devices. The excerpt below from a student essay combines comparison, contrast, statistics, and explanation in an attempt to persuade the reader that in an inflation the rich get richer and the poor get poorer.

One of the more painful aspects of inflation is the fact that in an inflationary economy the rich get richer and the poor get poorer. Nowhere is this more apparent than in the area of housing.

Figures released on April 10, 1977, by the Census Bureau and the Department of Housing and Urban Development showed that the median price of a single family home rose from $17,100 in 1970 to $47,500 in 1977, an increase of nearly 180 percent. During this same period, the median income for homeowners rose only 53 percent from $9,700 to $14,800. This placed the value of a single family home at about three times the income of its owner. When you add to this the cost of financing, it makes it virtually impossible for the average wage earner to purchase a first home.

The fact that inflation actually benefits the rich becomes apparent when one studies the report further. The report states that the housing/income ratio varies considerably accordingly to income level. While owners with incomes of $6,000 or less lived in housing valued at an average of four or five times that amount, the value of homes of those earning $25,000 or more was an average of less than two times income.

Furthermore, while renters paid about 25 percent of their annual income for rent in 1977 according to the study, the lower-income renter paid an average of 38 percent for rent, and the higher-income renter gave less than 10 percent of his earnings to landlords.

With permission of the writer, Joyce Jackson.

Contrast

While comparison points out similarities, contrast emphasizes differences. For example, there is an extreme difference between life in free and in totalitarian countries, between opera and rock, or between male and female (vive la différence!). The writer of the following editorial emphasizes the seriousness of our skyrocketing medical costs by contrasting a hospital visit in England with one in the United States:

What a Difference

A New York writer was in England last summer with his family. His four-year-old son became seriously ill, spent three nights in a private room in a hospital, had numerous tests and intravenous feeding. The boy's parents were given a room near him in the hospital.

Total cost was $7.80, for the parents' meals.

Foreigners in England are eligible, in emergencies, to receive the same treatment Britons get under their national health service.

On the other side of the coin — and the Atlantic — an Englishman visiting here last year was stricken and was rushed to a New York hospital. The hospital refused to admit him until it received a financial guarantee (he naturally had no private American health insurance coverage).

He died 16 days later. His wife received a bill for $12,000.

One point is not so much that a citizen of another country was treated shoddily here, bad as that is, but that many Americans would be in the same boat he was. The other point is that there are such things as health systems under which you can afford to get sick.

The Milwaukee Labor Press, November 18, 1971. With permission.

Contrast can be an effective attention-getter. Our language provides thousands of words which invoke striking contrasts. Life and death, love and hate, pleasure and pain, rich and poor, strong and weak, and fast and slow are just a few of the combinations that you have seen or heard. Charles Dickens uses the technique of sharp contrast in the opening paragraph of his novel, *A Tale of Two Cities:*

> It was the best of times, it was the worst of times, it was the age of wisdom, it was the age of foolishness, it was the epoch of belief, it was the epoch of incredulity, it was the season of Light, it was the season of Darkness, it was the spring of hope, it was the winter of despair, we had everything before us, we had nothing before us, we were all going direct to Heaven, we were all going direct the other way—in short, the period was so far like the present period, that some of its noisiest authorities insisted on its being received, for good or for evil, in the superlative degree of comparison only.

EXPLANATION

As a student you are probably involved more with explanation than any other supporting device. The textbooks that you read are, for the most part, written for the purpose of making ideas clear. Your teachers are primarily explainers. The answers that you give in class or in essay examinations are explanations.

Definition

Explanation can take several different forms. It can include definition, analysis, or description. One of the necessities in communicating is to be understood. If you plan to use a term that may be unfamiliar to your audience, either define it yourself or choose an appropriate definition by someone else. Do not fall into the habit of always using dictionary definitions; they are sometimes inappropriate for your specific context. If you can, keep your definition brief, clear, and geared to your audience's level of knowledge and experience.

For example, the definition of a "spinner" as "a cap that fits over the hub of an airplane propeller" would be more communicative and interesting to most people than the more technical definition of a spinner as "a fairing of paraboloidal shape which is fitted coaxially to the propeller and revolves with the propeller."

Malcolm X uses definition to clarify the word "revolution." Notice that in his definition he contrasts what revolution is with what it is not:

> This is a real revolution. Revolution is always based on land. Revolution is never based on begging somebody for an integrated cup of coffee. Revolutions are never based upon love-your-enemy and pray-for-

those-who-spitefully-use-you. And revolutions are never waged singing "We Shall Overcome." Revolutions are based upon bloodshed. Revolutions are never compromising. Revolutions are never based upon any kind of tokenism whatsoever. Revolutions overturn systems. And there is no system on this earth which has proven itself more corrupt, more criminal, than this system that in 1964 still colonizes 22 million African-Americans, still enslaves 22 million Afro-Americans.

Quoted in George Breitman (ed.), *Malcolm X Speaks,* p. 50; copyright © 1965 by Merit Publishers and Betty Shabazz. Reprinted by permission of Pathfinder Press.

Analysis

Analysis is the technique of breaking an idea down into its parts and explaining each part separately. It is essentially a process of answering such questions as: Who? What? Why? When? Where? How?

You use analysis when you demonstrate how to do something. While organizing a speech on "Swimming More Effectively," you might divide your speech into three parts: (1) the crawl stroke; (2) the body position; and (3) the flutter kick. An essay on how to plant a tree would probably be organized according to the steps involved: (1) digging the hole; (2) preparing the soil; (3) placing the tree correctly; (4) covering the roots and watering them down.

Evaluation is a form of analysis. The following student newspaper review uses the technique of analysis to comment on the record album, *Laverne and Shirley Sing.*

L&S's LP ho-hum

Laverne and Shirley have taken time off from their chores at the Schotz Brewery to record an album. The brewery's loss is our loss too.

Penny Marshall and Cindy Williams, who play the bumbling bimbos in the "Laverne and Shirley" TV show, have had the guts to title their album: *Laverne and Shirley Sing.* That's not quite what I would call it.

This alleged album consists of ditties—perhaps it could be called "Ditties for Bimbos"—produced in the 1950's style with shoo-be-doo-ahs and da-do-ron-rons dominating the proceedings.

The LP's most affected composition is "Five Years On," written by Michael McKean, who plays Lenny on the "L&S" program. A poignant lament, it tells of runaway lovers and the adjustments their abandoned mates have to make. Boo-hoo. Missing are songs by Squiggy and Carmine. But don't worry. Rumor has it that in the works is a new album, *Squiggy and Carmine Sing.*

"Da Do Ron Ron" and "Easier Said Than Done" are fast-moving fun songs. I give 'em a 75 'cause they're good to dance to. Heartwarming oldies such as "All I Have to Do Is Dream" are taken to new depths by the novice singers.

Background vocals and instrumentals tend to overshadow the efforts of Marshall and Williams and therefore provide high points in the album.

No doubt Marshall and Williams, who sound more like a men's clothing store than a singing duo, will make millions on this record. The fifties craze progresses toward 1980, unabated. I don't know where it's going to end, but I wish to hell it would end soon.

I promise in the future to write more serious, coherent reviews. But I have to stop here because I'm going to look up the word "bimbo."

By Janet Marie Dombeck. With permission of the *MATC Times*. From the December 10, 1976, issue of the *Times*.

Description

A third form of explanation, description, has been treated in Chapter 3. It makes use of the sensory appeals to give the reader or listener a clear picture of what is being communicated. The job of the writer or speaker who uses description as a form of support is to decide what to include and what to omit. Too much detail may bore your audience; too little may not communicate the picture you want conveyed.

The following excerpt from a TV speech delivered by President John F. Kennedy on October 22, 1962, makes use of each of the five supporting devices. The purpose of the speech was to persuade the audience that the steps the President was taking in regard to Cuba were prompted by sound reasoning and were consistent with this nation's principles. President Kennedy explained the situation to his audience, read the Soviet response to two separate protestations, reminded the audience of the lesson we learned from Hitler, indicated the steps to be taken, and dismissed the unacceptable alternative: submission.

1. *Explanation.* The President quickly moves to the business at hand. He explains that our promised surveillance of Cuba has revealed missile sites. These are *defined* as offensive missiles and *analysis* reveals that they provide a nuclear strike capability.

1. This government as promised has maintained the closest surveillance of the Soviet military build-up on the island of Cuba. Within the past week unmistakable evidence has established the fact that a series of offensive missile sites is now in preparation on that imprisoned island. The purpose of these bases can be none other than to provide a nuclear strike ca-

2. *Explanation / Examples / Statistics.* The number and range of the missiles is indicated (statistics). The *description* is made more graphic by the use of familiar cities as *examples* of targets within the missiles' range.

3. *Explanation.* The President uses all three forms of explanation. He *defines* the uncompleted sites as intermediate-range ballistic missles. He describes their strike capability, and he *analyzes* their presence as constituting an explicit threat to all the Americas.

4. *Testimony.* President Kennedy's use of direct quotations enables the audience to hear *exactly* what the Soviet government said about the missile sites. Note that the quote carries an implicit threat of Soviet rocket potential.

pability against the Western Hemisphere.

2.   The characteristics of these new missile sites indicate two distinct types of installations. Several of them include medium-range ballistic missiles capable of carrying a nuclear warhead for a distance of more than 1,000 nautical miles. Each of these missiles, in short, is capable of striking Washington, D.C., the Panama Canal, Cape Canaveral, Mexico City, or any other city in the southeastern part of the United States, in Central America, or in the Caribbean area.

3.   Additional sites not yet completed appear to be designed for intermediate-range ballistic missiles capable of traveling more than twice as far, and thus capable of striking most of the major cities in the Western Hemisphere. This urgent transformation of Cuba into an important strategic base by the presence of these large long-range and clearly offensive weapons of sudden mass destruction constitutes an explicit threat to the peace and security of all the Americas.

4.   The Soviet Government, publicly stated on September 11, that, and I quote, the armaments and military equipment sent to Cuba are designed exclusively for defense purposes, unquote, that there is—and I quote the Soviet Government— there is no need for the Soviet Government to shift its weapons for a retaliatory blow to

any other country, for instance, Cuba, unquote, and that—and I quote, the Government—the Soviet Union has so powerful rockets to carry these nuclear warheads that there is no need to search for sites for them beyond the boundaries of the Soviet Union, unquote.
That statement was false.

5. *Testimony.* The President includes this second quote for the benefit of those who might reason that what a government says publicly and what it says privately are two different things. He quotes the Soviet Foreign Minister at some length to supply additional background information to his audience.

5.   Only last Thursday, as evidence of this rapid offensive build-up was already in my hands, Soviet Foreign Minister Gromyko told me in my office that he was instructed to make it clear once again, as he said his Government had already done, that Soviet assistance to Cuba, and I quote, pursued solely the purpose of contributing to the defense capabilities of Cuba, unquote. That, and I quote him, "training by Soviet specialists of Cuban nationals in handling defensive armaments was by no means offensive," and that if it were otherwise, Mr. Gromyko went on, "the Soviet Government would never become involved in rendering such assistance."
That statement also was false.

6. *Comparison.* The comparison is drawn between this situation and Hitler's conquest of small countries in the thirties.

6.   The nineteen thirties taught us a clear lesson. Aggressive conduct, if allowed to go unchecked and unchallenged, ultimately leads to war.

7. *Explanation.* President Kennedy defines our objectives in terms of our commitments.

7.   This nation is opposed to war. We are also true to our word. Our unswerving objective, therefore, must be to prevent the use of these missiles against this or any other country; and to secure their with-

8. *Explanation.* After ' indicating his authority, the President combines description and analysis to explain the steps he will take to insure the withdrawal of the missile sites.

8.   Acting, therefore, in the defense of our own security and of the entire Western Hemisphere and under the authority entrusted to me by the Constitution as endorsed by the resolution of the Congress, I have directed that the following initial steps be taken immediately: To halt this offensive build-up, a strict quarantine on all offensive military equipment under shipment to Cuba is being initiated. All ships from whatever nation or port will, where they are found to contain cargoes of offensive weapons, be turned back. This quarantine will be extended if needed to other types of cargo and carriers.

9. *Psychological Proof.* The missiles are labeled as a clandestine, reckless, and provocative threat to *world* peace. Further, the missiles pose a direct threat to the *freedom* of every American. To back down on demanding a halt to this missile build-up would be like *surrendering,* which Americans never do.

9.   I call upon Chairman Krushchev to halt and eliminate this clandestine, reckless, and provocative threat to world peace. Let no one doubt that this is a difficult and dangerous effort on which we have set out. No one can foresee precisely what course it will take, or what course or casualties will be incurred. The cost of freedom is always high, but Americans have always paid it. And one path we shall never choose, and that is the path of surrender, or submission.

Vital Speeches, XXIX:3 (November 15, 1962), p. 66.

EXERCISES

I. Choose one of the following statements and support it with a short example of each of the supporting devices:

"Wear a seat belt. The life you save may be your own."
"The U.S. should have a standard drinking age of 18."
"Give yourself a break and quit smoking."

Model

The U.S. should adopt a system of national health insurance.

Comparison. National Health Insurance does the job in Denmark; it will also work in the United States.

Example. Fred Feldman's wife entered the hospital in January and died six months later. The next day Fred was given a bill for $27,000.

Statistics. According to a 1970 survey by the U.S. Department of Health and Welfare, the average American pays over $1,000 per year in medical bills.

Testimony. The U.S. Surgeon General warns that unless something is done to halt the spiraling cost of health care, only the rich will be able to afford it.

Explanation. If we had compulsory national health insurance, we could control doctor's fees and standardize practices for more efficient service.

II. Find an ad that combines explanation and statistics to sell its product. Analyze this use of supporting material. Are the statistics documented? Who compiled them? Are they accurate?

III. Indicate an authority that most of your classmates would respect as an expert in each of the following fields: education, pollution control, space exploration, crime prevention, medicine, professional football, and politics.

IV. Find an example of effectively used statistics in a current newspaper. Indicate why you think the statistics are effective.

GATHERING SUPPORTING MATERIAL

No doubt, for much of your writing and speaking you will gather supporting material from your own personal experience. However, there will be times when you will be asked to rely on other sources to insure the accuracy or objectivity of your papers and speeches. Research, the systematic gathering and documenting of this material, takes place mainly in the library. The pages which follow will deal with using the library, taking notes, and writing footnote and bibliography entries.

The Library

Your college or community library is the best place to go to gather supporting material for a speech or writing assignment. Because of the vast amount of information available today, libraries are becoming increasingly complex. Not only are more books available than ever before, but there is an increase of information being stored on microfilm, records, and video cassettes. Therefore, the more you know about how your library works, the more efficient you will become in gathering supporting material.

The Card Catalog   The card catalog consists of cases of drawers containing 3×5 inch cards. These cards list all of the books in the library alphabetically under three headings: title, author, or subject. Therefore, *What Did You Say? Second Edition* by Felber and Koch, can be located in at least three separate card trays. It can be found in the W's after *What*, the first significant word in the title; in the F's under Felber, the first listed author; and under English and/or Communication Skills.

The card catalog also lists the date the book was published, the publisher and place of publication, the edition of the book, and the call number of the book.

While works of fiction are usually filed alphabetically by the author's name, nonfiction books in the library are arranged on the shelves according to call numbers. Libraries organize these books in either of two different ways—the Dewey Decimal System or the Library of Congress System.

Dewey Decimal System   The Dewey Decimal System, as the name suggests, is divided into ten general categories:

000–099	General works	500–599	Pure Science
100–199	Philosophy	600–699	Technology
200–299	Religion	700–799	The Arts
300–399	Social Sciences	800–899	Literature
400–499	Language	900–999	History

Each of these general categories is further subdivided by tens:

600–609	Technology	650–659	Business
610–619	Medical Sciences	660–669	Chemical Technology
620–629	Engineering	670–679	Manufacturing
630–639	Agriculture	680–689	Other Manufactures
640–649	Home Economics	690–699	Building Construction

Library of Congress System   Library of Congress Classification numbers are arranged alphanumerically. The major categories are:

A. General works
B. Philosophy, Religion
C. History (General)
D. History (Old World)
E. History (American & U.S. General)
F. History (U.S. Local & American)
G. Geography, Anthropology
H. Social Sciences
J. Political Science
K. Law
L. Education

M. Music
N. Fine Arts
P. Language
   and Literature
Q. Science
R. Medicine
S. Agriculture
T. Technology
U. Military Science
V. Naval Science
Z. Bibliography,
   Library Science

Subject Guide to Books in Print   A second tool to use to locate books is the *Subject Guide to Books in Print*, which lists by subject all the books currently published in the United States, except fiction, poetry, drama, and bibles. The advantage to using this guide is that it lists *every* book presently in print in a particular subject area. If the library you use does not have a particular book in its collection, you can ask them to borrow the book from another library.

Periodical Indexes   Probably the best place to find short, current articles on a narrow subject is in a magazine or periodical. The most efficient way to search these publications is to use one of the available indexing services. Of these, the *Reader's Guide to Periodical Literature* is the most popular. It covers articles in over a hundred journals, listing them by subject and author, and it is published monthly.

Your library will also offer a great many other periodical indexes, specializing in such areas as photography, engineering, and applied technology. If you have a question about whether or not you are using the best possible index, ask a librarian for help.

The New York Times Index

Since 1913 the *New York Times* has published a monthly index which lists, by subject, all of the articles that have appeared in that paper. The index indicates the date, page, and column of the article. Therefore, you can either look up the article in the *Times*, or if the article is about an important event, use the date to locate a similar article in your local newspaper.

The Reference Room   Encyclopedias, dictionaries, atlases, almanacs, biographies—all books of general information are kept on open shelves in the reference section of your library. These books are labeled with an "R" for reference. They are so important for research that they must be used on the premises. Consult Winchell's *Guide to Reference Books* for the appropriate reference volumes. If you need help, don't be afraid to ask the reference librarian.

Bibliography Cards   If you are gathering your supporting material for research paper or speech, you should make one bibliography card for each source you will use. Use either a 3×5 or 4×6 inch card as your instructor directs. Your bibliography card should include the name of the author, the title, the call number of the book or periodical, the publisher, and the place and date of publication. You should also include a key number so your note cards can be "keyed" to the bibliography card.

Author's name (Last name first on bibliography card.)	Awad, Elias M. (13)
Title, place, publisher, and date of publication	Automatic Data Processing: Principles and Procedures. Englewood Cliffs, New Jersey Prentice-Hall, Inc., 1970.
Call number	651.2 A 962

Taking Notes

If you prepare your notecards carefully and accurately, you will save valuable time. Here are some simple rules to follow in taking notes. Observe them carefully and you will save hours of time.

1. *Use either 3×5 or 4×6 inch file cards for notes.* Notecards which are of uniform size are easier to work with.

2. *Include only one idea per card.* Don't copy large sections of the material because you are not sure of what you want. Spend some time in deciding what particular point you want to make. Then jot it down.

3. *Put the same key number on the note card that appeared on the appropriate bibliography card.* Since the full bibliographical information is on one card you won't have to rewrite the information again.

4. *Give each item a heading.* If you indicate the nature of the material with a topic heading, when you are ready to organize your cards into a paper, you can put them in piles according to topic.

5. *Follow the heading with information.* If the material is quoted exactly, use quotation marks. If you paraphrase, make sure you respect the author's meaning.

6. *Take accurate notes.* Be sure you have copied correctly the word order, punctuation and spelling of quoted material.

7. *Put down the exact page number from which your notes were taken.* You might have to refer to the source again to get a more complete statement. Besides you'll probably need the page number for your footnotes.

> Alphanumeric Data Representation
>
> "... although the user is interested only in decimal numbers as output, the internal operation of electrical computers is based on digits in various binary forms."
>
> p. 155
>
> (13)

Sample Note Card

Footnotes

There are two types of footnotes, reference and content. Reference footnotes give credit to the author for direct quotations, facts, or opinions. Content footnotes provide a place for explanations and supplemental information which you feel are important but would impede the flow of discussion if they appeared in the body of the text. Footnotes appear either at the bottom of the page that contains an entry to be footnoted or in a section at the end of a research paper between the text and the bibliography. In either case, footnotes consist of two parts: the footnote number and the data.

The key to effective footnoting is consistency. In order to make your footnotes consistent, you need to follow some conventional style. Below is a commonly used style of footnoting. Since footnoting styles vary, your instructor may ask you to use a different form.

Reference footnotes:

Book:

[1] George Soule, *The Theatre of the Mind,* (Englewood Cliffs, N.J.:Prentice-Hall, 1974), p. 7.

Periodical:

[2] George Adams, "Our Drug Culture," *Saturday Review* (January 20, 1978), pp. 48–50.

Newspaper:

[3] "Energy Crunch Continues," *The New York Times,* February 10, 1978, p. 4.

Content footnotes:

Supplemental Information Footnote: The author, title, publisher, place and date of publication are given in the first reference to a book. When a bibliography is provided, the name of the publisher is sometimes omitted.

When writing a research paper, you must often make subsequent references to a given source. For these references, you can use the author's surname and the page number provided that you are using only one book or article by that author. For subsequent references to newspaper or periodical articles, use the title (or shortened title) of the newspaper or periodical.

Examples:

[1] George Soule, *TheTheatre of the Mind* (Englewood Cliffs, N.J.: Prentice-Hall, 1974), p. 7.

[2] Soule, p. 19.

[3] George Adams, "Our Drug Culture," *Saturday Review* (January 20, 1978), pp. 48–50.

[4] *Saturday Review,* p. 49.

[5] "Energy Crunch Continues," *The New York Times,* February 10, 1978, p. 4.

[6] *New York Times* or *Times.*

Following are some common rules for footnoting:

1. If you are entering your footnotes throughout the body of your paper, type a line 1 1/2" long below the last line of the text to separate the footnotes from the text. Begin the line at the left margin and at least a double space below the last line of the text.

2. All footnotes should be single-spaced.

3. Footnotes should be numbered consecutively throughout the paper.

4. Footnotes are numbered with raised numbers placed one-half space above the line of type.

5. A double space should be left between footnotes.

6. Unless they are placed at the end of the text, footnotes must appear on the same page as the reference to them.

7. Footnote items should be separated from each other with commas; a period appears at the end of each footnote.

8. In a footnote the author's first name appears first.

9. Footnotes should run the full width of the page with the first line indented.

The Bibliography

A bibliography is a list of all the sources you have consulted in writing your paper. It is arranged in alphabetical order by author's last name. If there is no author, the source is listed by the first important word of the title. Since the bibliography is intended to show the reader where he can locate relevant material on the research topic, the first line is typed flush with the left margin (to make it more prominent) and the others are indented.

You can use the sample footnote and bibliography entries below as models. Make note of the major differences between the two.

A book by one author

Footnote:
[1]William L. Rivers, *Writing: Craft and Art* (Englewood Cliffs, N.J.: Prentice-Hall, 1975), p. 205.

Bibliography:
Rivers, William L., *Writing: Craft and Art*. Englewood Cliffs, New Jersey: Prentice-Hall, 1975.

A book by two authors

Footnote:
   [2] Stanley B. Felber and Arthur Koch, *What Did You Say?* 2nd ed. (Englewood Cliffs, N.J., 1978) p. 109.

Bibliography:
   Felber, Stanley B. and Arthur Koch. *What Did You Say?* 2nd ed. Englewood Cliffs, N.J.: Prentice-Hall, 1978.

A book with more than two authors

Footnote:
   [3] Anita Taylor et al., *Communicating* (Englewood Cliffs, N.J.: Prentice-Hall, 1977), p. 438.

Bibliography:
   Taylor, Anita, et al. *Communicating.* Englewood Cliffs, N.J.: Prentice-Hall, 1977.

An anthology

Footnote:
   [4] Alan Casty, ed., *A Mixed Bag: A New Collection for Understanding and Response,* 2nd ed. (Englewood Cliffs, N.J.: Prentice-Hall, 1975), p. 220.

Bibliography:
   Casty, Alan. ed., *A Mixed Bag: A New Collection for Understanding and Response.* Englewood Cliffs, N.J.: Prentice-Hall, 1975.

An article in a periodical

Footnote:
   [5] A. F. Williams, "Social Drinking, Anxiety, and Depression," *Journal of Personality and Social Psychology,* March 1976, p. 693.

Bibliography:
   Williams, A. F., *"Social Drinking, Anxiety, and Depression,"* Journal of Personality and Social Psychology, March 1976, pp. 689–693.

An article without an author

Footnote:
   [6] "Campus '65," *Newsweek,* March 22, 1965, p. 49.

Bibliography:
   "Campus '65," *Newsweek,* March 22, 1965, pp. 43–63.

An unpublished source

Footnote:
   [7] Irwin Stranz, "Marijuana Use of Middle- and Upper-Class Adult Americans" (Unpublished Ph.D. dissertation, School of Public Health, UCLA, 1971), p. 11.

Bibliography:
   Stranz, Irwin, *"Marijuana Use of Middle- and Upper-Class Adult Americans."* Unpublished Ph.D. dissertation, School of Public Health, UCLA, 1971.

A newspaper article

Footnote:
   [8] "Americans Take Big Chance In Hospital Emergency Rooms," *The Milwaukee Labor Press,* October 21, 1971, p. 2.

Bibliography:
   "Americans Take Big Chance In Hospital Emergency Rooms." *The Milwaukee Labor Press,* October 21, 1971, p. 2.

An interview

Footnote:
   [9] Interview with Joyce Jackson, Registered Nurse, Cudahy, Wisconsin, January 9, 1978.

Bibliography:
   Jackson, Joyce. Registered Nurse, Ackerman Clinic, Cudahy, Wisconsin. Interview, January 9, 1978.

A letter

Footnote:
   [10] Dr. Niels Nojgaard, letter dated June 10, 1963.

Bibliography:
   Nojgaard, Niels. Professor of Danish History, University of Kobenhavn, Denmark. Letter dated June 10, 1963.

EXERCISE

Use the card catalogue, the *Reader's Guide to Periodical Literature*, *The Subject, Author or Title Guide to Books in Print*, *The New York Times Index*, or other appropriate reference books to find the answers to the following questions in your local or school library. Along with your answers, indicate the source.

1. What books has J. Paul Getty written?
2. Who was the prosecuting attorney in the court-martial of William Calley?
3. Who won the gold medal in women's figure skating in the 1976 Olympics?
4. What is the name of the Arthur Miller play concerning a salesman?
5. On what day in 1974 did Richard Nixon resign?

6. How many acts are there in Hamlet?
7. What Washington, D.C., school did President Carter's daughter Amy attend in 1977?
8. From which college did Martin Luther King graduate?
9. Who wrote *Victory*?
10. Who won the Nobel Peace Prize in 1976?
11. How many books have been written about wolf children since 1962?
12. What is the title of a book about Lew Alcindor (Kareem Abdul-Jabar)?

Assignments

1. Develop a 1500–2000– word research paper as your instructor directs.
2. Prepare a 5–8 minute persuasive manuscript speech. Try to convince your audience to agree with the conclusions you came to as a result of your research.
3. Prepare a 5–8 minute extemporaneous speech based on your research project.
4. Answer the following questions about your school library.
   a. Which system of classifying books does your library use?
   b. To how many newspapers does your library subscribe? List them.
   c. What hours is your library open?
   d. For what period of time can a book be checked out?
   e. What is the name and title of the person in charge of the library?
   f. Where is the *Subject Guide to Books In Print* located?
   g. What fines are imposed for overdue books or records?
   h. What is the procedure for examining a periodical?

CHAPTER
8

Effective Sentence Structure

OBJECTIVES

After studying this chapter, you should be able to:

1. Classify sentences as simple, compound, complex, or compound-complex.
2. Distinguish among correct sentences, sentence fragments, and run-on sentences.
3. Recognize and correct errors in agreement of subject and verb.
4. Recognize and correct errors in agreement of pronoun and antecedent.
5. Recognize and correct errors in faulty parallelism.
6. Revise wordy sentences.
7. Revise sentences containing misplaced and dangling modifiers.
8. Analyze the sentence patterns found in *normal* sentences.
9. Expand the sentence patterns found in *normal* sentences through modification, coordination, and subordination.
10. Recognize and construct periodic, parallel, and balanced sentences.

SENTENCE VARIETY

The big league pitcher who threw nothing but fast balls would probably be batted out of the box in short order. A pitcher wants to keep the batter guessing, so he varies the pattern, throwing first a fast ball, then a curve, then a change of pace. The successful quarterback will, on occasion, throw the "bomb" when percentage dictates a power play into the center of the line. He, too, varies the pattern.

Sentence variety comes easily to the gifted writer. For those still striving to attain fluency, an understanding of different sentence classifications, both grammatical and rhetorical, will help to overcome the most common stylistic flaw in student writing—monotonous sentence structure.

GRAMMATICAL CLASSIFICATION

A clause is a word group containing both a subject and a predicate. A main clause (or an independent clause) makes sense when it stands alone. A subordinate clause is dependent upon, or subordinate to, a main clauses within a sentence or between sentences. An understanding of these relationships will enable you to recognize four basic sentence types: *simple, compound, complex,* and *compound-complex.*

The *simple sentence* consists of one independent clause.

1. John went to a rock festival. (one subject, one verb)
2. John and Mike went to a rock festival. (compound subject, one verb)
3. John and Mike went to a rock festival and met some interesting girls. (compound subject, compound verb)

All three examples above are simple sentences. Don't be confused by compound subjects and compound verbs. If the sentence contains only one main clause, it is a simple sentence.

The *compound sentence* consists of two or more independent (or coordinate) clauses. In order for a compound sentence to be effective, the ideas expressed in the main clauses must be of equal rank.

1. The doorbell rang, and John answered it. The doorbell rang; John answered it. (two independent clauses, separated by a conjunction or semicolon)
2. "The hum of talk came to him dimly, his rage blood pounded in his ears, and he burst through and strode away." (John Steinbeck, *The Pearl*) (three independent clauses, separated by commas and a conjunction)

Do not use compound sentences to express ideas of unequal importance.

Ineffective: John is a technical engineering student, and he has won a full-tuition scholarship.

Improved: John, a technical engineering student, has won a full-tuition scholarship. (*Note:* This is a simple sentence because it contains one independent clause.)

The *complex sentence* consists of one main clause and one or more subordinate clauses. Because it enables us to combine ideas of unequal rank in the same sentence by subordinating one idea to another, it is the sign of a sophisticated writer.

1. My brakes are defective.
2. I don't have any money to replace them.
3. I won't be able to drive home between semesters.

We could coordinate these three independent clauses in a single compound sentence, but that would only result in three parallel strands with nothing emphasized. The best solution would be to subordinate the first two clauses to the last in a complex sentence.

Because my brakes are defective and I don't have the money to replace them, I won't be able to drive home between semesters.

The *compound-complex* sentence combines the principles of coordination and subordination; consequently, it consists of two or more independent clauses and one or more subordinate clauses. Used too frequently, the compound-complex sentence can result in a cumbersome style, but, on occasion, it is an effective means of connecting interrelated ideas.

1. Get dressed and have your breakfast while we load the gear.
    (two independent clauses)   (one subordinate clause)

2. When we went on our picnic, I left my camera in the car and Mike went back to get it.
   (subordinate clause)   (two independent clauses)

EXERCISE

Indicate whether the following sentences are: (1) simple, (2) compound, (3) complex, or (4) compound-complex. Be prepared to explain your answers in class discussion.

1. When he smashed up his car, his wife became angry and the company cancelled his insurance.
2. Janet closed her eyes and rested her head on his shoulder.
3. George said he would return with the tickets, but I haven't seen him since noon.
4. My repeated attempts to talk him out of dropping English have fallen on deaf ears; nevertheless, I shall try again.
5. When the bell rings, leave quickly.
6. George Hays, the tallest player in the Conference, was dropped from the basketball team because of poor grades.
7. Before you report for your job interview, have your hair cut short and borrow your roommate's suit.
8. Jim's car, for which we couldn't obtain parts, had to be junked.
9. Before being wheeled into the operating room, the patient was given an anesthetic.
10. Being the only male in a class of nursing students must have its disadvantages, but I can't think of any.

Frequent use of complex sentences and an occasional compound-complex sentence can effectively link ideas of unequal importance. Our discussion of rhetorical classification will provide other equally effective techniques for achieving sentence variety. But before we proceed to this discussion, it would be well to pause and reflect upon the most basic type of sentence error: the inability to distinguish among complete sentences, run-on sentences, and sentence fragments.

Think back to your writing experiences in high school. Have your teachers ever commented on your inability to distinguish between a sentence and a nonsentence? Do you recall such symbols as *frag.* (sentence fragment) and *R.O.* (run-on sentence) in the margins of your compositions? If so, you may have a writing problem serious enough to affect adversely your chances for college and vocational success. Now is the time to resolve to correct that problem. Unless you plan to obtain remedial instruction, this will probably be your last classroom opportunity to learn to write a correct English sentence.

The following diagnostic test will measure your ability to distinguish among correct sentences, sentence fragments, and run-on sentences. If you achieve a score of 17 or better (out of a possible 20), you may skip the discussion of sentence fragments and run-on sentences and continue on page 148, beginning with *Agreement of Subject and Verb: Language Harmony.*

If you score below 17, review the material immediately following the Diagnostic Test, and then take the Post Test on pages 146–47. (The Diagnostic Test and the Post Test may be used interchangeably.)

DIAGNOSTIC TEST

For each of the following word groups, indicate C for correct sentence, R for run-on sentence, or F for sentence fragment.

1. When the moon comes over the mountain.
2. The moon comes over the mountain.
3. Don't worry, we will work it out somehow.
4. Hoping to hear from you soon.
5. Go!
6. Sam Jones, who is the oldest student in the class and the best swimmer in the school.
7. While running to the bus stop, I fell.
8. After buying her one ounce of fine French perfume and taking her to the best restaurant in town.
9. Then we arrived at our destination.
10. The books were neatly arranged, however, papers were scattered all over the floor.

11. Jogging for two miles before breakfast was his usual routine.

12. He quickly glanced to his right, then he sprinted for the finish line.

13. This car needs new brakes and new tires, nevertheless, it's a good buy for the money.

14. Working out on the parallel bars for three full hours each day.

15. My job, however, leaves much to be desired.

16. Leaving his place of employment promptly enabled him to avoid the rush hour traffic.

17. Wondering whether the cute blonde in his English class would meet him later on for a sandwich and a coke.

18. The interesting scenery, however, makes the drive to school relaxing.

19. I just can't feel sorry for him flunking out of school was his own fault.

20. Rereading the chapter increased his understanding.

The Sentence Fragment

The word *fragment* means a part broken off or detached. A sentence fragment is a part of a sentence, as in the following examples:

Fragment: 1. Martha did poorly in her history examination. *Although she spent all of her time studying.*

2. *Because my parents and kid sister are driving up for a visit.* I won't be able to have dinner with you tonight.

Explanation: Although both italicized examples contain subjects and verbs, they are incomplete. The words *although* and *because* introduce subordinate clauses which require main clauses to complete the context.

Combining the subordinate clause with a related main clause produces a grammatically correct, complex sentence.

Correction: 1. [Martha did poorly in her last history examination.]
main clause

[although she spent all of last week studying.]
subordinate clause

2. [Because my parents and kid sister are driving up for a
subordinate clause

visit,] [I won't be able to have dinner with you tonight.]
main clause

Review: Use the following subordinate clauses in complex sentences:

1. After we finished our dinner.
2. Even though summer jobs are very scarce.

Note: The subordinate clause may precede or follow the main clause.

Fragment: *Controlling exhaust emissions of the internal combustion engine.*

Explanation: Phrases, unlike clauses, are word groups which do not contain subjects and verbs; therefore, they are not complete sentences.

A phrase can, however, function as the subject of a complete sentence.

Correction: [Controlling exhaust emissions of the internal combustion engine] is one way of combating air pollution.
phrase as subject

engine] is one way of combating air pollution.

Review: Use the following phrases as subjects of complete sentences:
1. Watching televised football in color.
2. Studying for final examinations at the end of a busy day.
3. To play chess well.
4. The best dancer in our group.

Fragment: *To prevent loss of fuel vapors.*

Explanation: A phrase can modify a main clause.

Correction: [To prevent loss of fuel vapors,] [the gas tank should
phrase as modifier   main clause
always be tightly capped.]

Review: Use the following phrases to modify main clauses in complete sentences:
1. In order to decide which extracurricular activities to participate in.
2. Working as quickly as he could.

Note: The modifying phrase may precede or follow the main clause.

Fragment: 1. *Hoping to hear from you soon.*
2. *Walking in the rain.*

Explanation: A phrase can be converted into a main clause by adding a subject and a verb.

Correction: 1. I hope (am hoping) to hear from you soon.

2. I am walking in the rain.

Review: Convert the following fragments into correct sentences:

1. Giving my best whenever I compete.

2. Looking for a mutually satisfactory solution.

Fragment: *Jimmy Smith, the overwhelming choice for all-conference center.*

Explanation: We have a subject, *Jimmy Smith,* and a modifying phrase, *the overwhelming choice for all-conference center,* but a verb is lacking.

If we add a verb, perhaps as part of a complete predicate, our sentence would be complete.

Correction: [*Jimmy Smith,*] the overwhelming choice for all-con-
subject

ference center, [has received] an offer to play pro-
verb

fessional football.

Review: Convert the following fragments into correct sentences:

1. Deciding what to do next Saturday night.

2. Discussing yesterday's lecture with two of his classmates.

3. The new Student Union, a massive combination of steel and concrete.

4. Mr. Halloway, the best English teacher I ever had.

On occasion, you may find professional writers using fragments punctuated as complete sentences. Grammatical rules, like most other rules, have their exceptions. An accomplished writer will sometimes *knowingly* write a sentence fragment in order to achieve a particular stylistic effect. When a student *unknowingly* punctuates a fragment as a complete sentence, he tells his reader that he is unable to distinguish a sentence from a nonsentence.

It is generally a good idea to avoid fragments early in your college writing career. Once you have achieved a measure of linguistic sophistication, you may feel ready to deviate from some of the rules.

The Run-On Sentence

A *run-on* sentence contains two or more complete sentences punctuated as a single sentence. The two types of run-on sentences discussed in this section are the *fused* sentence and the *comma-splice.*

Run-on: Wait here we will see whether Tom is in his office.

Explanation: Two sentences are said to be *fused* when appropriate punctuation is omitted. This type of run-on sentence can be corrected as follows:

1. Place a period after the first sentence and begin the next with a capital letter.
2. Use a semicolon instead of a period if the two clauses are closely related.
3. Formulate a compound sentence by separating main clauses of similar rank with a conjunction.
4. Formulate a complex sentence by changing one of the main clauses into a subordinate clause.

Correction:

1. Wait here. We will see whether Tom is in his office.
2. Wait here; we will see whether Tom is in his office.
3. Wait here and we will see whether Tom is in his office.
4. If you wait here, we will see whether Tom is in his office.

Review: Correct the following fused sentence by using each of the four methods identified above:

> I purchased my cassette recorder many years ago it still gives me trouble-free service.

Run-on: Wait here, we will see whether Tom is in his office.

Explanation: When a comma is used to separate two complete sentences, the result is a *comma-splice,* another type of run-on sentence. The comma is not a terminal mark of punctuation; therefore, it cannot take the place of a period or semicolon. A comma, like a yellow traffic light, is a signal to pause and proceed with caution. Periods and semicolons are the "red lights" of punctuation; they are used to stop sentences from running into one another.

Correction: In order to correct a comma-splice, follow the same procedure previously indicated for the fused sentence.

(If the two main clauses are not of similar or equal rank, do not use the third technique involving connection with a conjunction.)

Review: Correct the following comma-splice. Attempt to use each of the four methods indicated above.

Let's have dinner at the Nantucket, they serve the best Kansas City strip steak in town.

Run-on: This semester I am taking a reduced program, therefore, I must take two additional courses in summer school in order to graduate.

My suitcases are already packed, however, I still have a few things to take care of before we leave.

Explanation: These two comma-splice sentences illustrate a particularly troublesome type of run-on sentence. The sentences can be corrected as follows:

1. Separate the two main clauses by placing a period after the first sentence and beginning the next with a capital letter.

or

2. Use a semicolon instead of a period if the two clauses are closely related.

Correction:
1. This semester I am taking a reduced program. Therefore, I must take two additional courses in summer school in order to graduate.

2. This semester I am taking a reduced program; therefore, I must take two additional courses in summer school in order to graduate.

3. My suitcases are already packed. However, I still have a few things to take care of before we leave.

4. My suitcases are already packed; however, I still have a few things to take care of before we leave.

Additional Explanation: The words *therefore* and *however* in the above sentences perform similar functions. Because they modify or qualify the first main clause and relate it to a second clause, they are called conjunctive adverbs. Some common conjunctive adverbs are:

therefore	**besides**	**consequently**
however	**then**	**furthermore**

Sometimes a comma-splice sentence containing a conjunctive adverb can be corrected by placing a conjunction before the conjunctive adverb:

First we plan to have dinner together, *and then* we will
see a play.   conjunction, conjunctive adverb

Do not confuse the conjunctions *and, but,* and *or* with
conjunctive adverbs:

Correct: The tree in our yard is huge, *but* it doesn't
              provide much shade.

Incorrect: The tree in our yard is huge, *however,* it
              doesn't provide much shade.

Correct: The tree in our yard is huge; *however,* it
              doesn't provide much shade.

Conjunctive adverbs separate main clauses. When
words such as *however* and *therefore* appear *within*
main clauses, they are separated from the words they
modify with commas:

Correct: Most rules, however, have their exceptions.

Correct: The train was four hours late. The team,
              therefore, forfeited the game.

Review: Make the needed corrections in the following:

1. I lost my notes, therefore, I cannot study for the following examination.
2. I have enough money to last until payday, however,
   I cannot afford to spend any of it foolishly.
3. I have enough money, however, to last until payday.
4. The game was dull, besides, the weather was terrible.
5. Rachel studied these pages carefully, consequently,
   she will do well on the following post test.

POST TEST

**For each of the following word groups, indicate *C* for correct sentence, *R*
for run-on sentence, or *F* for sentence fragment.**

1. After inviting him to dinner two consecutive Sundays and buying him a
   watch for his birthday.
2. Walking to Bill's apartment in this blizzard is folly.
3. Then we were ready to leave.
4. Losing his balance unnerved him.
5. Your directions were impossible to follow, otherwise I would have been
   here hours ago.

6. The extra money, however, paid for his tuition.

7. Jim Gibbons, who is the best punter and the fastest runner on the squad.

8. Because you aren't permitted to operate this machine without permission.

9. You aren't permitted to operate this machine without permission.

10. Conscientiously taking his medication after each meal enabled him to keep the problem under control.

11. Leaving me in charge of the automotive shop for the next three days.

12. Leave!

13. Try again, I'm sure you will be able to master the procedure shortly.

14. He said he would clean up after he finished the job, however, the house was a mess when he left.

15. Wishing you were here with me.

16. He checked his instruments and adjusted his helmet then he waited for the race to begin.

17. My plans, however, are still subject to change.

18. I hear the movie is excellent, besides, the concert has been sold out for more than a week.

19. Attempting to revise his plans so that he could visit his friend before the end of the semester.

20. Skating around the rink for the first time in years, I was surprised at how well I did.

Agreement of Subject and Verb: Language Harmony

Some years ago, a local department store advertised its annual sales event with the slogan: *Capacity Days Is Here.*

Some local partisans of grammatical purity were offended. How can the singular verb "is" be used with the plural noun "days"? The advertising agency responsible for the slogan rose to its own defense. They argued, quite logically, that while Capacity Days does, in fact, extend over a period of days, the term refers to *one* sale, the big sale of the year. Therefore, since Capacity Days refers to a single sale, the singular verb "is" is perfectly proper.

Certain elements of the population weren't convinced. The plural noun "days" followed by the singular verb "is" just didn't sound right. Rather than alienate prospective customers, the store compromised and adopted a modified slogan: *Capacity Days Is/Are Here.*

The basic rules of subject and verb agreement are simple and logical: Singular subjects require singular verbs; plural subjects require plural verbs. However, as we saw from the foregoing example, application of the rule can sometimes be troublesome. Let us take a closer look at a few of the more difficult situations:

Which verb form would you select in each of the following?

1. Jane, together with the other students in our English class, (was or were) offended by the instructor's sexist remarks.
2. Every student and faculty member (has or have) to carry an identification card at all times.
3. Neither Rachel nor the other bowlers on the squad (is or are) likely to finish the season with a 175 average.
4. The jury (is or are) still deliberating.
5. The value of the committee's decision (is or are) open to question.
6. An anthology of short stories (is or are) what Maggie would like for her birthday.
7. His height and agility (make or makes) him an ideal candidate for the basketball team.
8. Basic Economics (is or are) required for an Associate Degree.
9. Each of us who (is or are) enrolled in Communication Skills must write six papers this semester.

Now, let us see how well you did.

1. The subject is *Jane.* Don't be confused by the phrase beginning with "together with." When constructions such as *together with, as well as,* and *in addition to* intervene between the subject and the verb, the verb still agrees with the subject. *Jane . . . was* offended by the instructor's sexist remarks.
2. The indefinite pronouns—*each, every, everybody, nobody, neither, either, no one*—generally require singular verbs. *Every* student and faculty member *has* to carry an identification card. . . .
3. In either/or and neither/nor constructions, the verb agrees with the closer of the two subjects. Neither Rachel nor the other *bowlers are* likely. . . .
4. A collective noun—team, jury, class, public—requires a singular verb when the group is represented as a unit, a plural verb when the members of the group are acting as individuals. The jury *is* deliberating, but the jury *are* unable to agree on a verdict.
5. The subject is *value.* Don't be misled by *decisions,* the object

of the preposition. Since the subject, *value,* is singular, the value . . . *is* open to question.

6. Our subject is *anthology. Short stories* is the object of the preposition. Since the subject, *anthology,* is singular, an anthology . . . *is* what Maggie would like. . . .

7. Our compound subject — *height and agility* — requires a plural verb. Notice that while nouns generally add an *s* to form the plural, verbs frequently drop the *s* to form the plural. His height and agility *make* him an ideal candidate. . . .

8. Nouns that are plural in form but singular in meaning agree with singular verbs. Basic Economics *is* required.

9. The relative pronouns — *who, which,* and *that* — agree with singular or plural verbs, depending on their antecedents. Each of *us who are* enrolled in Communication Skills must write six papers. . . . The relative pronoun *who* refers to the antecedent *us,* which is plural; therfore, we use *are,* the plural verb form.

EXERCISE

Select the correct verb form in the following sentences:

1. Two weeks (is or are) too short a time for an annual vacation.
2. Neither my brothers nor my sister (is or are) as tall as I.
3. *Rocky* is one of the five movies that (have or has) been nominated for an Academy Award.
4. Mike, along with two of my other friends, (is or are) planning a trip to Florida during the spring recess.
5. Each one of us (is or are) entitled to be treated with respect.
6. Five dollars an hour (is or are) good money for inexperienced and untrained workers.
7. The committee (recommend or recommends) that the present policy be changed.
8. The worth of my photography courses (is or are) already evident.

Agreement of Pronoun and Antecedent: More Language Harmony

Which is correct? An antecedent is (a) the predecessor of the Honda Civic, (b) a long-lost aunt, (c) a small, blood-sucking insect, (d) the word to which a pronoun refers.

Just as subject and verbs must agree to achieve language harmony, so too, must pronouns and antecedents:

                     antecedent   pronoun

Singular: *Carol* enjoyed *her* dinner very much.

                     antecedent   pronoun

Plural: The *children* lost *their* way in the darkness.

Select the correct pronoun form in the following sentences:

1. Each person in this class should put forth (his or their) best effort.
2. Every man and woman should do what (he or they) can to conserve electricity.
3. When the national anthem was played, everyone rose to (his or their) feet.
4. (a) The team enjoyed (its or their) position in first place.

    (b) The team took (its or their) seats on the bench.
5. Either Rachel or her friends may miss (her or their) bus.

A singular pronoun is generally used with such indefinite antecedents as *each, every, everyone, everybody, someone, somebody, either, neither,* and *no one.* When the antecedent includes those of both sexes, a masculine singular pronoun is used. Therefore:

1. *Each* person in this class should put forth *his* best effort.
2. *Every* man and woman should do what *he* can to conserve electricity.
3. When the national anthem was played, *everyone* rose to *his* feet.

The above three problems of agreement of pronoun and antecedent illustrate the sexist nature of our language. Even though men and women are involved in all three situations, the masculine singular pronoun form is identified as the "correct choice." Language specialists have long deplored the fact that we have no word in our language that means *his or her.* You may choose to use alternate pronoun forms—*Every* man and woman should do *his* or *her* best—or reword your sentence—*People* should do *their* best. In informal English, the plural pronoun form is becoming increasingly commonplace: *Every* man and woman should do *their* best.

4. Collective nouns agree with singular pronouns when the group acts as a single unit: The team, therefore, enjoyed its position in first place. When the members of the group act as

individuals, the pronoun should be plural: The team took their seats on the bench.

5. When a pronoun refers to two antecedents, one singular and one plural, the pronoun agrees with the closer of the two: Either Rachel or her *friends* may miss *their* bus.

Let us examine a few additional pronoun references problems.

1. Jim told his friend that he would ace the exam.
2. Do not leave your machine unattended. This is an unsafe practice.
3. When one is ill, you should notify your supervisor as soon as possible.

In sentence 1 the antecedent of *he* is unclear. Does Jim mean that he will ace the exam? Or, does he mean that his friend will ace the exam? One way to clarify such sentences is to insert the proper reference immediately after the pronoun: Jim told his friend that he (Jim) would ace the exam.

In sentence 2, although the meaning of "this" is apparent, the pronoun reference is awkward because the antecedent is not specifically stated. Reword the sentence: Leaving your machine unattended is an unsafe practice.

Sentence 3 makes a needless shift in person. When *one* (third person) is ill, *you* (second person) should notify your supervisor. The pronoun shift from third to second person is awkward and unnecessary. When one (third person) is ill, (he or she) should notify (his or her) supervisor as soon as possible. Needless shifting should be avoided, not only within sentences, but within longer communications. If you are writing a narrative and you begin by relating an experience in the first person, try to follow through with the first person whenever possible.

EXERCISE

Correct any errors in agreement of pronoun and antecedent that appear in the following sentences:

1. Every member of this class should turn in his or her technical report before the end of the month.
2. After the delivery men removed the refrigerator from the crate, they discarded it in the village dump.
3. The class was making good progress with their semester project.
4. When one works and goes to school, I find it difficult to do justice to both.
5. Each member of the committee have specific responsibilities.

6. If a person wants to see your federal government in action, they should visit Washington, D.C.

7. If you don't remove the rat from the trap soon after the catch, it will start to smell.

8. I left Sam convinced that he lacked understanding.

9. Neither Bill nor the other members of the crew volunteered to work on their day off.

10. I rush to the refrigerator every time a commercial appears on the screen. That is not the way to stay trim.

Parallelism: "One of These Things Is Not Like the Others"

One reason for awkward sentences is lack of parallel structure. What do we visualize when the word "parallel" is mentioned? Some of us see railroad tracks; some see parallel bars in a gym; some see two parallel chalk lines on a blackboard. Whatever we visualize, the parallel elements are of the same length and the same material. When we have words or groups of words side by side in a sentence, they should be constructed the same way. This sentence, for example, lacks parallel structure:

(1)   (2)   (3)

He likes to play cards, to swim, and listening to music.

We don't even need to know any grammatical terminology to figure out what's wrong here; in the words of the Sesame Street song, "One of These Things Is Not Like the Others." The groups of words numbered (1) and (2) consist of *to* plus a verb, while (3) is an *ing* construction. To correct the faulty parallelism, we must make all three alike. We can say:

	to play cards,			playing cards,
He likes	to swim, and	OR	He likes	swimming, and
	to listen to music.			listening to music.

EXERCISES

The following sentences are awkward because of faulty parallelism. In each sentence identify the element that is not like the others. Then rewrite the sentences to eliminate the faulty parallelism.

1. The professor's lectures are dry, disorganized, and they are difficult to follow.

2. Super Woman is a beauty, can cook, and is also an electrical engineer.

3. I admire people who are honest, who are outspoken, and sticking to their principles is also admired.

4. To eat, drinking, and to make money are his goals.

5. Riding a motorcycle requires skill, coordination, and one has to have courage.

Supply the missing elements. Sometimes you may supply words, sometimes groups of words, but in any case your finished sentences should have perfect parallel structure.

1. I wish I had a job that _____

_____

_____

2. My idea of a fun evening is _____

_____

_____

3. TV programs would be better if _____

_____

_____

4. I disapprove of _____

_____

_____

5. Students who are doomed to failure are those who _____

_____

_____

Economy: Clearing the Air

The need for clarity is obvious. If a sentence isn't perfectly clear, if it doesn't make sense to the reader, what good is it? One of the enemies of clarity is wordiness. Too many unnecessary words may prevent the reader from getting the sense of the sentence — or at least getting it as quickly and easily as he should. But note the word "unnecessary." We aren't saying that sentences should be brief, short, or skimpy. We are merely saying that sentences should be stripped of useless verbiage and pretentious language.

Consider, for example, the following sentence: "I find myself in a state of regret because my present financial situation is so depleted that I will be unable to have the pleasure of accompanying you on your jaunt to the cinema." How much more quickly we get the point if the writer says, "I'm sorry I haven't enough money to go to the movie with you."

EXERCISES

Revise the following sentences, removing "deadwood" and pretentious language.

1. With regard to the high cost of transportation, I believe we should affiliate ourselves with a car pool whenever such an arrangement is feasible.
2. In my opinion I believe that the President has done a good job of leading the country in his first year in office.
3. By virtue of my interest in numismatic concerns, I recently purchased a subscription to *Coin World* for a period of three years.
4. The sizable and unexpected high cost of repairing my vehicle thwarted my plans for a relaxing and restful vacation in the vicinity of the Caribbean Islands.
5. She faithfully reads the newspaper *The Milwaukee Journal,* which is widely distributed throughout the State of Wisconsin.

Write sentences that are deliberately wordy. Exchange your sentences with those of a classmate. Now rewrite each others' sentences, getting rid of the "deadwood," without changing the original meaning.

Modification: The Case of the Misplaced Modifier

Another enemy of clarity is faulty word order. Words should always be near the words they modify; when they are not, the result is awkwardness and ambiguity. (If something is ambiguous, it has two or more possible meanings.) Now granted, particularly in poetry, we may want something to be interpreted on two levels, but when we speak of ambiguity we are talking about a variety of possible meanings that tend to confuse the reader or listener.

Consider, for example, the following sentence: "Tonight there will be a panel discussion about drug addiction in the student lounge." Does the writer mean that the discussion will be held in the student lounge, or that the discussion will concern drug addiction that is evident from student behavior in the lounge? If we change the word order and write, "Tonight in the student lounge . . ." we have the meaning that the writer probably intended. But the reader shouldn't have to juggle and guess.

Sometimes, in the case of what we call dangling modifiers, the words that the modifiers describe are not even present in the sentence. Consider the following: When only five, my father taught me how to swim. The words "when only five" are next to father, but when father was only five he obviously was not a father, nor was he capable of teaching swimming. To make the sentence make sense, we must insert the missing words: When I was only five, my father taught me how to swim.

EXERCISE

In the following sentences, the intended meaning is unclear. Revise these sentences so that all possible ambiguities are removed.

1. The fight was broken up before further damage was done by the security guard.
2. Hurrying to class, my wallet was lost.
3. A ham sandwich was in my lunch bag which I ate eagerly.
4. The milk spilled all over the kitchen floor that I had intended to drink for breakfast.
5. Jogging around the campus for forty minutes, my appetite increased.
6. He was carried out of the smoke-filled building by two attendents on a stretcher.
7. Discouraged by the score, the stadium began to empty.
8. I placed the chair in the corner of the room that I had recently purchased.
9. After sitting there awhile, it began to snow.
10. He gave the sweater to the girl that he had won in track.

RHETORICAL CLASSIFICATION

We have seen how the use of subordinate clauses in complex and compound-complex sentences helps add variety to our writing. Our discussion of rhetorical classification will provide other equally effective techniques for achieving sentence variety. Sentences may be classified rhetorically as *normal, periodic, parallel,* and *balanced.*

The Normal Sentence

The *normal sentence,* so called because it occurs more frequently than any other type, consists of variations of the following subject-verb patterns.

***Subject-Verb* (S-V)**   In this sentence pattern the verb is *intransitive,* meaning it does not require an object to complete the predicate.

1. The boy fell.   (S-V)
2. The boy fell (down the stairs).   (S-V-M)
3. Rachel sang.   (S-V)
4. Rachel sang (beautifully).   (S-V-M)

Modifying phrases or words do not change the basic sentence pattern.

***Subject-Verb-Direct Object* (S-V-O)**   In this pattern the verb is *transitive,* meaning that it requires an object to complete the predicate.

1. Bill hit a home run.   (S-V-O)
2. Janet bought a sweater for her boyfriend.   (S-V-O)

The modifying prepositional phrase, *for her boyfriend,* does not change the basic sentence pattern.

***Subject-Verb-Indirect Object-Direct Object* (S-V-IO-DO)**   Sometimes S-V-O sentences also contain indirect objects. When this is the case, the indirect object follows the verb, but precedes the direct object.

1. Mom bought Dad a new suit.
    S   V   IO   DO
2. Janet bought her boyfriend a new sweater.
    S   V   IO   DO

***Subject-Verb-Complement* (S-V-C)**   In this pattern a linking verb connects the subject to the complement. A complement functions like a direct object, but it always follows a linking verb.

1. Janet is a dental assistant.   (S-V-C)
2. Mary is beautiful.
3. Jim felt bad.

To be is the most common linking verb. Other verbs often used to connect subjects to complements are *to become, to feel, to taste, to touch, to smell, to sound, to grow, to appear, to seem, to remain,* and *to become.* If in doubt about whether the verb is linking, try to substitute a form of *to be* for the verb in question. If the meaning of the sentence remains essentially the same, the verb is linking.

1. The swimming pool became (was) rusty.
2. The hamburger tastes (is) great.

Two other commonly employed normal sentence patterns are the *expletive* and the *passive.* The *expletive sentence* begins with *there,* and the verb precedes the subject.

1. There *is a stranger* at the door.
       V   S
2. There *have been* no more *tickets* available for two weeks.
       V   S

The *passive sentence* is a variation of the S-V-O sentence in which the subjects and objects are interchanged.

1. Bill hit the ball.   (S-V-O)
2. The ball was hit by Bill.   (Passive)
3. Tom met Mary at the dance.   (S-V-O)
4. Mary was met at the dance by Tom.   (Passive)

Modifying phrases do not change the basic sentence pattern.

EXERCISE

Basic patterns may stand alone in simple sentences or be combined in compound, complex, and compound-complex sentences. Using the following abbreviations, identify each of the italic patterns.

S-V   S-V-O   S-V-IO-DO   S-V-C   E   P

1. *Players from both sides swarmed onto the field.*
2. *Some players become nervous before a game; others keep their cool.*
3. *There are twenty students in class,* and *all of them seem to be shouting at once.*
4. *The house had been sold by Mr. Potter,* but *the agent didn't know the selling price.*
5. *If you give him the ball, he will make the first down.*

6. *Ernest Hemingway's novels brought him international fame.*
7. *A sentence containing a subordinate clause and a main clause is complex.*
8. *There are many good motels in town,* but *the Elgin is the best.*
9. *When anyone asks Jim a question, he becomes hard of hearing.*
10. *Our cousins from New York arrived by plane this afternoon.*

Effective sentence combinations illustrate variations of these basic sentence patterns. Three rhetorical devices—modification, coordination, and subordination—help us to expand these basic patterns.

Modification   Two of the eight traditional parts of speech, adjectives and adverbs, function as modifying elements in the sentence. In addition, phrases and clauses also function as modifying elements. This principle has been illustrated in various examples of basic sentence patterns. Modification is an effective means of avoiding the choppy, monotonous sentence structure that makes for ineffective writing.

Weak: Dick Person is the first baseman for the Oshkosh Outlaws. He hit a home run on August 3. It was the longest home run ever hit in People's Stadium.

Improved: On August 3, Dick Person, the first baseman of the Oshkosh Outlaws, hit the longest home run ever hit in People's Stadium.

Weak: I have a new dog. His name is Willy. He is very intelligent.

Improved: My new dog, Willy, is very intelligent.

Coordination   Just as we combine independent clauses in a compound sentence, we utilize this same principle by coordinating subjects, verbs, objects, complements, and modifiers in any sentence to achieve economy of expression.

Weak: My new dog, Willy, is very intelligent. He is a beautiful animal.

Improved: My new dog, Willy, is intelligent and beautiful.

Subordination   As previously defined, subordination provides us with the means of linking ideas of unequal rank in the same sentence.

Weak: My brother is home on vacation. He attends the Milwaukee Area Technical College.

Improved: My brother, who is home on vacation, attends the Milwaukee Area Technical College. (Or, depending on which idea is emphasized: My brother, who attends the Milwaukee Area Technical College, is home on vacation).

Weak: My new dog, Willy, is intelligent and beautiful. He is not as good a watch dog as Rusty. Rusty is my friend's dog.

Improved: Although my new dog, Willy, is intelligent and beautiful, he is not as good a watch dog as my friend's dog, Rusty.

EXERCISES

Combine each of the following sets of sentences into one sentence by coordinating, subordinating, and modifying the various elements.

1. My little sister went to the store. She forgot to chain her bike to the railing. Her bike was stolen. She was afraid to tell my father.
2. Our regular English teacher is Mr. McCarthy. He is ill with the flu. Mr. Longrie is a substitute teacher of English. He has been temporarily hired to teach senior English until Mr. McCarthy returns.
3. My older brother lives in New York. His name is Ken. He is an engineer with Arco Industries. Last year we flew to New York to see him. We traveled via Northwest Airlines.
4. It was raining very hard. My windshield wipers were defective. My vision was severely hampered. My car swerved into the guard railing. I received a severe whiplash and I also broke my arm.

The Periodic Sentence

A *periodic sentence* must contain the rhetorical effect of building to a climax through a series of words, phrases, or clauses. Although the main idea of a periodic sentence is always withheld until the end, not every sentence in which the main idea is withheld is periodic. This somewhat confusing distinction might best be explained by example.

Not Periodic: When you go to the store, bring back some beer. (Although the main clause is withheld, the rhetorical effect of building to a climax is not present.)

Periodic: If you like authentic rock music, a sandy beach, picturesque Southern architecture, and lovely girls, you will love Fort Lauderdale.

Periodic sentences must be well-planned and properly executed if they are to be effective. They should be used more sparingly than any other rhetorical device if they are to add variety, rather than monotony, to your writing. The Reverend Martin Luther King, Jr., concluded his memorable *I Have a Dream* speech with the following periodic sentence:

> And when we allow freedom to ring, when we let it ring from every village and hamlet, from every state and city, we will be able to speed up that day when all of God's children—black men and white men, Jews and Gentiles, Catholics and Protestants—will be able to join hands and to sing in the words of the old Negro spiritual, "Free at last, free at last; thank God Almighty, we are free at last."

Douglas MacArthur's 1961 speech commemorating Philippine Independence Day provides the following example:

> In the effort to build a world of economic growth and solidarity, in the effort to build an atmosphere of hope and freedom, in the effort to build a community of strength and unity of purpose, in the effort to build a lasting peace of justice, the Philippines and the United States of America have become indivisible.

Shakespeare proves that a periodic sentence need not be lengthy to be effective.

> To die, to sleep; to sleep, perchance to dream;
> Aye, there's the rub. . . .

The Parallel Sentence

A *parallel sentence* is one which emphasizes coordinate elements—single words, phrases, or clauses—usually in a series. Anytime a coordinating conjunction (and, or, but) appears in a sentence, an element of parallelism is present. But for the purpose of our definition, a rhetorical effect different from that of a normal sentence must be achieved.

> . . . and that government *of the people, by the people, for the people,* shall not perish from the earth.   —*Abraham Lincoln*

> *We hold these truths to be self-evident, that all men are created equal, that they are endowed by their Creator with certain unalienable Rights, that among these are Life, Liberty and the pursuit of Happiness.*
> —*Declaration of Independence*

> *"Duty," "honor," "country"*—those three hallowed words reverently dictate *what you want to be, what you can be, what you will be.*
> —*Douglas MacArthur*

Frequently, the effect of parallelism is achieved by intentional repetition of key words or word groups through a series of sentences or paragraphs. Emphasis by repetition can be effective, it if is not overdone.

> *Dreyfus is innocent.* I swear it. I stake my life on it. I stake my honor. In the presence of this Court, the representative of human justice, before all France, before all the world, I now solemnly swear that *Dreyfus is innocent.* By forty years of work, by the authority it has given me, I swear that *Dreyfus is innocent.* By the name I have made, by my contributions to the literature of France, I swear that *Dreyfus is innocent.* May all the results of my life melt away, may my work perish, if Dreyfus is not innocent. *He is innocent!*   —*Emile Zola*

The Balanced Sentence

A *balanced sentence* emphasizes contrasting coordinate elements, usually two main clauses. It is similar to the parallel sentence in that it emphasizes coordination, but with one important distinction: the key to the balanced sentence is contrast. The conjunction "but" frequently serves as the fulcrum of the two contrasting ideas.

> The world will little note, nor long remember, what we say here, *but* it can never forget what they did here.   —*Abraham Lincoln*

> The true test of civilization is
> not the census,
> nor the size of the cities,
> nor the crops,
> no,
> but the kind of man the country turns out.
>
> —*Ralph Waldo Emerson*

> Survival is still an open question—not because of environmental hazards, *but* because of the workings of the human mind.
>
> —*Adlai Stevenson*

Notice how the elements of *parallelism* and *balance* are combined in the following example:

> It is time that we see this doctrine of guilt by association for what it is: not a useful device for detecting subversion, *but* a device for *subverting our constitutional principles* and practices, *for destroying our constitutional guarantees,* and *for corrupting our faith in ourselves and our fellow man.*   —*Henry Steele Commager*

A simple but striking method of achieving sentence variety is to vary sentence length. The paragraph from Zola given above is an excellent example. The sentences vary from three to twenty-six words. The shorter sentences at the beginning and end of the paragraph ring with finality. The longer periodic sentences in the middle build up to the same spirited conclusion—"Dreyfus is innocent."

We have touched on but a few of the many ways in which a writer may vary his sentence structure and thereby improve his writing. Because the sentence is our basic unit of communication, we have analyzed it, both grammatically and rhetorically, in the belief that this knowledge will enable the student to develop his own fluent and distinctive style.

EXERCISE

Examine a recent issue of *Vital Speeches*. Locate at least two examples each of periodic, parallel, and balanced sentences. Then, construct two original examples of each type.

CHAPTER 9

Effective Paragraphing

Short story writers and novelists utilize similar techniques in developing a narrative. Similarly, the planning and execution of paragraphs and longer compositions have much in common. For this reason, the paragraph has been referred to as a composition in miniature. Because of its brevity, the paragraph is an ideal subject for careful analysis. The techniques of careful paragraphing to be developed in this section apply to longer compositions as well.

PURPOSEFULNESS: A PLAN OF ATTACK

The principles of purposeful communication have already been detailed. Once your primary purpose is clear to you and you have tentatively selected your subject, you are ready to tackle the job of proper restriction. The brevity of most paragraphs makes adequate restriction particularly important. A subject not properly restricted invariably results in superficial writing. Having arrived at an adequately restricted subject, you should then formulate the main idea of your paragraph. Generally, this main idea is specifically stated in the paragraph; at times, however, it may be implied. The main idea of a paragraph is called the *topic sentence.* Here are some sample topic sentences:

1. Paperback textbooks are inexpensive and convenient.
2. A good dictionary is the most useful of all general reference books.
3. The phenomenal success of the instant 126 cartridge camera is due to its simplicity of operation.

UNITY: THE GUIDING LIGHT

We are often told that a topic sentence will assure unity in a paragraph. We are told that a topic sentence is the simple summary of ideas expressed in the paragraph, that it may come first, last, or at some convenient place within the paragraph or may be omitted entirely.

The beginning writer will find it wise to have a topic sentence in each paragraph, because unless he has fixed clearly in mind the central thought he wishes to develop, he may ramble off in different directions. He frequently begins his flight with uncertainty, pursues his course as if chasing a will-o'-the-wisp, and ends in a bog of confusion.

In the following paragraph, notice how the writer rambles from point to point. He apparently meant his first sentence to be his topic sentence, but it did not keep him developing in a steady line. As a result, he did not stress one central thought throughout the paragraph.

*The Battle of Bunker Hill showed that the Colonists were brave men.*They fearlessly stood their ground as the Redcoats charged up the hill. Bunker Hill is in Charlestown, Massachusetts, near Boston. Nearby is Breed's Hill, which was part of the same battle. Bunker Hill is famous as one of the first major battles of the American Revolution. Paul Revere made his brave ride a couple of months before the battle. The Colonists were under General Prescott. It was Prescott who said, "Don't fire until you see the whites of their eyes!" His men waited until the English soldiers under General Howe were right in front of them and then fired point blank. Their deadly volleys broke the advancing ranks of the Redcoats three times. The battle took place on June 17, 1775. General Gage was in command of the English, and he learned that the Americans meant to defend their principles. The Redcoats finally took the hill. The battle was the real start of the Revolutionary War. The war came to an end when Cornwallis surrendered at Yorktown on October 19, 1781.

The topic sentence of the above paragraph seems to have suggested to the student a number of ideas associated with the Revolutionary War. He talks about Bunker Hill, Cornwallis, the surrender at Yorktown, brave men, the battle, the principles of the Colonists, General Gage, and other things. He fails to realize that he should discuss only one idea in the paragraph, and he does not even recognize the one idea that the topic sentence, as he has worded it, seems to stress. What he should have developed was the idea "brave men" in terms of "the battle of Bunker Hill." The paragraph as written has good details, but since it lacks unity, it fails to be clearly developed.

Until we learn how to start with a definite idea and stick to it as we develop a thought, we should not ignore the only signpost that can give direction to our journey. Until we become experienced, we should include a topic sentence in the paragraph.

What, then, is a good topic sentence? It is a sentence that contains the topic or idea that the paragraph is to develop. Emphasis must be placed upon the words "topic" or "idea," for the paragraph will usually be about the "idea." In the topic sentence, "The Battle of Bunker Hill showed that the Colonists were brave men," the important idea is "brave men." The paragraph should be about that one idea. The rest of the topic sentence tells under what circumstance the men were brave, but the idea "brave men" was the writer's chief concern.

Such a topic sentence is rather general. The idea "brave men" permits the writer to use whatever details, illustrations, and reasons he believes will support his point. Sometimes, however, it may be well to word the topic sentence so that the basic idea is more limited. Instead of only "brave men," it may say "brave men despite every disadvantage." The paragraph will still be about the "brave men" at Bunker Hill, but the writer's chief concern now is to tell about the men who were brave "despite every disadvantage." Compare the original Bunker Hill paragraph with the following:

The Battle of Bunker Hill showed that the Colonists were brave men despite every disadvantage. Against superior numbers of Redcoats they held their ground on the heights. Against superior training they pitted their impromptu drills and primitive tactics. Against a seasoned officer like General Howe, they confidently backed their less experienced but courageous General Prescott. The colonial minutemen were limited in numbers and were poorly supplied with ammunition and provisions; the Redcoats were but a small part of the whole English army in and around Boston and could depend upon extensive reinforcement and adequate supplies.

All the material in this paragraph supports "brave men despite every disadvantage." The writer kept this idea clearly in mind and excluded from the paragraph everything that did not develop it. His paragraph, therefore, has unity.

We have just seen how an expression like "brave men" or a phrase like "despite every disadvantage" can be the basic idea of a topic sentence. Sometimes you may find that a whole clause is needed to express your basic idea; for instance, "The Battle of Bunker Hill showed that the Colonists were bravest when the odds were most against them." A paragraph developing this topic sentence would try to show that the Colonists were brave men during battle, especially "when the odds were most against them."

In writing a topic sentence, then, we should be sure that it contains a definite word, phrase, or clause that points out the chief idea of the paragraph. Sometimes the first written form of a topic sentence needs to be revised so that its chief idea is actually included or is given a place of greater prominence.

The difference between a topic sentence that contains a topic idea and one that does not is like the difference between a highway that is clearly marked and one that is not. Like the traveler, the writer (and the reader) needs a guide. Let us call this guide the *controlling idea.*

The controlling idea is the basic or topic idea which we have been discussing. There is a difference between a topic sentence as used by many students and a topic sentence containing a definite controlling idea. For a paragraph of average length, say about 150 words, many beginning writers would be satisfied with the following topic sentence:

Napoleon was one of the greatest generals in history.

With this as a topic sentence, they might proceed to discuss everything they could think of to explain the whole statement. They might tell how Napoleon led his men through several victorious campaigns, including the Battle of Austerlitz; how he was finally defeated at Waterloo and was banished to Elba; how he remained a heroic figure in the minds of his followers and of succeeding generations. They might even include examples of children in recent times who chose to be "Napoleon" while playing war.

What would such material, such a rambling discussion, actually make clear? What central idea could the reader get? True, all the statements would in some way be related to Napoleon, but really, what is the point behind them? When one is through reading them, what does he know of Napoleon as a general or a defeated leader, or an outcast, or an idol? Like the various foods in a supermarket, everything seems related, but there is no single purpose behind the selection, nothing like a specific picnic that prompts the choice of special foods. Suppose, on the other hand, a student had worded his topic sentence:

Napoleon proved to be a great strategist in the Battle of Austerlitz.

Such a topic sentence would limit what might be said about Napoleon to his abilities as a strategist alone. Furthermore, it would force the student to fix his attention upon "strategist" in terms of the "Battle of Austerlitz." Under such control, "strategist" in terms of the specific battle becomes the controlling idea of the paragraph. Finally, it is a far more suitable topic idea for a paragraph of some 150 words.

As we have seen, the controlling idea may be stated in a single word, a phrase, or a clause, depending upon what is needed to express the basic idea of the paragraph. It is the core of thought that is to be explained. Furthermore, the language expressing it is the guide to direct our thinking, the sign by which we choose this and that material from all the material available to us. In summary, *the controlling idea is stated in the word, phrase, or clause that announces the central idea that is to be explained in a particular paragraph.*

COMPLETENESS: WHAT DIDN'T YOU SAY?

Have your papers ever been returned with such comments as "support your judgments" or "further development needed"? Failure to support and develop your ideas adequately is an all too common characteristic of student writing. There are two main causes of inadequate development:

1. The writer *assumes* that his readers have knowledge about the subject that they do not, in fact, actually possess.
2. The writer *intends* to provide a more complete explanation than he does, but because of laziness or the inability to support his judgments, he fails to do so.

During the planning, execution, and proofreading of your writing, consider your readers and provide them with sufficient information to receive your message. Whether you are relating an incident from personal experience or dealing with a subject you have researched, it is incumbent upon you, as the expert, to supply sufficient details. If you must err, it is better to provide too much detail rather than too little.

See Chapter 7 for a detailed treatment of the five major supporting devices: Examples, Statistics, Testimony, Comparison Contrast, and Explanation. It would also be desirable to review President Kennedy's televised speech concerning the Cuban Crisis for an analysis of how these supporting devices are incorporated into a finished manuscript. The preceding pages contain examples of student writing which illustrate adequate generalization—support development.

Depending upon your approach to your subject, you might decide to use a combination of supporting devices or only one extended example. The quality of a communication cannot be judged by the number of supports used. One well-developed example of a heavy smoker who developed lung cancer because of his habit might be far more effective than a series of statistics and explanations.

EXERCISE

The following paragraphs are incomplete. Indicate why. Revise either, supplying additional supporting details for the topic sentence in order to achieve completeness.

1. After attending college for two semesters, I finally have discovered the way I can best earn good grades. Besides taking good notes in class, keeping good attendance, and doing assignments promptly, I have learned a good method to study for exams. I still have much to learn about good study habits, but now higher grades come much easier for me.

2. Regular reading of *Ms. Magazine* is a must for every career woman of the '70s. It is one of the finest magazines for and about women on the American newsstands today. If you have not seen it, you should go out and buy a copy now.

COHERENCE: KEEPING IT ALL TOGETHER

Effective paragraphs must be coherent; that is, all of the sentences must "stick together." After all, they form a unit of expression—the paragraph—and therefore must be related to each other as parts of a whole. Each sentence must carry the reader to the next for smooth reading. A paragraph that is coherent is one with transitions, or links, between every sentence. A number of useful devices can aid a beginning writer in providing these links from sentence to sentence in a paragraph.

1. Use transitional words and phrases.

   Again, also, and, besides, furthermore, in addition, likewise, similarly, at the same time, but, conversely, however, in contrast, in spite of, nevertheless, on the other hand, yet, therefore

2. Use enumerative devices.

   A good student must have three essential skills. *First,* he must take excellent notes; *second,* he must be a good reader; *third,* he must be able to take exams well.

3. Use parallel structures in successive sentences.

   When you are loaded, *your friends* love you. *When you are* broke, *your friends* avoid you. *When you are* collecting debts, *your friends* don't know you.

4. Use a pronoun to refer to a word in the previous sentence.

Joann knew she deserved a D in Communication Skills. What she did mind, however, was taking *it* all over again with the same instructor.

5. Repeat some key word from one sentence in the following sentence. For example, the direct object of the first sentence may be used as the subject of the second.

Leonard *did* not want to admit his *drug addiction* to his wife. *Drug addiction* was not something he was proud of, but he was still unwilling to hurt his family with the truth.

6. Use the same subject in the successive sentences, employing identical words, synonyms, or pronouns.

Alcoholism is not a crime. *Alcoholism* is a sickness.

EXERCISE

In the following paragraph, identify the devices used to achieve coherence.

Although the bodies of our cameras do the same job, the similarities end there. My parents' Instamatic camera is large and made of plastic. It's not all that rugged, and a good jar would leave it cracked or damaged. My camera, on the other hand, is small and compact. Its all-metal design makes it a strong, dependable piece of equipment. It also houses a film buffer assembly that holds the film on which the image is to be formed perfectly flat. The instamatic has no such buffer; therefore, the image produced is not as sharp.

Since paragraphs are also part of a larger whole (the essay), they must also be linked together to show their relationship. The following suggestions will help us provide transition between paragraphs to attain a coherent essay.

1. Conclude a paragraph with a sentence that introduces the next phase of the action.

Example: A week later, the students decided to take action and occupy an office in the "O" Building.

2. Use a connective or a transitional word or phrase in the first sentence of a paragraph: *furthermore, therefore, as a result, in addition, on the contrary.*

3. Begin a paragraph with a sentence that refers clearly to a statement at the end of the preceding paragraph or its topic idea.

Example: Many high schools, then, are not giving the students adequate preparation for college-level writing. Should this be ignored by the colleges, or accepted as a real challenge?

(The first sentence summarizes the idea of the preceding paragraph. The second sentence introduces the controlling idea of the paragraph.)

ORGANIZATION: SEQUENCE OF IDEAS

Unity, completeness, and coherence are further aided by a logical plan of development suited to the material. Each paragraph has its own order or sequence of ideas. An essay may take advantage of several types of paragraph orders to achieve variety. The examples of organization given below are taken from student writings.

General-to-Specific Organization

Effective communication involves adequate generalization — support development. When the topic sentence stating the generalization or main idea appears at the beginning of the paragraph and the supporting details follow the topic sentence, a general to specific organizational pattern is employed.

Of the four basic organizational patterns, the general to specific is by far the most popular. Why? If you begin with your topic sentence and remain conscious of your main idea as you develop and support it, it is almost impossible to stray from your purpose.

MAIN IDEA

Although at first glance a final exam appears to be nothing more than a series of sloppily mimeographed, vaguely worded questions, *it is really a conspiracy aimed at students everywhere.* It is a third degree with no safequard against self-incrimination, a mismatch with no time out between rounds, a sentence to solitary confinement without bread or water, and a parachute jump without a parachute. While purporting to test a student's knowledge of subject matter, the final

SUPPORTING DETAILS

exam measures, instead, his ability to withstand the ill effects of poor ventilation and bad circulation in an overcrowded classroom. It forces the student to sit between a rhythmic sniffer and a compulsive cougher while he is serenaded from behind by a nervous throat-clearer and carefully watched by a sadistic proctor. Temporary relief is just around the corner, but the establishment figure in charge views with suspicion the student who attempts to relieve the tension through the only avenue open to him: a brief, but glorious visit to the John.

MAIN IDEA   *Loving someone for a long period of time is like breaking in a new pair of denim jeans.* At first they are scratchy and stiff, constricting your movements, making you constantly aware of their presence. Very gradually they begin to loosen up; the color changes from intense navy to pale blue, more easy to live with; the material molds to your contour, becoming almost like a **SUPPORTING** second skin. As you continue to wear them, they be-**DETAILS** come inextricably linked to your experiences. You have spilled coffee on them, cried on them, and spit up on them. You have sat in them, crawled in them, and slept in them. Soon they are so much a part of you that you take them for granted, almost forgetting they exist. So, you have a brief fling with your high-styled, high-waisted, elephant bell cuffs and feel flashy and attractive. But you always go back to the comfort and security of your blue jeans. You've spent too much of your life with that piece of denim to toss it away.

Specific-to-General Organization

At times you might attempt to achieve a specific stylistic effect by beginning your paragraph with a series of details which lead up to your generalization. When the main idea or topic sentence is withheld until the end of the paragraph, a specific-to-general organizational pattern is utilized.

     Do you often take in a movie or watch television when you should be doing assigned reading? Do you **SUPPORTING** enjoy having bull sessions with your friends into the **DETAILS** early hours of the morning when you should be getting your rest? Would you rather tackle a ski slope on a winter afternoon than crack a novel assigned by your English instructor? Do you prefer a burger, fries, and a Coke to a well-balanced meal? Are you more interested in campus social life than you are in the pursuit of knowledge? Do you view a college degree as a passport to the good life? Have you puffed on an occasional joint and given some thought to the hard stuff? **MAIN IDEA** Are you frequently bored and occasionally stimulated by class lectures? If so, cheer up; *like thousands before you, you're college material.*

SUPPORTING DETAILS

One night in a fit of idiocy I counted the number of times I have moved. It came to twenty-one times in the twenty-three years that I have been on this earth! This, of course, does not include vacations and trips, of which there have been many. If I were to count all of the hours spent in preparation for travel, hours spent using some mode of transportation and hours spent readjusting to new surroundings, I am afraid I might become more than a little hysterical. It is best left untotalled and uncounted. Let us just say that I never want

MAIN IDEA

to move again, but I know I will. *I am very tired of it all; I have moved too much.*

Chronological Organization

When you employ a chronological pattern of development, you relate a series of incidents according to the order in which these events actually occurred. Narration and exposition are the two forms of discourse most frequently organized chronologically.

NARRATION

Just before sunrise I awoke, quietly dressed, shook Mike, my son, and went outside to start the coffee. A few minutes later Mike came bounding out of the tent raring to go. We had decided the night before to get some fishing in before breakfast. After shoving off we maneuvered our raft into the deep water. Mike got a bite almost as soon as his bait struck water. Seconds later, the tip of my pole went down under the weight of a catch at the end of my line. When I reeled in the line and started to pry the hook from the walleye's mouth, Mike started to laugh. As I looked up I noticed that we had drifted back to shore. The gentle breeze had carried our anchorless raft halfway across the lake. Mike baited my hook, as I paddled back to the deep water.

Our morning was busily occupied by the activities of catching fish, rebaiting, and paddling back to the deep water. After this cycle had been repeated many times, I noticed my wife waving us in to shore. As we headed for land, Mike and I held up our stringers of fish and Mike proudly hollered, "This should make a delicious breakfast." "Breakfast," my wife exclaimed; "it's time for lunch!"

NARRATION

The first move that I can remember took place when I was four years old. We moved by streetcar from one Chicago neighborhood to another. I don't remember caring much one way or another about the moving, but I was thrilled by the streetcar ride. I bounced gaily from seat to seat, gazed out of the windows, and tried to see everything. There were to be many moves following that one. Each one was both exciting and heartbreaking, but perhaps the most poignant was the last move we made as a family. We left the first real home we ever had to the wreckers who tore it down to make a larger football field for Marquette High School. A young woman drove her own car away from that house, and unlike the little girl on the streetcar, she did not gaze out the window, but stared straight ahead and tried very hard not to cry.

EXPOSITION   *The phenomenal success of the instant loading 126 cartridge camera is largely due to its simplicity of operation.* First swing the back open and insert the cartridge into the camera. Then close the camera and advance the lever clockwise, repeatedly, until it locks. You are now ready for your first exposure. Compose your picture carefully, using either a horizontal or vertical format, whichever better suits your subject. Then squeeze the shutter release, taking care not to jerk the camera. Continue to advance the lever, compose carefully, and avoid excessive camera movement for your remaining exposures. Provided your lighting is adequate, a series of pleasing snapshots will be your reward.

Spatial Organization

An organizational pattern is spatial when the progression of details is arranged according to some logical arrangement in space. Placing gravel, plants, and ornaments in your new aquarium, arranging an attractive floral display, and describing a place with which you are familiar are subjects that would lend themselves to this pattern of development.

MAIN IDEA   Tucked away on the north east corner of our unpretentious second story flat, *my 10' x 12' room houses all my possessions, treasured and otherwise.* As I enter the room my maple bed, placed adjacent to the north wall, is immediately evident. My matching nightstand, to the left of my pillow, supports my clock radio, a recent birthday gift, and a hand-me-down lamp with a battered pirate ship for its base. The remainder of the

**SUPPORTING
DETAILS**

west wall surrounds the only window in the room, my window on the outside world. There I sometimes sit for hours watching the early morning traffic entering the city or the late afternoon traffic returning to suburbia, thinking thoughts, dreaming dreams of life styles so very different from my own. Beneath the window sits my desk, antiqued blue years ago by my father. The cigarette burns and chipped corners are usually hidden from view by the ever present textbooks and clutter of papers. Opposite the window my mirror-topped dresser is placed in the middle of the east wall, surrounded by the sports banners and autographed pictures of my youth. My black wrought iron bookcase, covering the two feet of wall space between the door and the closet of the south wall, is crammed with the paperbacks, magazines, and records that enable me to escape, if only temporarily, my commonplace surroundings.

NARRATION

As I walked down the stairs to the basement — that's where the completely equipped kitchen was supposed to be — I passed by the empty Pepsi and candy machines. On the other side of the Pepsi machine was the door leading into the kitchen. As I walked through the doorway and entered the kitchen, the first thing I saw was the electric stove. Right across from the stove was a large refrigerator; both were of recent vintage. The cupboards and countertops were both of stainless steel, and the sink was also stainless steel. From my first glance around the kitchen, everything appeared spotless.

Order-of-Importance Organization

News stories appearing in our local newspapers are generally organized by order of importance. Reporters know that when stories are cut, they are likely to be cut from the bottom up; therefore, it is important that the really significant information appear in the earlier paragraphs.

News stories are not, however, the only communications that are suited to order-of-importance organization. For a variety of informative and persuasive situations, you may find it advantageous to lead off with the most important evidence or argument, followed by others in descending order of importance. In the following example, the student lists reasons why he believes he should be exempt from the introductory courses in communication skills. Reason one, he surmises, might be sufficient to produce the desired result. However, since he has two other arguments, almost equally compelling, why not list all three in order of importance? The combined effect, he reasons, should enhance his chances of persuading the Dean to grant his request.

Dear Dean _____:

In support of my request for exemption from English 151 and 152, I offer the following reasons for your consideration:

1. I have completed two semesters of Freshman English and one semester of Introduction to Speech at State University with grades of "B" in all three courses. A copy of my official transcript is attached.

2. For the past two summers I worked for radio station WMTC editing news and filling in for announcers on vacation. Mr. Roger Stone, Station Manager, will be happy to verify my competence in written and oral communication.

3. Should my request be granted, I intend to enroll in Technical Report Writing, a course which should be of great help to me since I plan to obtain a two-year degree in Photo Instrumentation Technology.

Sincerely yours,

_____

Pro-Con Organization

The pro-con pattern can be a very effective method of organizing persuasive communication. When you are for or against a proposal or when two or more alternative solutions to a problem are being considered, lead off with the arguments or solutions of your adversaries. If these arguments contain some advantages, summarize them honestly. Intentional distortion is unethical. Furthermore, such distortion weakens your creditability, particularly with a knowledgeable reading or listening audience. Conclude by pointing out weaknesses in opposing arguments and summarizing your position, presumably the best solution to the question under consideration. Think of the pro-con pattern as a method of "setting up" your opponent by summarizing his position first, then "knocking him down" with the weight of your point of view.

> Proponents of the proposal to restrict our suburban high school's enrollment to children who reside in our district claim that their plan will save taxpayer dollars and maintain quality education. "Why," they argue, "should those of us who moved to the suburbs to insure better schools for our children subsidize those who remain behind?" They also point out that the overcrowded classrooms that could result will harm all children, suburban and city.
>
> Should the open enrollment plan be adopted, the increased cost to suburban taxpayers would be minimal, only 75 cents per $1000 of assessed valuation. In return for this slight expenditure, we would provide increased educational opportunities for minority students who live in the city. In addition, we would give our children the opportunity to mingle with and befriend other children of varied backgrounds and life styles. Our children will become the new culturally disadvantaged if we restrict their contacts to their suburban counterparts.
>
> The open enrollment plan I support has a built-in safeguard: out-of-district student enrollments would be limited to 40 students each year. Since our high school is operating at only 70 percent of capacity, the "overcrowded classroom" argument is merely a smokescreen aimed at keeping our schools racially segregated.
>
> I urge all of you—for the sake of our cities, ourselves, and our children—to support the open enrollment plan.

Question-to-Answer and
Effect-to-Cause Organization

Still another method of organizing your paragraphs involves answering a question asked at or near the beginning of your paragraph or stating an effect and then indicating its cause. The question-to-answer or effect-to-cause pattern is particularly suited to expository or persuasive communication. Notice how, in the following paragraph, the "fib" about the "funny-looking church" (effect) is clarified for the reader through effect to cause development:

> **EFFECT**   What happened in the "funny-looking church" with the hard benches, dark walls, and the stained glass windows, brought many changes to my life. It wasn't a church at all you see; it was a court room. It took many years to figure out why my first mom and dad told a fib
>
> **CAUSE**   about the church. They weren't in the habit of lying to me; it just wasn't their way. Perhaps they were, in a

> sense, lying to themselves because they didn't want to
> believe what was happening. I had been theirs since I
> was ten days old and now four years later this was all
> to change. Calling it a church hadn't helped at all; the
> man in the long black robe just didn't see things their
> way. The woman who had given birth to me had not
> signed the papers, so their four years did not count for
> anything in this court of law.

The foregoing discussion is not intended to be inclusive of all patterns of development. As you become more proficient in your organizational ability, you may elect to vary some of the patterns. In general-to-specific organization, for example, you might restate your topic sentence at the conclusion of your paragraph. Or you might modify or qualify your initial statement with new insights. The patterns summarized above are guidelines for developing organizational skills, not gospel to be rigidly followed.

EXERCISES

Study the following essay. Identify the pattern of development employed in each of the paragraphs.

Why do I question my God and my religion? Why do I demand answers to a multitude of questions which plague my mind about my religion in my life? Perhaps it is my search for a convenient and unfailing crutch. Perhaps this crutch is the insecurity of the life I lead and the responsibilities I face. I often feel a strong and demanding desire to define all the reasons for my existence, my religion, and my purpose in this frustrating world.

I begin by asking myself why I practice the religion of my parents. I wonder what choice I had as an infant being baptized to decide my own faith. Upon reaching seven years old, I was promptly enrolled in a parochial school. Eight years of religion in this grade school were followed by four more years in a parochial high school. Parochial schools can give a very precise and unyielding point of view concerning God and religion. After leaving school, I first began to really evaluate and examine my religion.

And today, I have difficulty discussing my evaluations and thoughts with members of my own family. My father cannot seem to understand why his youngest son has turned into a heretic. My mother refuses to believe I could sustain any doubts about my religion and casts off my questions as typical of a "growing" stage. And of course my older brothers and sisters can't begin to answer my questions, so they turn their backs to me as if I've fallen victim to some sort of disease.

All this seems very amusing, I suppose, but consider my own feelings on Sunday mornings as I walk through the glass doors of my church. The light is very dim inside this house of God as I walk down the long center aisle towards the huge marble altar in the front of the church. The high walls on each side of me hold stained glass windows in the forms of saints and angels. The carved statues high on their pedestals along these walls seem to bow their heads in shame as I walk by. And most of all, the figure on the large wooden crucifix high above my head refuses to give me the answers I need, to feel as though I, too, belong in this church—this religion.

PARAGRAPH ANALYSES

Paragraph A

It is 6 a.m. of a winter Sunday in Putney, a crossroads town in southern Vermont. There is a foot of new snow, but lights go on in the houses as families arise and start to pack picnic lunches. Minutes later the lights go off, doors open and laughter fills the crimson dawn. Toddlers, kids and adults snap onto narrow touring skis and, bodies bent and arms swinging, glide off through the fields. As the sun rises and twinkles on icy peaks, more people join the parade. Children call to each other as they disappear into the silent forest, their voices muted by the powdery snow.

Excerpt from "The Magic of Ski Touring," by Jean George, *The Reader's Digest*, February 1972. Copyright © 1972 by the Reader's Digest Assn., Inc.

Analysis

1. Which organizational pattern is employed?
2. Locate a simple sentence, a compound sentence, and a complex sentence.
3. Locate a parallel sentence.
4. Show how two of the sentences in the paragraph illustrate the principle of modification.
5. Is the paragraph effective? Explain your answer.

Exercise: **Describe a seasonal scene, organizing your paragraph chronologically.**

Paragraph B

Frequently, some belligerent, anti-law enforcement elements of our society refer to police officers as "pigs." Obnoxious four-letter words are shouted at policemen, and the familiar chant, "Off the Pigs," meaning "Kill the Police," is a prominent cry wherever these groups assemble. Further, cartoons and publications depicting police officers as pigs are common fare, even for children. The ridiculous statement, "The only good pig is a dead pig," is a slogan of violent protesters. Such deplorable epithets can be gratifying only to little minds.

By J. Edgar Hoover. Reprinted with permission of the FBI Law Enforcement Bulletin.

Analysis

1. Identify the topic sentence and the organizational pattern.
2. Hoover describes policemen as "officers," a term having favorable connotation, while bemoaning the fact that certain elements in society refer to them as "pigs." Complete the following table, supplying favorable and unfavorable terms for the neutral words given:

Favorable	Neutral	Unfavorable
Officer	Policeman	Pig
_____	Teacher	_____
_____	Lawyer	_____
_____	Housewife	_____
_____	Student militant	_____
_____	Salesman	_____
_____	Politician	_____

3. How do connotative words reveal the attitudes and values of the communicator?

Exercise: **Write a paragraph giving your point of view about a word having a strong connotation, either favorable or unfavorable. Use either a general-to-specific or specific-to-general organizational pattern.**

Paragraph C

Fashions in what society considers proper fluctuate wildly. A number of words Chaucer used in the *The Canterbury Tales,* one of the great masterpieces of the language, couldn't possibly be printed today in a book like this one, and though they have only very recently again been permissible in contemporary fiction, they have also helped set off controversy about the "degeneracy" of the modern novel. In contrast, our Victorian forbears were "proper" in public to a degree that seems fantastic to us today. "Legs" were unmentionable, for instance. The decent word for them, especially on ladies, was "limbs," but it was no doubt preferable not to have to mention them at all. It was during this era that the "breast" of chicken became "white meat," to avoid any unpleasant suggestivity in mixed company. At about the turn of the century Owen Wister wrote a story entitled "Skip to My Loo," set in Texas, in which much is made of the disapprobation of the local people for names like "boar," "stallion," "rooster," and "bull," euphemisms being employed in their stead. I myself have heard an old timer refer to a bull as a "he cow." (Incidentally, dancing was frowned on as quite sinful by the people in this story, though they enjoyed a game set to music, remarkably like dancing, which was called Skip to My Loo, and hence the name of the story.) I remember that during my boyhood something of this attitude lingered on in the more primitive backwaters of the West, where I was raised, and I was punished once for using the word "belly" and again for calling my younger brother a "liar." In this latter instance it wasn't my attitude toward my brother that was considered wrong— calling him a "story teller" would have been all right—but the coarse, bald, ugly word "liar" itself.

Ray Past, *Language as a Lively Art* (Dubuque: Wm. C. Brown Co., 1970), p. 274.

Analysis

1. Identify the topic sentence and the organizational pattern.
2. Identify and illustrate the methods of support.
3. Explain the "controversy about the 'degeneracy' of the modern novel" referred to in the paragraph. Does this controversy extend into other art forms?
4. What is a euphemism? Give at least three examples not found in the paragraph.
5. How does the author's point about euphemisms relate to the preceding Hoover paragraph?
6. Give three examples (other than those mentioned in the paragraph) of words that have graduated to positions of respectability.

Exercise: **In a paragraph relate an experience, preferably personal, involving the changing nature of the English language. Employ whatever organizational pattern you deem appropriate.**

Paragraph D

Contrary to the widespread notion that people go through a divorce with a minimum of psychic disturbance, divorce is generally an emotionally, psychologically, and socially traumatic experience, which leaves its marks and scars on the personalities involved. To begin with, many individuals experience a sense of personal rejection, which is painful. Even when there is mutual agreement that the divorce is necessary, each may feel that he was not wanted or desired by the other. Furthermore, there may be a profound feeling of having failed in a personal sense. It is as though the couple "should have made it work" in spite of any obstacles in their path. The extent to which one is disturbed by a divorce is frequently increased when one member of the former marriage decides to remarry. For the remaining individual the remarriage of his former spouse may prove to be rather traumatic. This is particularly so when one member of the relationship continued to hope, as many do, that somehow even after the divorce "they would get back together." Sometimes these people become martyrs, waiting for the mate to return. In other instances they may desperately plunge into a new relationship prematurely in order to prove that they are still lovable and desirable.

Herman R. Lantz and Eloise C. Snyder, *Marriage: An Examination of the Man-Woman Relationship* (New York: John Wiley & Sons, Inc., 1962), p. 410.

Analysis

1. Identify the topic sentence and the organizational pattern.
2. Identify the principle method of support. Are any other supporting devices employed?
3. Do you agree that a "widespread notion that people go through divorce with a minimum of physic disturbance" really exists? Discuss.
4. Define in context: *psychic, traumatic, martyr.*
5. Discuss the effectiveness of the foregoing paragraph.

Exercise: **Take issue with a commonly held belief, employing a general-to-specific organizational pattern.**

Paragraph E

In a troubled corner of the country, something vaguely subterranean is welling up. It seems, at once, an apprehension of the final catastrophe or the huge breathing of a vast organism, or perhaps the anonymous mobility of some mute ghost that yearns to make itself known. The American South—a land of labored fables, shared glories, soil, blood, brassy vanity and souls spun tight together in patterns of tradition—remains an intricate, fugal overlay of clashing passions: Gentility and violence, humanism and hatreds, beliefs and brutalities, obscurities, incongruities, cadenzas of humor, Sweet Jesus and unknowable madness. Add to this an infinitude of traumas and small transformations, multiply by 38 million whites, 11 million blacks plus every possible variable of the past, the present, the climate and the terrain, and you extract today a place where nothing whatever is the same. Yet you draw from this, too, a people who in being forced to find pragmatic new realities of their own, may well forge prophetic insights into the very root of all human hearts.

With permission of Cowles Communications, Inc.

Analysis

1. Identify the topic sentence and organizational pattern.
2. As what part of speech is *welling* used in the first sentence? The word *well* is an excellent example of *functional shift*, meaning that a word shifts its function or part of speech in different contexts. With the help of your dictionary, indicate how *well* can be used as five different parts of speech. Then illustrate each use in a separate sentence.
3. Define in context: *subterranean, mute, fugal, humanism, incongruity, cadenza, pragmatic, prophetic.*
4. Identify and illustrate the methods of support.
5. State the purpose of the paragraph.

Exercise: In a paragraph, give your impression of a place with which you are thoroughly familiar: a neighborhood, a favorite hangout, a vacation retreat, a school, a place of employment. As in the foregoing example, provide your readers with insights into the people who occupy the place you describe.

Supply a caption for each of the following photographs. Then, using one of the captions as your subject, write a paragraph or a longer essay, as your instructor directs.

Used with permission of the photographer, Arnold Gore.

Used with permission of the photographer, Elliott Schnackenberg.

Used with permission of the photographer, Stanley Felber.

With permission of the photographer, Randy Klauk, and the MATC Times.

CHAPTER 10

The Business Letter

The business letter may be a different form of letter writing from what you are used to. Up to now most of the letters you have written have been simply "newsy notes" to loved ones, communication to inform about things that have happened to you that you think will interest your reader. These letters are spontaneous rather than preplanned. You sit down, begin writing, and as thoughts occur to you, jot them down.

In writing the business letter, however, you are faced with a specific problem—how to evoke a desired response from your reader. For this reason your letter must be carefully planned and clearly and correctly written. If your letter creates a poor impression, your chances of getting that desired response are lessened. If your letter is unclear or lacks some necessary information requiring additional letters, time and money are wasted.

The first part of this chapter deals with business letter form. Although there are a number of forms for business letters, the two most common are the full block (page 200) and the semiblock (pages 196, 199). In the full-block form, the heading, inside address, salutation, body, complimentary close, and signature begin at the left margin. In the semiblock form, the inside address, salutation, and body (with each paragraph indented) are flush with the left margin, and the heading, complimentary close, and signature are on the righthand side. (This is the form referred to in the discussion below.) The second part deals with the content of business letters by discussing examples of different types.

This chapter was written by John D. Lewinski.

PARTS OF THE BUSINESS LETTER

A business letter should contain *six* distinct parts: the heading, the inside address, the salutation, the body, the complimentary close, and the signature.

The Heading

The heading is located in the upper right-hand corner and should include the writer's full mailing address and the date the letter was written. Both are important. The full address gives the reader a return address right on the letter, facilitating his reply. The date, which establishes the time the letter was written, can be referred to in future letters. Notice that the writer's name appears at the bottom of the letter, not in the heading.

> 507 Main Street
> Cudahy, Wisconsin   53110
> March 1, 1978

Many organizations have stationery designed for them with an engraved or printed letterhead. These letterheads often include the title of the organization, its full address, phone number, officers, and in some cases a brief description of what the organization does.

UWEX UNIVERSITY OF WISCONSIN–EXTENSION

929 NORTH SIXTH STREET   MILWAUKEE, WISCONSIN 53203   (414) 224-1891

DEPARTMENT OF BUSINESS AND MANAGEMENT

Management Institutes ● Correspondence Study ● Special Classes

If letterhead stationery is used, the date should be typed in two spaces below the letterhead at either the center of the page or the right margin.

The Inside Address

The inside address is placed at the left margin and at least four spaces below the date. It contains the full name and address of the person or organization to whom you are writing. It is identical to the address on the envelope.

The inside address indicates exactly to whom the letter is sent. In many large organizations, the mail is originally opened by someone other than the addressee, perhaps a secretary or mail sorter. If the name of the person or department to whom you are writing is not on the letter, it may be misplaced or sent to the wrong person. The more complete the information is in the inside address, the greater the likelihood your letter will reach its proper destination. Include the full name and position of the intended reader, if known, and the department or division of the organization to which you are writing. Remember, your chances of getting a desired response are always better if your letter is addressed to a specific person. If, for instance, you are writing a letter applying for a job at a specific company, it would be in your best interest to call the company office and find out the name of the personnel director.

> Mrs. Judy Miller
> Personnel Director
> Acme Welding Company
> 1472 North 35th Street
> Chicago, Illinois   60684

The Salutation

Place the salutation two spaces below the inside address at the left margin. While the salutation is the greeting, it is a bit more formal than a simple "Hello." In a business letter the sex of the reader and the tone of the letter will determine the title to use. Here are some acceptable choices:

For Men	*For Organizations*	*For Women*
Dear Sir:	Gentlemen:	Dear Miss _____ :
Dear Mr. _____ :	Ladies:	Dear Mrs. _____ :
		Dear Ms. _____ :

Another function of the salutation is to set the tone of the letter. Consider the difference between a letter asking for a job interview and a letter complaining about a faulty product. You can set the tone of the letter by choosing the proper title and by adding or deleting the words "My" and "Dear". Here are some examples:

For a letter of stern tone:
Sir: or   Madam:

For a letter of neutral tone:

Dear Sir: Dear Madam:
Gentlemen: Ladies:

For a letter of friendly tone:

Men	*Women*
My Dear Mr. _____ :	My Dear Mrs. (Miss, Ms.) _____ :
Dear Mr. _____ :	Dear Mrs. (Miss, Ms.) _____ :
Dear *(First Name)*:	Dear *(First Name)*:

Although the salutation involves only a few words, it should be obvious that its proper use is an important aspect of the business letter.

The Body

The body of the business letter begins two spaces below the salutation. It is written in paragraphs that are single-spaced. A double space is used between paragraphs. The body, which contains the message you want to convey, is the heart of the letter. Since the purposes of different types of business letters are so varied, it is difficult to discuss the content of the body in any detail. However, some general rules apply:

1. Preplan the letter. Decide what and how much you want to say. Then write it out in a natural, to-the-point way. Be yourself. Efforts to sound impressive usually result in an awkward, stilted style.

2. Make the letter "reader-centered." Write with the reader in mind, address yourself to his problems and needs. Try to anticipate what his reaction will be to your letter. Ask yourself, "Would I do what I suggest if I were the receiver of my letter?"

3. Organize your letter, keeping the main points together in neat paragraphs. Generally, you begin by stating your purpose in a simple, straightforward way. Then, clearly explain the details the reader will need to respond correctly to your letter. Your conclusion should indicate what you want to occur because of your letter. Your tone should not appear to dictate what it is you want done. Rather, it should lead the reader naturally to your desired response.

The Complimentary Closing

The complimentary closing is the writer's way of saying "goodbye" to his reader. It is located two spaces below the last paragraph of the body and slightly right of the center of the page. The way you close your letter is again determined by the tone and subject. Here are some suggestions:

For formal or stern letters:
Respectfully   or   Respectfully yours,

For neutral letters:
Very sincerely yours,   or   Very truly yours,

For friendly letters:
Sincerely yours,   or   Cordially yours,

The Signature

The signature is important in making the letter a personal communication. Because it should be both legal and legible, it should appear in two forms: signed and typed. The typed signature assures legibility. Make sure your signature does not overlap either the complimentary closing or the typed signature.

Sincerely,

James Johnson

James Johnson

SOME DO'S AND DONT'S

1. *Do* type your letter. No matter how neat your handwriting, it is common practice to type the business letter.
2. *Do* preplan the letter. This will not only improve the content; it will help you space the elements properly on the page.
3. *Do* keep a copy of your letter. In the event of a question concerning your letter, you will be readily able to answer it.
4. *Do* try to keep your letters as brief as possible. Letters of no more than one page are best, whenever possible. If you do not attempt too many things with a single letter, chances are you will be successful.
5. *Do not* send your letter before carefully proofreading it. Errors in spelling, grammar, or typing reflect negatively on you, the writer. Further, they can cause misunderstandings or communication breakdowns.

EXERCISE

Rewrite the following letter in an accurate semiblock form:

```
                              George Krall
                              2730 Lake Dr.
                              Kenosha, Wis.  53140



     Renata Smith, Mgr.
     Church Supply Co.
     4730 East Morgan St.
     Chicago, Ill. 60607

     Dear Mrs. Smith:

          I wish to thank you for recommending me to Mr. Karl
     Stoll.  I have just received word that I am to begin work
     June 7.

          Mr. Stoll mentioned that you had given me an excellent
     recommendation which had much to do with my getting the job.
     I want to thank you for taking time out of your busy schedule
     to write a letter for me.  I hope that I will live up to your
     faith in me.

     Sincerely yours,

     George Krall

     George Krall
     6/1/78
```

TYPES OF BUSINESS LETTERS

Because the purposes, forms, and lengths of business letters are so varied, representative samples of different types are included on the following pages.

Job Application

Perhaps the most important business letter you will ever write is a letter of application for a job. Because many jobs require interviews, the applicant must be able to write a formal letter requesting one.

Sally Johnson, a commercial arts major at a large Midwestern junior college saw this ad in her local newspaper.

WANTED: Talented young artists to work for
a national advertising company. Contact:

Mr. Edward Brown
Syndicated Talent, Inc.
P.O. Box 1131
Chicago, IL 60607

She wrote the following letter:

3535 East 3rd Street
Milwaukee, Wisconsin 53202
March 14, 1977

Mr. Edward Brown
Syndicated Talent, Inc.
P.O. Box 1131
Chicago, Illinois 60607

Dear Mr. Brown:

I read your ad for young artists that appeared in the
Milwaukee News-Review. I would like to apply for one of
those positions.

I am presently a second year student majoring in
commercial arts at Columbia College in Milwaukee. I am
presently the Art Editor for our campus newspaper, The
Columbian. For the past three years I have worked for a
local advertising agency, Midwest Marketing Corporation,
as an advertising artist.

While my class schedule is rather restricting, I am
available for an interview on Friday afternoons, and Satur-
days. I would appreciate an opportunity to call at your
office for an interview. Please notify me if these times
are convenient for you.

Sincerely yours,

Sally Johnson

(Miss) Sally Johnson

Notice how Sally indicated in her first paragraph how she heard of
the position, and why she was writing. She then gave a few of her
qualifications for the position. She concluded her letter by indicating
her desire for an interview and requesting a response from the employer. These are wise practices for such a letter.

Along with her letter, Sally sent the accompanying resume.

RESUME

I. Personal Data

       Name: Johnson, Sally M.
       Address: 3535 East 3rd Street
                          Milwaukee, Wisconsin 53203
       Phone: 414-555-1324
       Health: Good
       Date/Birth: August 10, 1957
       Place/Birth: Wauwatosa, Wisconsin
       Marital Status: Single
       Height: 5'6"
       Weight: 130 lbs.

II. Education

       1975-1977 Columbia College, Milwaukee, Wisconsin
                 Degree Sought - Associate of Arts
                 Major - Commercial Art
                 Minor - Advertising
                 Grade Point - 3.75
                 Grade Point in Major - 4.00
                 Favorite Courses:
                     Commercial Art I - A
                     Commercial Art II - A
                     Display - A
                     Photographic Principles - A
                 Extracurricular activities:
                     Art Editor - College Newspaper
                     Secretary - Student Government
                     Queens Court - 1976 Homecoming

       1971-1975 St. James Academy, Wauwatosa, Wisconsin
                 Degree - High School Diploma
                 Graduated 7th in a class of 147
                 Studies included:
                     Art 101 and 102 - A in both
                     Commercial Drawing - A
                     Business Math - A
                     Accounting for Business - B
                 Extra Curricular Activities:
                     Art Editor - School Newspaper
                     Assistant Artist - School Yearbook
                     Set Designer - Drama Club

-2-

III. **Experience**

1974-1977 - Advertising Artist
Midwest Marketing Corporation
103 Downer Plaza
Milwaukee, Wisconsin 53204

1972-1974 - Stock Person
Milwaukee Artist's Supply
1414 Penn Avenue
Wauwatosa, Wisconsin 53213

IV. **References**

Mr. Paul Scoggins, Manager
Midwest Marketing Corporation
103 Downer Plaza
Milwaukee, Wisconsin 53204

Sister Mary Louisa,
Art Instructor
St. James Academy
4525 River Road
Wauwatosa, Wisconsin 53213

Professor Mary Bennett,
Commercial Art Department
Columbia College
613 North University Drive
Milwaukee, Wisconsin 53207

V. **Occupational Goal**

Someday, I would like to be managing art editor for a
national magazine or company. In the interim, I wish
to learn all I can about the world of commercial art.

Soon Sally received a response from Mr. Brown, indicating a date and time for an interview. She then wrote this letter to confirm the appointment.

```
                              3535 East 3rd Street
                              Milwaukee, Wisconsin 53202
                              April 2, 1977
```

```
Mr. Edward Brown
Syndicated Talent, Inc.
P.O. Box 1131
Chicago, Illinois 60607
```

Dear Mr. Brown:

Thank you very much for your letter of March 27 offering me an interview on Friday, April 8, 1977. I shall be most happy to talk with you at 2:00 P.M.

At this interview, I will bring some samples of my previous work, as you requested.

I am looking forward to meeting you and learning about your company.

```
                              Sincerely,

                              Sally Johnson

                              (Miss) Sally Johnson
```

Now, Sally began to prepare for her interview. First, she found out what she could about the company. She called the Better Business Bureau, and she discussed the company with her boss at Midwest Marketing and her college teachers. Next, she selected an appropriate outfit, nothing too dressy, but neat and clean. She realized that personal appearance is a big part of an interview. Finally, she considered how she would respond to some of the more common questions that interviews ask.

Why are you interested in this field?

Why are you interested in this company?

What are your occupational goals?

What hours would you be willing to work?

What salary would you require?

What special likes and dislikes do you have?

What special strengths and weaknesses do you have?

She also made a list of questions that she would like to have answered.

What are the job requirements?

What salary and fringe benefits are available?

What are the possibilities for advancement?

What are the hours, and when would she start the job?

During her interview, naturally Sally was nervous. But she kept her composure. She listened carefully to what Mr. Brown asked, and she responded honestly and briefly. She brought a copy of her resume to refer to, as well as several samples of her previous work. When Mr. Brown asked if she had any questions, she asked several polite ones. After thanking him, she left the interview feeling that it had gone well.

Sally knew that she was not the only person being interviewed for the position. So, when she returned home, she sent the following letter to Mr. Brown:

```
3535 East 3rd Street
Milwaukee, Wisconsin 53202
April 12, 1977


Mr. Edward Brown
Syndicated Talent, Inc.
P.O. Box 1131
Chicago, Illinois 60607

Dear Mr. Brown:

I want to thank you for the opportunity to discuss the posi-
tion of Art Consultant with your company. After our Friday
interview, I felt I had learned a great deal about the real
world of commercial art.

I especially want to thank you for your kind words about my
pictorial display entitled, "Winter's Wonder." It is nice
to know that someone in the business of commercial art appre-
ciates my work.

I hope that you have heard from my references, and that I
may hear from you soon.

Thank you again for taking the time to talk with me.

Sincerely,

Sally Johnson
(Miss) Sally Johnson
```

Notice how Sally refreshes the interviewer's mind about her interview and indicates her continued interest in the job, as well as thanking Mr. Brown.

We don't know whether Sally got the job or not. But we do know that she followed the proper letter-writing and job-application procedures. If you follow her example, your chances for finding that job will be enhanced.

Other Business Letters

In this section we will consider two additional types of business letters: the letter of adjustment or complaint and the letter of inquiry. As our society grows more complex and depersonalized, the need to seek redress or to obtain additional information increases. A clear and concise business letter is generally the most practical means to that end. Consider the following:

A. In September, James Wilson saw an advertisement on television for a collection of hit records from the 1960s. Since there were several songs on the album that he liked, he placed an order for the album with the Zapp Record Company in New York. To save the $2.25 C.O.D. charge, James sent a personal check for the full amount with his order. Then he waited. In October, his check cleared his bank, but still no record arrived. He waited all through November, but he never received the album. On December 5, he sent the following letter:*

```
                          2765 Washington Avenue
                          Los Angeles, California 90009
                          December 5, 1976



Zapp Record Company, Inc.
1465 Park Avenue
New York, New York 10019

Gentlemen:

On September 14, 1976, I placed an order for one copy of
your 2-record album, "Swinging Sixties."  I enclosed a per-
sonal check for $10.95, which was the full amount of the
advertised album, plus shipping and handling.  That check
was paid by my bank on October 8, 1976, and I have the can-
celled check.  However, to date I have not received my
order.

Your advertisement says to allow 6 to 8 weeks for delivery.
I have now waited over 11 weeks.  Is there some problem
that would account for this delay?

I would appreciate it if you would check on my order, and
notify me of its situation at your ealiest convenience.  A
response from you will prevent any further action on this
matter.

                          Respectfully yours,

                          James Wilson

                          James Wilson
```

---

*In this variation of the semiblock form the paragraphs are not indented.

Notice that, while the letter is not angry or insulting, it is also not as friendly as the letters Miss Johnson wrote. The salutation and closing are much more formal in tone.

Also notice how James handles the message. In the first paragraph, he identifies the reason for the letter. He mentions names, dates, and amounts, so that the company can check its records. In the second paragraph, he reminds his reader that the company has not fulfilled its obligations, but he does this in a polite way. James concludes his letter by indicating what he expects from the company. While he suggests that he is prepared to follow this matter through, he doesn't directly threaten legal action or the like. If the company doesn't respond, he can then take more firm action.

Before he sent the letter, James did two more things, which are very good practices in this kind of situation.

1. He made a copy of the letter.
2. He sent the letter certified mail and attached his receipt to the copy of the letter.

While this procedure costs a little money, it is an inexpensive way of keeping a record of the whole transaction. We assume that the record company will explain the delay, and James will get his album. If he doesn't, he has a record of what he has done.

B. Often a person needs to obtain additional information about a product, an organization, or a situation. In this next example Betty Meyers, a student at a local junior college, is trying to decide what University she should attend to complete her education. While she has a good deal of information about the course of study she is interested in pursuing at Kennedy University, Betty still has some questions about the area, the housing situation, and job opportunities. She writes a letter of inquiry (see page 203).

Several things should be noted in Betty's letter. Notice how the tone is much more friendly than that of Mr. Wilson's letter of complaint. The first paragraph explains the purpose of the letter, and the next two ask the questions. Also, notice how Betty doesn't ask Mrs. Moore to answer the letter directly; she doesn't make a great demand on a person who is probably quite busy. Mrs. Moore may answer the questions herself, or she may refer Betty to the Director of Housing and the Director of Student Placement. In either case, Betty will probably get the answers she seeks.

Finally, notice that Betty has decided not to thank Mrs. Moore in advance. When she gets the response from Mrs. Moore, she may want to write a thank-you letter, similar to the one Miss Johnson wrote earlier.

```
12527 West Longwood
East London, Maryland 01212
April 8, 1977


Mrs. Margaret Moore
Director of Admissions
Kennedy University
Boston, Maryland 02109

Dear Mrs. Moore:

I am currently a sophomore at East London Junior College,
planning to graduate this June with an Associate of Arts
Degree in Computer Technology.  I have applied for admis-
sion to your University, and am awaiting word on my appli-
cation.  In the meantime, several questions have arisen
concerning my enrollment, and I feel it important to ask
for your assistance.

First, I notice in your literature that you allow upper
classmen to live in off-campus housing.  Since I will be
entering as a junior, and will be 21 years old, I feel
that I would prefer this arrangement to dormitory living.
My problem is that I am unfamiliar with the area in which
Kennedy is located, and have no idea about where to live
and what to expect to pay.  Could you possibly suggest
someone I could contact?

Second, not being wealthy, I will probably need to find
a part-time job in the area.  I have had two years of ex-
perience as a key punch operator, and would like to find
something in the general field of computer technology,
if possible.  Do you also know of any one I could contact
to help me with this problem?

I am looking forward to several rewarding years at K.U.
I hope you will be able to give me some assistance on these
matters.

Sincerely yours,

Betty Meyers

(Ms.) Betty Meyers
```

Don't simply assume that "the establishment" won't respond to the needs of the individual. A clear, concise, and purposeful business letter can serve to remind the largest corporation or institution that its continued success is dependent on customer satisfaction.

EXERCISES

1. **Find an ad in the help wanted section of your local newspaper for a job in your chosen field. Write a job application letter in response to the ad.**
2. **Write a letter to a former teacher or employer asking for permission to use his name as a reference on your resume.**

3. Write a letter thanking a prospective employer for a job interview.

4. Write a letter of complaint about a product or service you found unsatisfactory. Indicate exactly what you would like done to solve the problem.

5. Write a letter to one of your governmental representatives expressing your opinion on a current local, state, or national issue with which he is connected.

CHAPTER 11

The Technical Report

It is estimated that mankind's technical knowledge doubles every ten years; in some technologies, the rate of growth is even more rapid. The old woodburning stove of the 30s was replaced by the gas and electric ranges of the 50s and 60s. Now these are being replaced by heatless radar ranges. In 1903, two brothers flew the first heavier-than-air machine. Less than 70 years later, mankind landed on the moon. Today computers do everything from bake bread to pay bills. People who cannot deal with these advances in technology are lost in our modern world.

One of the ways to understand and participate in this technological world is through the technical report. In this chapter, you will learn how to communicate technical data through this special writing form.

WHAT IS A TECHNICAL REPORT?

Technical reports have two general characteristics: they deal with technical subjects, and they are primarily informational. Both of those characteristics are difficult to define clearly. A technical subject is one that deals with the industrial arts or science. However, because almost every business has a special terminology that applies to it alone, reports that deal with those terms and subjects can be considered technical reports. The word "report" implies that the main purpose of the paper should be to inform. A technical report should have as its primary goal increasing the knowledge, awareness, or understanding of the reader.

This chapter was written by John D. Lewinski.

TYPES OF TECHNICAL REPORTS

Because a technical report can be something as simple as a time card, or as complex as a 1000-page manual, there is no one example we can describe as typical. However, we can identify some general characteristics of all technical reports. There are three basic types: informal, semiformal, and formal.

Informal Reports

Informal technical reports, the type utilized most frequently, include time cards, invoices, progress reports, memos, business letters, and project analyses. An informal technical report generally has four sections: the *heading*, the *introduction*, the *findings*, and the *conclusion*. While each of these sections may be expanded to include other data, the basic requirements are:

1. The *heading* must contain the date, name of the submitter, name of the person to whom it is submitted, and a title or indication of subject.
2. The *introduction* is a two- or three-sentence statement of why the report is being made and what it deals with.
3. The *findings*, or body, containing the actual data, usually comprise the longest section of the informal report.
4. The *conclusion* indicates the result of your study and, on occasion, includes recommendations.

Semiformal Reports

The semiformal report usually is longer and contains more sections than the informal report. Semiformal reports are quite common in business and industry, although not as common as informal reports. Often, a semiformal report follows an informal report on the same subject. While the informal report takes care of the many daily or repetitive communication chores, the semiformal often represents the completion of a specific project or the results of a longer study. Although semiformal reports vary greatly, most experts agree that they should contain at least six sections, as follows:

1. Title page
2. Summary

HEADING	TO:	Mr. Gene Rogers, Chairman, City Planning Commission	
	FROM:	Ross Bennett & Associates	
	DATE:	March 24, 1977	
	SUBJECT:	Feasibility of Additional Seating at Central Arena	

INTRODUCTION   As per your request, my associates and I have completed a preliminary analysis of the possibility of adding additional spectator seating to the present Central Arena. Following is a summary of our major findings. A full report will be issued within the next 30 days.

FINDINGS   Available area for expansion: 4,400 sq. ft.

Number of additional seats possible:

Plan 1	Type A Seating	-	300
	Type B Seating	-	700
	Total		1,000
Plan 2	All Type B Seating	-	1,100
Plan 3	Bleacher Seating	-	1,700

Approximate cost for completion:

Plan 1	Type A Seats	$15,000
	Type B Seats	28,000
	Installation Costs	$47,000
	Total	$90,000
Plan 2	Type B Seats	$44,000
	Installation Costs	41,000
	Total	$85,000
Plan 3	Bleacher Seats	$17,000
	Installation Costs	31,000
	Total	$48,000

Sample Informal Report

-2-

<u>Projected additional gross revenue per home</u>
<u>game (full usage)</u>:

Plan 1	Type A Seats	$ 3,000
	Type B Seats	5,600
	1 Game	$ 8,600
Plan 2	Type B Seats	$ 8,800
Plan 3	Bleacher Seats	$ 6,800

CONCLUSIONS

1. Plan 3 offers the largest increase in seating for the smallest expenditure.

2. Plan 2 offers the highest gross revenue per game.

3. Plan 1 would be most consistent with present seating arrangements.

3. Introduction
4. Discussion
5. Conclusions
6. Recommendations

Title   In the semiformal report, the heading is replaced by a title page containing the title of the report, the name of the person or company that prepared the report, and the date. It may also include a number or classification to help with its distribution and filing.

Summary   The summary—also called an abstract, précis, preface, or synopsis—is considered by many experts to be the most important part of the report. Its purpose is to tell the reader what the report is about, identify the major points, and indicate conclusions and/or recommendations. It is intended to tell the reader at a glance whether he should read the report in detail or forward it to someone else in the organization for study. It must be informative, but it must also attract attention to the content. It must be aimed at the busy executive who receives dozens of reports daily, yet it must be comprehensible to many employees.

Although it generally appears first in the report, the summary should not be written until the rest of the report is complete. Only then will you know the highlights you will want to emphasize and the conclusions you will want to leave with your readers. Your job, then, is to make the summary both interesting and informative.

Introduction   Do not confuse the introduction with the summary. The summary covers the whole report in a few sentences; the introduction presents, in detail, the material that the reader must understand at the outset. The introduction should accomplish the following things:

1. Identify and clarify the purpose of the report.
2. Define the scope of the report. Only rarely can a short report cover an entire subject completely. Your report will most likely be limited to a specific problem or set of circumstances. Identify these carefully in the introduction.
3. Give necessary background data. You must assume that your reader is not as familiar with or aware of the subject as you are. Take some time to define your terms, and explain the situations that led you to write this report.
4. Identify the method of research used. Tell the reader how and where your material was gathered. If the introduction accom-

plished these goals, the reader will be ready to more fully digest the remainder of the report.

Discussion   The discussion section of a technical report is similar, at least in purpose, to the body of a research paper. It will be the longest part of the paper but one of the easiest parts to write.

The discussion contains all the data, evidence, facts, test results, and other material that you have found. The key to an effective discussion is organization. You must organize your material so that the reader can receive the information clearly and concisely. The patterns or organization will depend on the type of material and problem you are reporting on, but they are the same as for a paragraph or the body of a research paper.

Conclusion   The conclusion is the part of the report that tells the reader what you have proven and what inferences can be drawn from all the data that have been presented. While you may feel that the conclusion is obvious, it must tell the reader, clearly, what the report proves. No new evidence is included in the conclusion. If more than one conclusion may be drawn from the data, arrange the conclusions in order, from what you feel is the most valid or important to the least.

Recommendations   Sometimes technical writers confuse this section with the conclusion. In the recommendation section, you indicate what you think should be done about your report. Your conclusions are logical facts supported by the data. Your recommendations are personal suggestions or opinions about what should come next. While your conclusions cannot be ignored, your recommendations might well be. Your boss may well decide not to follow your recommendations, but he must accept your conclusions, provided you have done your work properly.

Formal Reports

In addition to the six elements already identified for the semiformal report, the formal report generally contains the following items:

1. Cover
2. Table of Contents
3. Bibliography
4. Appendix

Cover   The cover, containing the title, is usually an attractive binding of some harder material.

Table of Contents   The table of contents lists the subject matter and indicates the overall organization of the paper.

Bibliography   The bibliography, which may also be called "References," contains a list of all the sources referred to in preparing the report.

Appendix   The appendix contains the visual materials that support the facts presented in the discussion. Items such as charts, graphs, photographs, drawings, and tables are often difficult to incorporate into the discussion. But because they are necessary to prove the validity of the conclusions, they are included at the back of the report.

In addition to these four elements, formal reports may also have some attachments that help in the proper description and distribution of the report. They are as follows:

1. Distribution list—identifies the people who should read the report. It usually appears near the bibliography or appendix.
2. Cover letter—introduces the report and explains why it has been sent to a particular person or department. It is arranged like a typical business letter and attached to the front of the report. It is never included inside the cover.
3. Letter of transmittal—often written by someone other than the report writer. It may reflect the management's evaluation of the report and include suggestions or recommendations. Sometimes it may take the place of the summary. It is always bound inside the cover, either before or immediately after the title page.

WORDING OF TECHNICAL REPORTS

A common problem that you as a technical report writer will face is selecting appropriate vocabulary. How do you write about highly technical material in a way that both technicians and nontechnicians understand? The answer is: Write for your primary reader and use technical language only when necessary!

By "writing for the primary reader," we mean adapting your vocabulary to the technical abilities of the person for whom you are writing. The concept of jargon or "shop talk" is a bothersome one for the average technician. Often he may not realize he is using technical jargon. The terms are so much a part of his everyday life, that he just assumes everyone will know to what he is referring. Think about this when you write. If you don't know about computers, you may not understand terms like "interface," "program," "terminal," and "data bank." Any computer technician will use these terms so commonly that he will have a difficult time realizing that his reader might not understand them. But the reader might be an accountant who can understand terms like "debit," "credit," "trial and balance," "capital investment," and "depreciation"—terms which are just as foreign to the computer technician as the computer language is to the accountant. So—try to understand your reader, and write accordingly.

Certain parts of the report require technical vocabulary. Others do not. Match the vocabulary to the purpose of the particular section you are writing. The heading and the summary should be nontechnical; the introduction, conclusions, and recommendations should be partly technical; and only the findings, discussion, and appendix should be fully technical. If the report is a formal one, the distribution list and cover letter should be nontechnical, and the other formal elements— cover, title page, table of contents, bibliography, and letter of transmittal—need be only partly technical.

BASIC SKILLS

In addition to the format and the appropriate level of language, a technical report must also be an example of good written communication. The basic writing skills of proper grammar, punctuation, sentence construction, and spelling must be employed.

Is it fair to expect the technician to be able to write properly? To answer this question, you only need consider the consequences if he doesn't. A misspelled word is like a big flashing sign that says "mistake—mistake—mistake." Not only does it cast doubt on the capability and intelligence of the technician, but it also makes the reader wonder, "If he can't even spell properly, how reliable is this report?"

The same is true for a grammatical error. While you don't expect your reader to have a Ph.D. in English, you must expect him to have a certain degree of intelligence. Glaring grammatical errors reflect adversely on the the intelligence of the writer and the validity of the report.

When it comes to punctuation and sentence construction, the problem is more serious than just credibility. Errors in punctuation or poor sentence construction can actually cause the wrong message to be sent.

A REPORT ON THE

FEASIBILITY OF ADDITIONAL

SEATING IN CENTRAL ARENA

Prepared by:

Ross Bennett & Associates
April 15, 1977

Prepared for:
City Planning Commission

Sample Semiformal Technical Report

SUMMARY

The City Planning Commission wants to increase the
seating capacity of Central Arena. It has already been
determined that the building is structurally sound and
capable of holding additional seats. This report discusses
three plans for such expansion. Plan 1 will maintain the
present scheme of seating, at a slightly higher construction
cost than that of Plan 2. It is aesthetically the best.
Plan 2 will provide the highest return on the initial investment, with minor changes in the present seating pattern.
Plan 3 is the least expensive, but will change the present
seating pattern most significantly.

The plan that we recommend is Plan 2, since it
achieves the highest economic return with the least change
to the present seating scheme.

INTRODUCTION

Owing to increased interest in sports and other spectator shows, the City Planning Commission desires to increase
the seating capacity of Central Arena. A previous study by
this firm, dated November 12, 1976, has determined that the
building is structurally capable of accommodating up to 2000
additional spectators, with no danger to the building and its
occupants and no violations of city codes. Based on this
study, the City Planning Commission retained this firm to
explore possible plans to achieve this increase in seating.

This report will suggest the three plans we feel repre-
sent the best options. Each plan has advantages and disadvantages that require consideration. A previous report,
dated March 24, 1977, was submitted to Mr. Gene Rogers, Chairman of the City Planning Commission. That preliminary report
outlined the three plans and gave some general recommendations.
This report will further clarify the data in the preliminary
report and make a more comprehensive recommendation.

Throughout this study, the following criteria were considered:

1. Present seating pattern

2. View of arena floor

3. Maximum use of available space

4. Maximum economic return on investment

5. Maximum comfort and convenience for spectators

DISCUSSION

General Considerations:

After careful analysis of the available space, it was determined that 2200 square feet at each end of the floor was available for additional seating. In addition, bench or bleacher type seating could be added to the upper levels of the present side seats. However, the cost of such installation would be extensive, and the economic return would be minimal; therefore, this option was not explored further. Elimination of this option meant that the maximum expansion could reach as high as 1700 additional seats. This figure is well within the limits of structural and code requirements.

PLAN 1:

Plan 1 would be most consistent with the present seating pattern. Plan 1 involves the installation of 300 type "A" seats, 150 at each end of the floor, and 700 type "B" seats, 350 at each end. (See Figure 1.)

(Type A seats are identical to the present highest priced seats in the arena.)

(Type B seats are identical to the present lower priced seats in the arena.)

The total increase in seating under Plan 1 would be 1000.

The total cost of Plan 1 would be $90,000, computed on the following basis:

```
300 cushioned Type A seats
            @ $50/seat          = $15,000

700 noncushioned Type B seats
            @ $40/seat          = $28,000

Installation costs              = $47,000

Total                           $90,000
```

Possible increase in revenue, based on full occupancy:

```
300 Type A seats @ $10/seat     = $3000
700 Type B seats @ $ 8/seat     = $5600
Total/event                     = $8600
```

Analysis:

Advantages:

1. Maintains present seating pattern throughout the arena

2. Offers increased "comfortable" seating

Disadvantages:

1. Is most costly of plans to install

2. Requires spectators to pay top prices for end of floor seating

PLAN 2:

Plan 2 would change the present seating pattern slightly.

Plan 2 involves the installation of 1100 Type B seats, 550 at each end. (See Figure 2.)

Plan 2 represents an increase of 1100 seats over present capacity, and 100 more than Plan 1.

The total cost of Plan 2 would be $85,000, computed on the following basis:

```
1100 Type B seats @ $40/seat      = $44,000

Installation costs                =   41,000

Total                             = $85,000
```

Possible increase in revenue, based on full occupancy:

```
1100 Type B seats @ $8/seat       = $ 8800/event
```

Analysis:

Advantages:

    1. Lower initial cost than Plan 1

    2. Higher revenue per event than Plan 1

Disadvantages:

    1. Violates present seating pattern slightly.

    2. Does not increase number of higher-priced seats.

PLAN 3:

Plan 3 would change present seating pattern significantly.

Plan 3 involves the installation of 1700 bench or bleacher type seats, 850 at each end (See Figure 3.)

Plan 3 represents an increase of 1700 seats over present capacity, 700 over Plan 1, and 600 over Plan 2.

The total cost of Plan 3 would be $48,000, computed on the following basis:

```
1700 bench seats @ $10/seat       = $17,000

Installation costs                = $31,000

Total                             = $48,000
```

Possible increase in revenue, based on full occupancy:

1700 bench seats @ $4/seat   = $6800/event

Analysis:

Advantages:

    1. Lowest initial cost of all plans

    2. Greatest increase in seating

Disadvantages:

    1. Represents a radical departure from present seating pattern

    2. Returns lowest amount per event

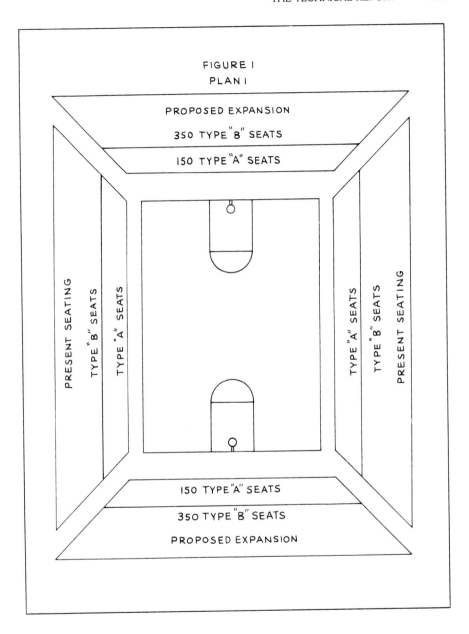

FIGURE I
PLAN I

PROPOSED EXPANSION

350 TYPE "B" SEATS

150 TYPE "A" SEATS

PRESENT SEATING   TYPE "B" SEATS   TYPE "A" SEATS

TYPE "A" SEATS   TYPE "B" SEATS   PRESENT SEATING

150 TYPE "A" SEATS

350 TYPE "B" SEATS

PROPOSED EXPANSION

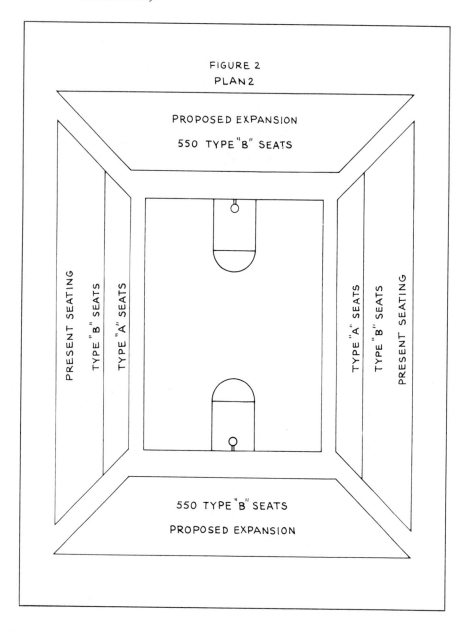

FIGURE 2
PLAN 2

PROPOSED EXPANSION

550 TYPE "B" SEATS

PRESENT SEATING

TYPE "B" SEATS

TYPE "A" SEATS

TYPE "A" SEATS

TYPE "B" SEATS

PRESENT SEATING

550 TYPE "B" SEATS

PROPOSED EXPANSION

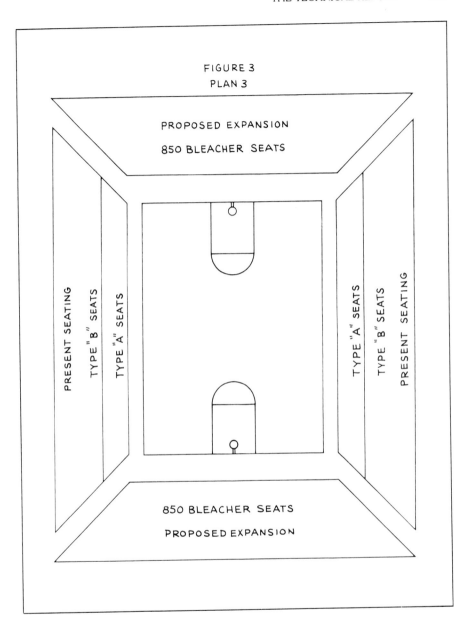

FIGURE 3
PLAN 3

PROPOSED EXPANSION

850 BLEACHER SEATS

PRESENT SEATING   TYPE "B" SEATS   TYPE "A" SEATS

TYPE "A" SEATS   TYPE "B" SEATS   PRESENT SEATING

850 BLEACHER SEATS

PROPOSED EXPANSION

CONCLUSIONS

While all three plans are feasible, each has separate and distinct advantages and disadvantages. What the Commission should decide depends on the criteria that are most important to them.

If it desires to maintain the aesthetic symmetry of the arena, Plan 1 offers the best way to increase seating. Plan 1 also provides an acceptable level of return on expenditures; however, it is the most expensive of the three options.

If the Commission desires the greatest return for the money invested, Plan 2 is preferable. However, Plan 2 does change the present seating pattern slightly.

If the Commission is most concerned with increasing the capacity to the maximum with the lowest initial cost, Plan 3 is recommended. However, this option changes the existing seating patterns greatly and has the lowest per event return.

RECOMMENDATIONS

We recommend Plan 2 for the following reasons:

1. It maximizes seating with the least damage to the existing seating pattern.

2. Its initial cost is lower than that of Plan 1.

3. Its return per event is highest of all three plans.

4. Spectators may be reluctant to pay higher prices for end seating.

5. Spectators may be reluctant to sit on bench or bleacher type seats.

In the event that Plan 2 is not the Commission's choice, our second recommendation is Plan 1, for the following reasons:

1. It maintains the present seating pattern.

2. It represents a reasonable return on the initial investment.

3. It increases the number of cushioned, higher-priced seats.

Plan 3 is the least desirable for the following reasons:

1. While it maximizes seating, it returns little revenue.

2. It would radically change the appearance of the seating.

3. Comfort in such seats is minimal, which might cause spectator dissatisfaction.

EXERCISES

Below is a list of some typical communication activities. Indicate what type of technical or nontechnical paper each would be, using the following symbols:

> N   – Nontechnical paper
> I.T. – Informal technical report
> S.T. – Semiformal technical report
> F.T. – Formal technical report

1. A letter requesting information about a new product.
2. The annual stockholders report of a large corporation.
3. A six-page manual explaining the operation of a new electrical generator.
4. The monthly report of expenses for a department of a larger company.
5. A weekly progress report on a continuing process.
6. A letter requesting an interview for a job as a chemical engineer.
7. A student's report on a one-day science experiment.
8. A student's paper on a semester's biological project.
9. A governmental study of the effects of air pollution on plants for a five-year period.
10. A student's report on the symbolic use of color in a novel.

Technical Reports – Assignments

1. Bring to class several examples of informal, semiformal, and formal reports. Be prepared to discuss the similarities and differences among them.
2. Select five terms from your technical field. Prepare a working definition for each that a nontechnical reader would understand.
3. Prepare a drawing of a tool or machine that is used in your field. Label the important parts.
4. Prepare an informal technical report related to your occupational interest.
5. Prepare a semiformal technical report related to your occupational interest.

CHAPTER 12

Speech Content

OBJECTIVES

After studying this chapter, you should be able to:
1. List the six steps to follow when preparing the content of your speech.
2. Discuss the procedure to follow when choosing a speech subject.
3. Explain the reasons for approaching speech as an audience-centered activity.
4. Write a clear and precise speech purpose statement.
5. Identify three broad sources of material to be used in your speech.
6. Demonstrate an ability to record material accurately.
7. Outline the three main parts of a speech.
8. Discuss three main characteristics of a communicative style.

If you are like most students, you probably face the thought of getting up to deliver a speech in front of a group of classmates with some apprehension. Perhaps you are not entirely clear as to how to develop an effective speech. You might be concerned with whether what you want to say will be interesting to your audience. You could be afraid that you will forget part of your speech, or say the wrong thing, or say it badly. You might even feel, "Why should I learn how to deliver a formal platform speech? I'll probably never have occasion to deliver one."

Although you may be called upon to make a formal public speech only a few times in your entire lifetime, the same skills are indispensable to effective face-to-face communication. People generally tend to equate ability to speak well with ability to think well. Therefore, the impression you make on others, even your own circle of friends, depends upon your ability to express yourself clearly and effectively in an easy, natural way.

Although there is no single formula that must be followed to be effective as a public speaker, two broad guidelines can help insure success: (1) say something worthwhile, and (2) say it in an easy, natural way.

SAYING SOMETHING WORTHWHILE

When you prepare a speech, you are concerned with two things: what you want to say, and how you want to say it. What you say is called the *content* of the speech, which includes the subject, the way you organize your material, the types of attention factors you choose, and your choice of words. While you should choose a subject from your own area of interest so that you know what you are talking about and have some enthusiasm for it, you must do so with your audience in mind. An audience will find your speech worthwhile if it is either interesting or useful to them. If the subject you choose has little to offer your audience in terms of usefulness and is not interesting of itself, your job is to make it interesting by handling your material in an imaginative and attention-getting way. It should be noted that although you are often free to choose any subject for a speech, the less interesting or useful the subject, the more difficult it will be to make the speech interesting. For example, unless you were in a class of music students, a speech on classical opera would require more imagination and effort than a speech on sky diving. The latter means daring, danger, thrills, and excitement to many; while opera might evoke similar responses in a few, it does not have nearly as broad an appeal.

Similarly, your classmates would be more inclined to see the usefulness of a speech on how to take a better snapshot than one on how to tune a guitar. Almost everyone takes snapshots, and most of us do not do so as effectively as we might. Consequently, a speech on how to improve this ability would be useful. On the other hand, probably the only person who would see the value of learning to tune a guitar would be someone who has just started learning how to play one. Anyone who knows how to play a guitar knows how to tune one, and the person who neither plays the guitar nor has a strong interest to play couldn't care less.

SAYING IT IN AN EASY WAY

The way in which you say something is called *delivery*. Delivery includes such things as platform manner, voice, eye contact, and facial expression. Effective delivery should seem easy and natural. Other than an increase in volume for a larger audience, the *principal difference* between platform speaking and ordinary conversation should be in content. Since a platform speech is more carefully prepared than everyday conversation, your subject will, no doubt, be handled more imaginatively and your words chosen more carefully. Be sure to avoid using languge with which you are unfamiliar. Use your own vocabulary, but eliminate words which might be inappropriate to the occasion.

An advantage to using your conversational style of delivery in front of an audience is that you will feel comfortable with it. If you try to change your way of speaking, your style will seem stilted and unnatural. The key to effective delivery is to be yourself. At first this might seem difficult—how do you get up in front of your classmates, many of whom you haven't met before, and be yourself? You will probably meet most of your fellow students during the semester on an individual basis anyway. Meeting others casually involves spontaneous, unplanned conversation. By delivering a carefully thought-out speech that deals with your own areas of interest, you show your classmates your best side. When listening to them, you get to know something about their interests. Both of you have, in effect, put your best foot forward, which should result in a clearer understanding of each other.

PREPARING SPEECH CONTENT

Specific instructions on how to prepare your speech for delivery will appear in the next chapter. Presented below are the six steps to follow when preparing the content of your speech.

1. Choose a subject.
2. Analyze the audience.
3. Determine the purpose.
4. Gather the supporting materials.
5. Organize the speech.
6. Word the speech.

Choose a Subject

It may be that when you are given your speech assignment, you immediately think of a subject that you are interested in and that you feel will be interesting to your audience. If this happens, you can move right on to step two, analyzing your audience. However, if you find you don't know what to talk about, take out a piece of paper and jot down as many as you can of the things that you are interested in or have experience with. There is no better place to look for a subject than in your own back yard. Have you grown up on a farm? Did you go to school in a different part of the country? Were you in the armed forces? Do you have an unusual job? Are you turned on by a particular religion? Do you have special skills in music, photography, theater, auto mechanics, or fashion design? With a little imagination and some hard work, you can make these subjects interesting to your audience. Detailed instructions on how to select and restrict your subject are found in Chapter 2.

Analyze the Audience

The process of communication involves a sender, a message, a medium, a receiver, and a response. Whenever a breakdown in communication occurs, it is at one or more of these points. Breakdowns in speech communication often occur when the speaker fails to consider carefully both the receiver and his response. As a result, too many speeches end up with the speaker talking about matters of self-interest, with little regard for the needs or interests of his audience. An effective speech must be audience-directed. Man is basically a self-centered creature; nothing interests him so much as himself. He relates to others in terms of their concern for him. A speaker whose purpose is simply self-expression or personality enlargement has little chance of holding the interest of his audience. He must show his listeners that he is concerned with their interests and needs.

Knowledge of your audience will help you plan a speech designed specifically for them. Find out as much as you can about them: their age, sex, educational background, and common interests. The more you know about an audience, the more likely you will be to establish a common ground of interest and information.

Contrast, for an example, an audience of college students with an audience of golden-agers. College students tend to be liberal, objective, willing to take a chance, interested in performance sports, and familiar with the language, music, personalities, and problems of their own generation; golden-agers are more likely to be conservative, cautious, subjective, interested in spectator sports, and more concerned with problems of security and health than with current issues. A subject that would be highly interesting to one group might be quite boring to the other. Chapter 5, which deals with audience analysis, will help you plan a speech with a specific audience in mind.

Decide on a Specific Purpose

After you have chosen your subject and analyzed the audience, you are ready to choose a purpose for your speech. For most of the speech assignments in this course, you will be given a general purpose: to inform, to persuade, or to entertain. Your job now is to determine a *specific aim* or purpose for your speech. What exactly is it that you are going to inform your audience about? What specific action do you want your audience to take as a result of your speech? For each speech, develop a specific purpose in a single sentence that states clearly and precisely what you want to accomplish. For a complete discussion of purpose, read Chapter 2.

Gather Supporting Material

The key to finding effective supporting material is to begin early. Finding good ideas takes time. There are no shortcuts. Decide on your subject as soon as possible after you are given the assignment. This will greatly increase your chances of finding effective supporting materials. As we said earlier, the first place to look for materials is in your own back yard. What are your thoughts on the subject? Jot them down. Can you enliven your speech with a story from your own experience? By all means include it.

Another source of materials for writing or speaking is mass communications, radio, or television. Talk shows, documentaries, news broadcasts, news analysis, and on-the-scene coverage of major events are just some of the kinds of programs that offer worthwhile material on a wide range of subjects.

Finally, the widest selection of speech materials can be found in the library. Every good library contains hundreds of sources. Newspapers, magazines, professional journals, pamphlets, yearbooks, textbooks, and reference books can often provide all the necessary supporting material for a successful communication. If you are not already, you should become familiar with the various guides to research that the library has available to you. For example, *The Readers' Guide to Periodical Literature* will help you locate articles written on thousands of subjects in magazines since the turn of the century. You can pick up the phone and call the ready reference section of your local library to get information ranging from who played free safety for the Green Bay Packers in 1964 to the present form of government in Greece.

Here is a final tip. Form the habit of recording the material you have gathered promptly and accurately. Some students prefer to keep the details of their readings in notebooks; for convenience of collecting, recording, and filing, however, the use of note cards is best.

When preparing note cards, observe the following rules:

1. Use a 3 × 5 or 4 × 6 inch file card.

2. Include only one idea per card.

3. Give each item a heading.

4. Follow the heading with the information. If the material is quoted exactly, use quotation marks. If you paraphrase, make sure you respect the author's meaning.

5. Indicate the exact source from which the information comes.

```
For new CIA Chief,
     a big rebuilding job.

As director of the Central Intelligence
Agency, Adm. Stansfield Turner will
face two stern challenges.

1.  How to revive confidence in the CIA.

2.  How to weigh accurately the strate-
    gic balance of power between the U.S.
    and the Soviet Union.

U.S. News and World Report, February 21, 1977
```

A Sample Note Card

EXERCISE

Find the answers to the following questions in your local or school library. Along with your answers, indicate the source.

1. At this date, how many states have ratified the Equal Rights Amendment?
2. What is the name of the "Son of Sam" killer captured August 11, 1977?
3. What was the date of the first public performance of *Jesus Christ Superstar?*
4. What were the names of the first men to land on the moon?
5. Which was the first country to be occupied by the Nazis in World War II?
6. How many acts are there in the play *Macbeth?*
7. Locate the title of a 1976 *Ms.* magazine article about Ted Kennedy's wife, Joan.
8. From which high school did Martin Luther King graduate?
9. Who wrote the novel *Of Mice and Men?*
10. Who won the Nobel Peace Prize in 1973?

ORGANIZING THE SPEECH

The function of organization is twofold. First, an audience can more easily understand and appreciate a message that is set in a clear framework. Second, an organizational pattern helps the speaker to eliminate wordiness, i.e., material that is unnecessary to the realization of his purpose. All speeches are divided into three parts—the introduction, the body, and the conclusion. The introduction should direct your audience's attention to the subject and make them want to listen. The body should communicate your ideas in a clear, meaningful way, and the conclusion should tie these ideas together in a neat package.

Introduction

The introduction to a speech has much to do with its success or failure. If a speaker fails to capture the attention of his audience in the introduction, he has little chance of regaining their interest. An introduction can have three purposes: (1) getting the audience's attention, (2) indicating the usefulness of the subject, and (3) indicating the purpose of the speech and its main idea. Although an introduction will often include all three of the above, at times one or two of them may be omitted.

Besides fulfilling these purposes, a good introduction has other characteristics. It must be appropriate to the purpose and main idea of the speech. A humorous introduction to a serious speech, for example, might cause the audience to feel that the speaker was not sufficiently concerned with his intentions. The introduction must lead naturally and easily into the body of the speech. Because the job is not only to get the attention of the audience but to hold it throughout the speech, a transition should be provided between the introduction and the body. Finally, an introduction should make an audience want to listen to the rest of your speech. The first impression you make is very important, so develop your introduction with your audience and subject in mind. Suggestions for developing an attention-getting introduction are found in Chapter 6. Some of the more commonly used methods are listed below:

1. Begin with humor.
2. Refer to a recent happening.
3. State the main idea.
4. Ask a rhetorical question.
5. Refer to a previous speaker.

6. Refer to the occasion.

7. Begin with a startling statement.

8. Begin with a brief illustration.

Body

The body of a speech develops the speaker's ideas in detail. It should contain a statement of the main idea and supporting material that clarifies or reinforces the main idea. The first step in developing the body of the speech is to formulate a main idea statement. In order to do this, carefully consider the subject and purpose of your speech. What is your restricted subject? Your specific purpose statement? Next, write down exactly what you want to say in one sentence. When you have done this, ask yourself these questions: Does this say what I want to say in the best way possible? Will this statement be clear to my listeners? You may have to make several revisions before you come up with a statement with which you are satisfied. However, this step in your preparation is vital. Keep at it until your sentence states the main idea as well as it can be said.

Once your main idea statement is ready, you can begin arranging the supporting materials for your speech. In order to organize your ideas clearly and interestingly, you should have a plan. You might compare developing a speech to building a garage. Not many people would begin building a garage from a pile of lumber without a blueprint to guide them. The information you have collected is like a pile of lumber. Before you begin putting your material together, find a plan or pattern you can follow. Basic patterns of organization are discussed in Chapter 9. Once you discover the correct pattern for your speech, details will fall into place and you will acquire a sense of direction.

Conclusion

No matter how short your speech is, it must have a conclusion to round it off. Many experienced speakers feel that the conclusion is the most important part of the speech, since it leaves the listener with his final impression.

An effective conclusion should leave an audience with a sense of completeness. Usually involving a summary or restatement of the main idea, a conclusion should be brief, to the point, and developed in the same style as the rest of the speech. Both the language and mood of the introduction and body must be continued in the conclusion. (A humorous conclusion to a serious speech would reflect on the sincerity of the speaker.)

One final note. New material should never be introduced in the conclusion. Such an action will give your audience the impression that you have failed to plan your speech carefully and have added the new material as an afterthought. A number of methods for concluding a speech are listed below:

1. Summarize the important points.
2. End with an appropriate anecdote.
3. Present recommendations.
4. End with a quotation or poem.
5. End by restating the main idea.

STYLE

The manner in which a person expresses himself in language is called his style. This book has stressed the use in speech of conversational style, with its frequent employment of the personal pronoun, which gives it an air of familiarity, as if the speaker were talking to close friends. To achieve a conversational style, make frequent use of the terms "us," "we," "our," and "you and I." Think of your speech as talking "with" your audience, not "to" them.

The level of usage in conversational style will vary according to the occasion. In general, the more formal the occasion, the more formal will be the language of the speech. However, regardless of the language used, a style, to be effective, must be communicative. A communicative style has three characteristics: clarity, interest, and appropriateness.

Clarity

Communication does not take place unless the listener understands the message. Too many speakers are concerned with what the audience will think of them rather than with whether they are communicating. By using multisyllabic words and flowery phrases, they try to project what they feel is the image of a successful orator. This is a mistake, because the effective speaker never tries to impress the audience with his vocabulary; he communicates, whenever possible, with a common vocabulary. If you want an effective speech style, choose terms that are appropriate and easily understood. If too much of what you have said is missed or misinterpreted, communication has failed.

For example, if a writer uses the word "exigency" in an essay, the reader unfamiliar with it can look it up; a listener has no such opportunity. Unless he knows the word or can determine its meaning from the context, he misses part of the message. This is avoided by the speaker who chooses a more familiar word, such as "urgency."

Unless you are delivering a formal speech, you should present your ideas in relatively short, uncomplicated sentences. Today's listeners may not spend the time or effort to search for your meaning. For example, a half century ago, when one-hour sermons were common, congregations were impressed with the verbal gymnastics of their clergy. Today the average sermon lasts about 15 minutes because the modern churchgoer demands directness and simplicity.

Interest

Clarity and interest are closely related to each other, since a listener or reader is more inclined to pay attention to a message that he can easily understand. To insure clarity a speaker must explain abstract terms which are important to the understanding of his subject. While this can be accomplished through definition, a more interesting way is through illustration or comparison. Note how interestingly Martin Luther King clarifies the abstract concept of equal opportunity by comparing it to a paycheck:

> In a sense we have come to our nation's capital to cash a check. When the architects of our republic wrote the magnificent words of the Constitution and the Declaration of Independence, they were signing a promissory note to which every American was to fall heir. This note was a promise that all men, yes, black men as well as white men, would be granted the unalienable rights of life, liberty, and the pursuit of happiness.
>
> It is obvious today that America has defaulted on this promissory note insofar as her citizens of color are concerned. Instead of honoring this sacred obligation, America has given the Negro people a bad check, which has come back marked "insufficient funds."
>
> But we refuse to believe that the bank of justice is bankrupt. We refuse to believe that there are insufficient funds in the great vaults of opportunity of this nation. So we have come to cash this check—a check that will give us upon demand the riches of freedom and the security of justice.

From "I Have a Dream," reprinted from *Rhetoric of Racial Revolt* (Denver, Colorado: Golden Bell Press, 1964), by permission of the publisher.

Another way of achieving clarity and interesting style is to choose the specific rather than the general. This is especially important in description. When the word "dog" is mentioned, what comes to mind? A collie? A poodle? A St. Bernard? Obviously, you can respond in various ways. With the more specific term "boxer" you get a clearer mental picture. This can be improved even more with added modification, e.g., "Cruncher, the boxer next door." If you want to be clear and interesting, be specific. Don't say, "a man came toward me," if he "staggered," "lurched," "ran," "stumbled," or "crawled."

Sometimes a word can appear to be specific and yet be difficult to visualize. Words that deal with statistics or measurements fall into this category. For example, it is estimated that last year 37 million people died of starvation, most of them children. Although it is specific, this figure is difficult to visualize. To say, "10,000 people die each day" is more vivid, since the number is easier to comprehend. An even more vivid and, therefore, more interesting image, is provided by saying, As you listen to these words, seven people have died of starvation."

Appropriateness

You must use language appropriate to your audience. It would be obviously inappropriate to use medical terminology in presenting a speech on cancer research to a group of laymen. Not so obvious would be the use of technical terms (even though simple) in discussing carburetor adjustment to a general group of students. Since most people are unfamiliar with auto mechanics, you would probably be confusing some in your audience.

In most cases, it is best to avoid off-color stories or profanity. Although modern novels and movies tend to belie this, most listeners will consider the speaker who uses off-color material guilty of poor judgment. While you might draw the attention of your audience with the startling use of a four-letter word, any advantage you gain will be negated if some find the word offensive.

Finally, unless it is apparent that you are deviating for deliberate effect, observe the rules of good grammar. An audience will probably overlook or even miss an occasional grammatical slip, but if your speech is filled with errors, they will think less of you. Whether they are justified or not, an audience tends to judge a person's intelligence by his use or misuse of language.

The accompanying speech evaluation form is designed for both student and instructor evaluation. It lists those characteristics of delivery and content which should be considered when evaluating a speaker.

It is important that a speaker be able to evaluate his performance objectively. Fill out a self-evaluation form (see page 240) after each speech you deliver. This will help you to clarify your strengths and weaknesses as a speaker.

Name_____Section_____Speech #_____Date_____

SPEECH EVALUATION SHEET

Grade_____

	Poor –	1	2	3	4	– Excellent	COMMENTS
A. DELIVERY							
1. Platform Manner							
2. Eye Contact							
3. Enthusiasm							
4. Confidence							
B. VOICE							
1. Volume							
2. Articulation							
3. Variety							
4. Quality							
C. CONTENT							
1. Introduction							
2. Use of Supports							
3. Knowledge of Subject							
4. Audience Analysis							
5. Conclusion							
D. LANGUAGE							
1. Clear							
2. Interesting							
3. Appropriate							

SELF-EVALUATION FORM

NAME_____ DATE_____ GRADE_____

SPECIFIC PURPOSE_____

_____

STRENGTHS

_____

WEAKNESSES

_____

AUDIENCE RESPONSE

_____

WAYS TO IMPROVE

_____

COMPARE YOUR EVALUATION
WITH EVALUATION OF THE
INSTRUCTOR AND OTHERS
_____

DID YOU FULFILL
YOUR PURPOSE?

_____

CHAPTER 13

Speech Delivery

OBJECTIVES

After studying this chapter, you should be able to:

1. Name the four principal methods of delivery.
2. Explain why extemporaneous speech is the best method for most occasions.
3. List five techniques for controlling speech tension.
4. Identify the nonverbal aspects of platform manner.
5. Discuss the four reasons for maintaining eye contact.
6. List and explain the five different characteristics of voice.
7. Demonstrate your ability to use note cards effectively when delivering a speech.
8. Discuss at least five suggestions you have found helpful in practicing your speech for delivery.

You have finished the hardest part of your job when you have developed the content of your speech. However, the work you have done in analyzing your subject and organizing your material may be wasted if you fail to deliver your speech effectively. Good delivery demands preparation and practice. There are four principal methods of delivery: (1) manuscript, (2) memorized, (3) impromptu, and (4) extemporaneous.

While the way in which you present your speech will vary according to audience and occasion, the best method for most occasions is the extemporaneous speech, spoken with preparation but not written out or memorized. Let us consider each of these methods of delivery separately.

MANUSCRIPT

In formal situations, where the oral presentation must be very precise, you may find it best to read your manuscript verbatim. Be careful to avoid overusing the manuscript speech. While this method offers security to the speaker afraid that he will forget what he wants to say or say it badly, it has three disadvantages: (1) it is difficult to maintain eye contact with the audience while reading, (2) it takes skill and practice to read a speech in a spontaneous and convincing manner, and (3) it is almost impossible to change the language or content of a manuscript speech to fit the mood or reaction of an audience.

Although you may be tempted to accept these disadvantages in return for the security of a manuscript speech, the best advice is to read a speech only when its content demands exact word order, as would research papers and technical data. To deliver a manuscript speech effectively, consider the following suggestions:

1. Edit your speech by reading each sentence aloud. Avoid overly long or involved sentences. No matter how complex or technical your material, it must be communicated clearly.
2. Type the manuscript speech in capital letters, triple-spaced to allow easy reading. Type on only one side of the paper.
3. Become familiar with your material by practicing it aloud; this will help you to obtain maximum eye contact. Even though you are reading, you must read "to people."
4. Indicate pauses and places of emphasis.
5. Use gestures and bodily action to enliven your delivery.

MEMORIZED

While the memorized speech appears to offer ease of eye contact along with the advantages of a manuscript speech, it has two distinct weaknesses: (1) it takes a skillful actor to present memorized material in a natural, spontaneous way, and (2) the speaker who delivers his speech from memory runs the risk of forgetting. Unless you have complete confidence in your ability to deliver a speech naturally without losing your place, memorizing a speech is a risky method.

IMPROMPTU

An impromptu speech is one developed on the spur of the moment. Since it seldom allows opportunity for advance thought or preparation, it demands a great deal of the speaker. Unlike the writer of an impromptu theme, who can rephrase a clumsy sentence, the speaker finds it awkward to correct himself once he has said something. His audience receives his message the moment it is delivered. He has little time to analyze his subject, audience, or occasion, and must think on his feet as he chooses and organizes his material. While the impromptu method can often impart directness and spontaneity to the speaker's delivery, handling material that is not carefully thought out can often result in a rambling presentation. Experience in the planning, preparation, and delivery of extemporaneous speeches will provide guidelines for greater effectiveness in impromptu situations.

When you are called upon to deliver an impromptu speech, consider the following advice: (1) make sure that your central idea and specific purpose are absolutely clear to your audience, (2) keep your speech short and to the point, and (3) handle only one main point.

EXTEMPORANEOUS

Like the written or memorized speech, the extemporaneous speech is carefully planned and rehearsed with the difference that the speaker does not deliver the speech in a predetermined word order. He decides on his exact wording at the moment of delivery. Thus, the extemporaneous method offers the same directness and spontaneity as the impromptu method without the danger of the speaker's rambling off the point or repeating himself unnecessarily. You might compare extemporaneous speech delivery with the telling of a detailed funny story. Most people tell a funny story that they are familiar with extemporaneously. They know how the story is going to unfold, but they haven't memorized the word order. As long as they include those details necessary to make the humor clear, they can tailor the story to fit the occasion. The result is a relaxed, spontaneous style, which is the main advantage of extemporaneous delivery.

STAGE FRIGHT

You may be saying to yourself, "How can I say it in an easy, natural way when I'm scared to death up there?" If you feel this way, you have probably at one time or another experienced a case of stage fright. Stage fright is the fear that you will not do as well as you would like to in front of an audience. The symptoms may be any combination of the following: dry mouth, rapid pulse, quivering voice, uncontrollable trembling, loss of memory, sweaty palms, or queasy stomach. If a person is afflicted with stage fright what can he do about it? We suggest a two-way approach: (1) become familiar with the causes of stage fright, (2) use specific techniques to control tensions.

Causes of Stage Fright

When you deliver a speech in your communication course, you are communicating in a friendly situation. You are speaking to a classroom

A CASE OF STAGE FRIGHT?

Have you ever had a case of stage fright?

If you're an undergraduate theater student or a secondary school drama teacher, your stage experience has probably included at least one case of stage fright.

If so, you're just the person we're looking for.

The Durham Summer Theater's fourteenth season is only months away, and we're beginning our national search for talented, energetic students and teachers to study in our acting, management, and technical workshops and join our repertory company at the University of New Hampshire.

Of course, we can't promise a cure for stage fright. But the theoretical knowledge and practical training you'll receive will increase your confidence in your abilities, on stage and off.

Apprentices in the Undergraduate Theater Workshop undergo a rigorous eight-week schedule of classes in acting, voice and diction, scenic arts, lighting, costuming, and management. Secondary school teachers follow a similar program and also attend seminars on directing, production, and teaching theater techniques.

All workshop participants will have the opportunity to join the resident professionals on stage in the company's six major productions.

Workshops are held in the Paul Creative Arts Center's two air-conditioned theaters: Johnson Theater, a 721-seat proscenium theater, and Hennessy Theater, a 250-seat theater-in-the-round.

When you're not involved with workshops or performances, you'll find plenty of things to do close by. The University of New Hampshire is situated near some of New England's finest beaches; fresh-water lakes, the White Mountains, and Boston are all within easy driving distance.

Final plans for the 1977 Durham Summer Theater schedule are still being completed, but this season's productions are expected to include *South Pacific, Much Ado About Nothing, A View from the Bridge, Arms and the Man, Celebration,* and *The Real Inspector Hound.*

The Durham Summer Theater at the University of New Hampshire

Undergraduate Theater Workshop/June 26-August 19/ 8 credits (transferable)/some high school apprentices accepted

Undergraduate auditions/New York—Americana Hotel, April 14-16/Chicago—Loyola University, April 21-23/Los Angeles—by arrangement/University of New Hampshire—by arrangement, April 1-May 30

Theater Workshop for Teachers/Session I—June 26-July 22/Session II—July 25-August 19/teachers may enroll for one or both sessions/acceptance through application/enrollment limited

Information and applications/Linda L. Spohn, Managing Director, Durham Summer Theater, Paul Creative Arts Center, University of New Hampshire, Durham, NH 03824

Concept/Ken Silvia—Photo/Jack Adams, University of New Hampshire

245

of students who are pulling for you and expect you to make mistakes, just as they will. In this kind of situation a speaker should feel relaxed and at ease—but many don't. Why? Many beginning speakers see the situation as threatening rather than friendly. They see their egos in jeopardy. They worry about others' seeing their weaknesses and imperfections, real or imaginary. Worrying too much about what other people will think of you is what causes stage fright.

A student has good reason to be fearful if he gets up to deliver a speech he has done little to prepare or practice. He not only has to worry about losing his place or forgetting what he was going to say; he has the added burden of having wasted the audience's time. Few of your classmates will react favorably to your presentation if they feel you are taking advantage of them. Sometimes a person may be well prepared but experience stage fright when speaking to what psychologists call "significant others." A student might find it easy to speak in a history or psychology class but freeze up in a communications course because the instructor is evaluating his performance. A Sunday school teacher may be relaxed and at ease when teaching class but be filled with fear when addressing the congregation.

Stage fright also occurs when risk is involved in the situation. Your instructor, for example, may become much less fluent when his supervisor drops in on the class to evaluate his performance. A young man might feel self-conscious and ill at ease when asking that special someone for a first date. You may, for example, have no difficulty communicating with your boss until it comes time to ask for that raise.

Finally, stage fright can occur because the speaker is in a depressed mood. Perhaps something tragic has recently happened to a friend or loved one, or there might be a problem hanging over his head that seems unsolvable. It could be that a person is down without even knowing why. In any event, whatever effects the speaker's personality effects his speech.

How to Control Tensions

Since most speakers experience some nervousness when they appear before an audience, you probably will, too. Here are some suggestions on how to keep your nervousness at a minimum.

1. Develop an attention-getting introduction. It is important to get off to a good start with your audience. A novel or humorous introduction will put your audience in the right frame of mind and help you relax as well. Suggestions on how to develop attention-getting introductions are found in Chapter 6.

2. Instead of worrying about your own speech, listen carefully to the speaker you are going to follow. Perhaps there is something in his speech that you can refer to in your introduction. This will take your mind off of your own plight and start you on the right foot. Your audience will be impressed with your imagination.

3. Make sure that you carefully develop a speech that is audience-centered. If you feel that you have something worthwhile for your audience, chances are your concern will shift from yourself to the ideas you are trying to communicate. Suggestions for developing an audience-centered speech are found in Chapter 5.

4. Practice your speech from three to five times. The idea is to practice enough so that your ideas can be recalled quickly and easily but not so much that you unconsciously memorize it. When you are well prepared, speaking is fun.

5. Develop a positive mental attitude about speaking. It is natural to be nervous when standing before an audience. As you get more and more practice in speech making, you will find that this nervous energy can be transferred into making your speech more vibrant and enthusiastic.

PLATFORM MANNER

In a broad sense, platform manner can include all of the speaker's nonverbal communication—the way he walks up to and away from the platform, his facial expression, posture, gestures, and attire. The speaker who approaches his audience in a positive way says to his listener, "I have something to offer that I think you will find rewarding." An audience begins evaluating a speaker as soon as he comes into their line of vision. If you want to create the right impression, walk to the speaker's platform in a firm, energetic way. Good posture projects alertness and self-confidence. After you have reached the lectern, pause briefly and look out at those in your audience in a friendly, interested manner. If a smile is in order, by all means smile. The important thing is that your facial expression should be appropriate to your subject matter; it should set the mood for your speech.

It is usually a good idea to maintain good posture when addressing an audience. Speakers who slouch over the lectern or affect too casual a pose tend to receive an indifferent response.

There will be times when it will be necessary for you to move around in front of your audience, to walk to a chalkboard or map, to demonstrate a way of doing something, or simply to move closer to them to develop a more intimate mood. There is one simple rule to follow when you are in front of an audience. Anything you do, whether it is sitting on your desk or walking to the window, is acceptable as long as it does not call attention to itself. A movement is unacceptable when the audience thinks, "I wonder why he's doing that?"

Gesture is another characteristic of platform manner. In casual, relaxed conversation we habitually employ a wide range of gestures. We nod our heads, shrug our shoulders, wrinkle our brows, or wave our hands to emphasize what we have to say or to describe something.

If, when presenting your speeches, you find it difficult to use gestures successfully, wait until you feel the urge to use them. To be effective, gestures must come naturally and instinctively. A beginning speaker is often overly conscious of his audience. It is better to wait with your gestures until you are more relaxed in the speaking situation, since an awkward gesture is worse than no gesture at all.

The clothes worn by a speaker should suit the occasion. For a classroom speech, wear what you would normally wear to class; for a more formal occasion, dress accordingly. In both cases your clothes should be cleaned, pressed, and in good repair. Clothing which does not call attention to itself is always the best choice.

The conclusion of your speech should be carefully planned so that you can finish with your eyes fixed on the audience. After a brief pause, leave the speaker's platform with the same air of confidence with which you approached it. Don't indicate by your facial expression or gesture that you were at all dissatisfied with your performance. Let your audience evaluate you.

EYE CONTACT

Good eye contact is an aid in holding attention, and necessary for feedback from the audience. In general, your eye contact will be effective if you look slowly from one individual to another; if your eyes dart rapidly from person to person, the effect will be shifty or unnatural. Although it isn't necessary to look at each individual in your audience, be careful to include persons from all parts of the group. Do not develop the habit of looking mostly to one side of the room or at just those nearest you.

Eye contact is an aid to holding your audience's attention for a number of reasons. First, we indicate our interest in others by looking them in the eye. One of the most important things a speaker can do is to convince each listener that he is addressing him as an individual. An audience will tend to respond to a speaker who demonstrates that interest.

Second, eye contact is thought of as an indication of straightforwardness and honesty. We look people right in the eye when we are open and aboveboard, and avoid someone's eyes when we are saying something dishonest or embarrassing. Looking your audience right in the eye will convince them of your honesty and sincerity.

Third, we speak to our audience nonverbally as well as verbally. We say a great deal to them with our facial expression, especially the eyes. Facial expression can aid greatly in making meanings clear, giving emphasis, and expressing moods. Obviously, an audience will have difficulty seeing your facial expression if you are staring out the window or at your notes.

The final reason for establishing eye contact is to obtain feedback from the audience. We look at people while communicating to them because we are interested in their reaction to what we are saying. They indicate this through changes in facial expression, posture, and gestures. This feedback tells us how well we are communicating, whether our listeners are interested or bored, clear or confused, friendly or hostile, thus giving us the opportunity to respond appropriately.

VOICE

The very least a listener can expect of a speaker is that he speak in a voice loud and clear enough to be heard and understood. It takes too much effort to listen to a speaker who mutters or speaks too softly. However, if you want to be an effective speaker, you must do more than the bare minimum. Your voice must be an asset to you; it must help to make what you say more interesting and meaningful. The different characteristics which express meaning and add variety to your voice are: volume, rate, articulation, quality, and pitch.

Volume

Volume refers to the loudness or softness of your voice. Obviously, you must increase your volume to be heard in a large room or in a situation with a high degree of surrounding noise. Don't be misled by the fact that you can hear yourself adequately. If it takes effort on the part of the listener to hear you, you are probably not communicating effectively.

Rate

Rate, the speed at which a person speaks, is dependent upon two elements — duration and pause. Duration is the length of time a word is prolonged. It is an effective way to emphasize, and is often used in conversation, particularly to accentuate modifiers, e.g., "He has a *fabulous* record collection — we had a *fantastic* time." Pause, together with duration, determines the rate at which a person speaks. If a person cuts his words off short and allows little pause, his rate will be rapid. Most beginning speakers tend to speak faster than they should, because a person tends to increase his rate when he is nervous or excited. In addition, many people tend to associate pause with nonfluency, with the idea that a person pauses because he does not know what to say. Ironically, this attitude toward pause as an indicator of nonfluency is often formed while a child is being taught to read in the primary grades. The child who reads slowly and haltingly, pausing before words with which he is unfamiliar, is thought of as a slow learner. The child who reads at a fairly rapid rate with few pauses is considered bright and given praise. The result is that the student is taught to avoid pause.

Articulation

We learn to speak by imitating the speech of those close to us. Consequently, our habits of speech often resemble the speech habits of those we have imitated. If we are lucky, and those we learn from speak distinctly, we tend to speak distinctly. However, if those we learn from tend toward indistinct speech, the chances are that our speech will also be indistinct. Unless the problem is physical, indistinct speech is caused by poor articulation, which is the process of forming the consonant and vowel sounds of words. It is a necessity for successful communication, since if you fail to articulate your words clearly, you will be difficult to understand.

The two common errors of articulation are substituting one sound for another and leaving off the endings of words. For example, "this" becomes "dis," "student" becomes "stoont," and "asked" becomes "ast." An audience forms an unfavorable impression of a speaker who says things in a careless way. If the impression you give to others is important to you, make sure your articulation is precise.

Improving your articulation may not be easy if bad habits are ingrained in your speech. The first thing you must do is become aware of your weaknesses. What are your specific problems — running words together? Leaving off word endings? Substituting sounds? Although you can become aware of your problems by listening carefully to yourself as you speak, it is preferable, if you have the opportunity, to record your voice with a tape recorder or video tape. Tape yourself not only while practicing your speech but during ordinary conversation as well. Once you have determined your problems, make a list and study them.

Quality

A pleasant voice is free from undue harshness, huskiness, hoarseness, breathiness, and nasality. Unless a person has some problem caused by a disease or physical defect, he should be able to speak in a voice which is pleasant to listen to. Serious speech problems should be handled by a trained speech therapist. For those with minor difficulties, Jeffrey and Peterson make the following suggestions:

1. The speaker should learn to hear his voice as others hear it. An almost universal reaction of persons upon hearing a recording of their voice for the first time is, "That's not me. There must be something wrong with the recorder." But, of course, there is nothing wrong with the recorder and the recording, as classmates or friends will verify, is a faithful reproduction of the individual's speech. The speaker's initial reaction reveals that most people do not hear themselves as others hear them. This is in part because some of the sound is carried from the voice box to his ears through the cheek and neck bones. But it is also in part because most people have become so accustomed to hearing their own voice that they really do not listen to themselves carefully or analytically.

   Quite clearly, the first step in learning to hear one's voice as others hear it is for the speaker to record and listen to his speech frequently. The second step is to develop an awareness at all times of how it sounds.

2. To avoid strain, one should speak at a comfortable pitch level.

3. The speaker should maintain adequate breath support.

4. He should remain relaxed while speaking.

5. If strain or hoarseness occurs regularly, the speaker should consult a speech correctionist.

   Robert C. Jeffrey and Owen Peterson, *Speech: A Text with Adapted Readings* (New York: Harper & Row, Publishers, 1971), pp. 385–86.

Pitch

Pitch refers to the highness or lowness of a speaker's voice. Everyone has a natural pitch level at which he can speak most comfortably. Problems in pitch can occur when a person tries to speak at a pitch which is higher or lower than his natural level. Suppose, for example, that a young man with a natural tenor voice feels that a bass voice is more masculine. His attempts to speak in a lower voice result in a husky and rasping sound. Instead of his natural, resonant voice, he produces a voice with an unpleasant quality, lack of adequate volume, and monotony in pitch. The size and length of your vocal chords determine the tone of your voice. If you want to avoid problems with your voice, speak at your most comfortable pitch level.

A natural conversational style is characterized by a variety of pitches. In normal conversation, these inflections come spontaneously. The best way to insure that your inflection will be interesting and meaningful is to choose a subject which you desire to communicate to your listeners. When you are concerned with expressing your true feelings, your inflection will come naturally.

PREPARING THE SPEECH FOR DELIVERY

An extemporaneous speaker delivers his speech from notes which include his main ideas and supporting materials. Many experienced speakers put their individual ideas on separate note cards rather than together on the same page. An individual note card isolates an idea so that it can be seen at a glance; after the speaker has dealt with the idea, he can move on to the next card. Although your audience expects you to use notes in an extemporaneous speech, you should do so unobtrusively. Remember, anything that calls attention to itself can distract from what you are saying. Note cards are much easier to handle if you must deliver the speech without a lectern. You can hold them in one hand and still be able to gesture freely. However, in most platform situations a lectern will be available to you. Once you have reached the lectern, put your notes down and leave them there; notes are to remind you of what to say, not to read verbatim. When you finish with a note card, move it to one side as unobtrusively as possible.

There is one instance when you should call attention to your notes. When reading a direct quotation, hold your notes up so that your audience can see that you are taking special care to be accurate.

Be sure that you can read your notes easily. Notes are easy to read when they are typed in capital letters, and double- or triple-spaced. Use only one side of the paper, since turning over your notes is both awkward and time-consuming. Each note card or page should be clearly numbered to prevent you from losing your place.

Avoid writing your notes in too much detail. Coming to the

speaker's platform with an overly detailed guide may tempt you to read your speech, thereby defeating the whole purpose of the extemporaneous method.

Finally, don't let the fact that you are using a guide inhibit your gestures or facial expression. Spontaneous, convincing delivery requires bodily action and expressiveness.

Following are two types of note cards prepared for a student speech on diabetes. Create similar copy of your own to see which type is most effective for you.

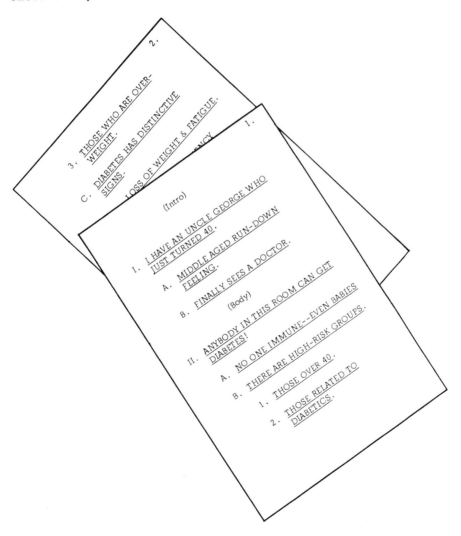

Practicing the Speech

The key to effective delivery is practice. Few experienced speakers would deliver an extemporaneous speech without practicing at least two or three times. Practice offers an additional benefit to you as a beginning speaker. While practicing in a relaxed atmosphere to improve a specific speech, you can take stock of your strengths and weaknesses as a speaker.

After you have practiced your speech a few times, deliver it as if you were in front of an audience. Doing your best in practice will give you a good idea of the quality of your ultimate performance. If possible, deliver your speech to someone who can evaluate it objectively. If it is possible to tape record or videotape yourself, by all means do so. Self-evaluation is a prerequisite to improvement. Below are specific suggestions for practicing your speeches.

Suggestions for Practicing Your Speech

1. Practice delivering your speech from three to five times. The idea is to practice enough so that you will feel confident and relaxed when it comes time to deliver your speech, but not

so much that you unconsciously memorize it. In other words, practice enough to develop fluency in the way you express your ideas, but not so much that you lose spontaneity.

2. Don't try to deliver your speech the same way twice. Become reconciled to the fact that you might forget something during practice. The important thing to remember is that if you practice your speech carefully, you will have no difficulty in remembering the main ideas when you deliver it. After all, if you forget a statistic or example during the speech, who is going to know besides you?

3. Go through the entire speech during each practice. Inexperienced speakers often stop and go back to the beginning after they have made a few mistakes. This is unwise. Accept the fact that some hesitation or groping for words is inevitable and continue through to the end. If the rough spots don't work out by themselves, you can work on them before you practice the speech the next time.

4. Practice as if you were actually delivering your speech to an audience. If at all possible, try to practice with the same volume and animation you will use when it comes time to deliver your speech. There is a certain amount of acting involved in giving a speech. Develop this "performance" attitude in practice, and you will do a much better job when it comes to the real thing.

5. Practice with the same note cards or manuscript you plan to use when delivering your speech. If you are planning an extemporaneous delivery, don't practice from a manuscript or outline and then walk up to the speaker's platform with a set of notes you have never used before. Also, don't practice from notes you have scribbled changes and comments on and then type up a brand new set to use in class and expect to do a good job with them. Make sure that the notes you bring on the day of delivery are the same ones you used in your last practice.

6. Don't practice individual gestures. It's fine to gesture naturally while practicing, but don't decide that at a certain place in your speech you will pound your fist on the lectern or point your finger at the audience. To be effective, gestures must be spontaneous.

7. Practice with the aids you will use in your speech. One guaranteed way to cause butterflies in the stomach is to stand in front of an audience with a visual aid that doesn't work. Fur-

thermore, it might take you longer to demonstrate something with an aid than you thought it would. Finding this out in practice could prevent an embarrassing situation.

8. Time your speech in practice. Develop your speeches so that they fall within the time limit of the assignment. Mark Twain told the story of going to listen to a minister he had heard was one of the finest in the area. After listening to him for the first fifteen minutes he was so impressed he decided to leave twenty dollars in the collection plate. Another thirty minutes passed, and he lowered it to ten. Finally, one hour later when the sermon was over and they passed the plate around, he took out five dollars and stalked out.

9. Whenever possible, practice in front of a live audience. Even if you have to bring your little brother and his friend into the room, it helps to practice delivering your speech to a listener. If you can find a listener who will give you some constructive evaluation, all the better.

10. Tape record or video tape your practice when possible. If you have access to recorders at home or in school, by all means make use of them. They are excellent aids to self-evaluation.

EXERCISES: SPEAKING ASSIGNMENTS

Following the suggestions given on the preceding pages, prepare and deliver whichever of these assignments your instructor chooses.

INTRODUCING A CLASSMATE

Interview a classmate, questioning him about his hobbies, likes and dislikes, goals, attitudes, or anything you feel will be of interest to the class. Take careful notes. Then, have your classmate interview you. After class, review your notes selecting the information you believe is most interesting. Arrange this information in an order which will be easy for you and your audience to remember. Deliver this speech to class as your instructor directs.

Suggestions

1. Make sure you pronounce your classmate's name *distinctly* and *correctly*.
2. Be accurate. Don't try to make your classmate out to be someone he is not.
3. Be as friendly and interesting as you can.
4. Be familiar with your material. If you need a note card, use only one.

A LETTER TO THE EDITOR (An expression of viewpoint; 2–3 minutes)

Write to the "Letters to the Editor" column of one of your local newspapers expressing a point of view. It will be helpful if you familiarize yourself with these columns in order to be aware of the rules and format to follow. A reader will judge you on your style and grammatical correctness. A simple, to-the-point style must still be interesting.

Delivery: This speech will be delivered in the manuscript method of presentation. Remember, the successful speaker reads as though he were speaking extemporaneously. Practice to deliver this speech in a spontaneous, convincing manner.

Suggestions

1. If you are writing in response to a published letter, read it so that your audience is clear as to what you're disagreeing with.
2. Write as if you were speaking—in an informal, direct way.
3. Read the letter aloud to a friend or two.
4. Become familiar enough with the letter to develop good eye contact.
5. Proofread your letter to eliminate weaknesses in style and grammatical errors.

THE IMPROMPTU SPEECH

Deliver a 2–4 minute impromptu speech. Your purpose may be to inform, persuade, or entertain. You will either be given a subject or allowed to choose one from a list made available to you shortly before you will begin speaking.

Delivery: Use the limited time available to you to decide on your purpose and specific intent. Make sure that both are absolutely clear to your audience. Keep your speech short and to the point. Handle only one main point in the body and restate your central idea at the conclusion.

Sample Topics

1. Honesty as the best policy
2. My views on socialism
3. The ideal wife (husband)
4. The most useful profession
5. If I had it to do over again
6. What I consider a good movie
7. City versus country living
8. The most useless profession
9. A day I would like to forget
10. Thirteen, my lucky number

READING PROSE OR POETRY

Choose a selection of prose or poetry. Study it carefully in regard to meaning and mood. Practice it until you can deliver it effectively. In order to read well, a person must understand the meaning and mood of the material, and be able to convey that meaning and mood to his audience.

Suggestions

1. *Choose your reading carefully.* Pick something interesting that you can handle intelligently.
2. *Time your reading.* Your selection must fall within a 2–3 minute time limit.
3. *Insure understanding.* Preface your reading with any information that will contribute to your listener's understanding.
4. *Use effective speaking techniques.* Speak clearly and distinctly, using variations in rate, pitch, and volume to convey the author's meaning and to make the reading more interesting. Know your selection well enough so that you can maintain adequate eye contact with your audience. It might be a good idea to copy your selection double-spaced on note cards or half sheets of paper.

Model

The reader's job here is to communicate the attitudes of the two speakers in the poem.

SLOW DOWN?

Slow down, black man, you tell me.
You're moving much too fast
At the rate you're going
You surely cannot last.
You're entitled to your rights,
You're going to get them too.
But, you're rushing things too fast
And, that ain't good for you.
Sure you're demonstrating,
You're picketing and such
I know you want your rights.
But, you're crowding things too much.
Slow down, black man, Slow down.
Heed the words I say
You're injuring your cause
This is not the way
Things will be all right.
You haven't got to worry.

But, slow down, black man. Slow down.
Don't be in such a hurry.
I get the Message white man.
It's coming in loud and clear.
But, you ain't saying nothing.
It's like, Mister, I can't hear.
How long you been a black man?
How long you been a "boy"?
What rights does the nation have
That you cannot enjoy?
It's easy for you to say,
"Black man, take it slow."
But, do you know segregation?
Have you ever met "The Crow"?
You don't fool me, Mr. White Man.
You ain't dealing from the top.
You don't mean "slow down."
You mean, damn it, "NIGGER"

STOP! Slow down, black man, you tell me.
Man you got your gall.
You've never cried for justice
You don't understand at all.
Have you ever lost a brother
To the fury of a mob?
Has the color of your skin
Stopped you from getting a job?
Slow down, black man, you tell me.
Well, mister, that's all right.
It's easy for you to say.
Who've never known a slight.
I have been going slow
For more than five score years
And yet and still I know
The same old hate and fears.

Have your brethren been lynched?
For the crime of being white?
Have you seen your mother tremble
When the klansmen rode at night?
I've been patient, Mr. White Man.
The Lord knows I have been
But, I ain't as good as Job
My patience has an end.
You bomb my house of worship.
You kill my babies, too.
Slow down, black man, you tell me.
Well, man, that's up to you.
I'll slow down, Mr. White Man.
I promise you I will,
When jimcrow is interred—
And we stand on freedom hill.

With permission of the author, Ben Anderson, Mt. Vernon, New York.

READING A COMMERCIAL

Read a 1–2 minute radio or TV commercial that you have written yourself or picked up from a local broadcaster. Study it carefully to decide how best to indicate meaning and emphasis. Practice it so that you can deliver it easily and naturally.

Delivery: It is important that you communicate sincerity to your audience. You can do this best by using a conversational style. Be yourself. Try to inject color and feeling into your words and phrases by being enthusiastic about the product. Smile when you speak.

Model

MISTER DONUT

(Establish and fade background for announcer.)

ANNCR: Before he opens his own shop, each MISTER DONUT owner goes through a rigorous 5-week training course on how to make the finest and freshest donuts a man can buy. That's why they're able to make over 100 varieties of fresh donuts . . . honey dips, chocolate, bavarian cream, toasted coconut . . . even fancy pastries like eclairs and bismarks and blueberry bursts. Why, these fellows have such good looking fancy donuts, some of them look as good as miniature wedding cakes. Come on in to Mister Donut and buy a dozen . . . for the kids, or your guests or the gals at the office.

Visit the Mister Donut Shop, at 3151 South 92nd Street . . . or . . . the Mister Donut Shop, at 9230 West Capital Drive . . . in Milwaukee.

(Music to fill)

Used with the permission of Mister Donut of America, Inc. and The Sycamore Corporation.

A SPEECH OF CRITICISM

Deliver a 2–4 minute speech or write a 250–500 word essay in which you criticize a person, policy, or organization. Pick a subject that really annoys you. Express your views in a direct, to the point manner, emphasizing your annoyance with the language you use. If you deliver this as a speech, underline your irritation with facial expression, gestures, and tone.

Delivery: This speech should be delivered extemporaneously. The more spontaneous and direct you are in your presentation, the more clearly you will communicate your conviction and sincerity to the audience. This is an expression of *your* viewpoint. Indicate your attitude with emphasis, intensity, and force.

Suggested Topics

1. Let's end our hypercritical attitude toward (censorship, segregation, communism, religion, etc.).
2. Welfare is another word for stealing.
3. People who brand all long-haired teenagers as hippies are ignorant.
4. Let's get the bigots out of our judicial system.
5. When are we going to stop kidding ourselves about America being a free country?
6. Allowing students to protest is undermining the principles upon which our colleges and universities were founded.

Model

WHERE DOES THIS HERO REST?

Mr. Conyers: Mr. Speaker, not too long ago a young black American named William Terry volunteered to serve in the U.S. Army. Proudly he assumed the uniform of his country, and willingly took his training and was sent to Vietnam.

Private First Class Terry wore his uniform proudly, even though it may have been woven by a company which would not have hired or promoted him. And he fought for his country, even though he and 24 million of his countrymen were denied the rights due to them as full-fledged American citizens. And, not long afterwards, Private First Class

Terry, only 20 years old, gave his life to his country—killed in action in defense of a government that renounced the same freedoms he was told he was fighting for.

Bill Terry did not think of the slave ships, the auction blocks, Jim Crow, or Judge Lynch. He did not allow himself to be swayed by those who would destroy the dreams of himself and his fellows, by those who would segregate his schools, isolate his jobs, hurl threats, or even bombs at his doorways. Instead, he thought only of what he conceived to be his duty to his country. He fought for what he thought right and he died for it.

And then, in a Government-issue coffin, he came home to his family—in Birmingham, Ala.

His family asked that he be buried in Birmingham, in a place called the Elmwood Cemetery. But the Elmwood Cemetery said no, only white people could be buried there. So, because he was black, Bill Terry was buried in another cemetery outside of Birmingham, where only blacks were interred. And he was buried in an unmarked grave.

Just as it is a source of pride to relatives of others who lie with him that he is there, so it is a source of shame to our country that he was forced to lie there. What was he to America, even in death? What was his family to America? And now, what is America to them?

In recent days we have heard much of patriotism and our country. Many speeches have been delivered. With all those flags flapping in the breeze, I wonder whether all those speakers included Bill Terry in their thoughts. Did they count him in? Did they care?

Maybe Bill Terry even heard them, there in that place where he rests.

Congressional Record. Speech given by Hon. John Conyers, Jr., of Michigan in the House of Representatives, November 25, 1969.

RELATING A PERSONAL EXPERIENCE (To entertain)

Deliver a 2–5 minute speech or write a short narrative of 300–500 words in which you relate a personal experience. Describe the situation in enough detail to create a mental picture for the reader or listener. Develop your material informally, with emphasis on details of action.

Delivery: This speech should be delivered extemporaneously. An audience will expect you to have almost total eye contact when talking about your own experiences. The more spontaneous and relaxed you are, the more your audience will enjoy your presentation.

Suggested Topics

1. My last day on the job
2. A visit to the Internal Revenue Service
3. My uncle George

Model

One day, a few friends and I were in my basement playing cards and drinking beer. One of them was an avid parachutist. I don't recall how it happened, but I soon found myself making a bet with this skydiver, Tom, that I would not be afraid to jump. The deal was, if I would jump, he would pay for it but if I didn't jump, I would pay him five dollars. I asked him where we would be jumping and he said "out at the airport."

We left the next morning for what I thought would be a major airport. It wasn't. It was a shabby pasture with one beaten-down path for a runway and a rundown shack. I had figured on this jump being highly supervised by qualified personnel. Now that I saw where we were going, the tension started building.

We went up to the shack, and Tom started pulling out a number of chutes and helmets, trying to decide which ones he was going to use. I went into the building to pay the five dollars for the ride up. I asked the man at the desk for my parachute, and he directed me to a dusty corner where a pile of packed chutes were. I picked up a chute and he said, "No, not that one, that one don't work." So I picked up another one and he said, "Yah, that's a good one." I said, "Well are you sure?" He said, "Yah, don't worry, that one works." So I picked it up and I noticed a clean spot underneath it, amid all the dust. Now I was really getting nervous.

We got over to the plane and it was obvious that it wasn't one of the latest models. In fact, it almost looked obsolete. The pilot started the engine, and it wasn't the soft purr of a finely tuned engine that I had expected. It sounded like an old, oil burning, sputtering piece of junk. It was running for about a minute, and then of all things, it conked out. I thought to myself, "Aw this is ridiculous." The pilot was cursing and trying to start the plane again, and I noticed a hole in the back wall of the plane. I said to Tom, "what happens if this plane conks out up there?" And he says, "Well, we'll just glide down." I said, "No Tom, if that plane conks out up there we're going straight down." Then he said, "Ah, don't worry, nothin'll happen."

The pilot got the plane started again and we piled in, me first, because I was to jump last. Next, I found myself in the back of the plane with four people pressing against me, right next to that hole that I saw from the outside. There was no doubt about it now—my knees were shaking and I was scared.

Well up we went. When we got to about 6,500 feet the first three guys jumped. With each jump the plane rocked and swayed. The wind was rushing in my face as I hung on to my back corner seat with an iron grip. Tom told the pilot that he wanted to go up another thousand feet, and I began to think that my friend was nuts. When we got to the right altitude, Tom asked me to come over to the open door and view the target. We were so far up that I couldn't even see the airport. Tom got out on the wing, smiled at me, and down he went . . . just like a bullet. I never saw anyone drop so fast. He was doing summersaults, both forwards and backwards with the seconds going by. He kept falling and falling and I started to think that he had better open that chute pretty soon. Finally, he popped his chute, and I thought to myself, "This is nuts." When the pilot looked back at me and asked me if I wanted to go up another thousand feet, I said, "Hell no, I want to go down."

By the time we landed, Tom was floating to the ground. I walked up to him, gave him the five dollars, and never went near the place again.

Robert Wojs. Used with permission of the speaker.

RELATING A PERSONAL EXPERIENCE (To persuade)

Deliver a 2–4 minute speech or write a short narrative of 300–500 words in which you relate a personal experience to persuade. Describe the material in enough detail to create a mental picture for the reader or listener. Develop your material informally, with emphasis on details of action. A personal story is an excellent means of reinforcing or clarifying your ideas.

Delivery: This speech should be delivered extemporaneously. An audience will expect you to have almost total eye contact when talking about your own experience. The more spontaneous and relaxed you are, the more your audience will enjoy your presentation.

Sample Topics

1. Getting involved can pay off
2. Don't depend on the other driver
3. The grass is always greener on the other side
4. Sometimes it pays to be ignorant
5. A first-aid course could save a life

Model

I used to feel that a lot of what people learned in classes at school was unnecessary. I remember thinking that about a course in first aid that I had to take as part of my naval reserve requirement. That all changed one evening about four years ago. I was sitting in our living room with my uncle George, watching the Wednesday night fights on television. During a particularly exciting round I heard a thud. Looking around I saw that my uncle had fallen to the floor. I rushed over to him and found that he wasn't breathing. Remembering what I had been taught in first-aid, I immediately rolled him on his back, put his head on a pillow and to the side and loosened his collar after I checked to see if he had anything in his mouth. I rushed to the phone and called the rescue squad. When I returned to my uncle I found that he was not only not breathing but that his heart had stopped too. I began giving him mouth-to-mouth resuscitation and external heart massage at the same time. Almost miraculously I remembered the instructions for both as if they were being given to me by the instructor again. "Exhale into the person's mouth and push down sharply on the sternum, release, count to ten and begin again." Finally, after what seemed like an eternity, uncle George responded and began breathing. By the time the rescue squad arrived, some of the color had returned to his cheeks and he had regained consciousness.

To this day whenever I think of a course as being of doubtful value, I think of my uncle George and work at it a little harder.

SPEECH TO INFORM

Choose a subject in which your main job as a speaker is to present information. Present your material in such a way as to hold and maintain audience attention so that they can readily understand and remember.

Delivery: **This speech can be delivered either with manuscript or extemporaneously. Keep the pattern of development simple so that you move from one idea to another smoothly.**

Suggestions

1. Decide whether your audience is listening to the information out of curiosity or need.
2. Present material that is unknown by relating it to what is known.
3. You may need to summarize from time to time to make your points absolutely clear.

Sample Topics

1. The Koala bear
2. Today's average student
3. The real story of Howard Hughes
4. Planting a garden
5. The native American

Model

BLACK HISTORY WEEK

Mr. Anderson of California: Mr. Speaker, the black man's history in the United States, although often neglected in our history books, is one of great achievement and accomplishment. The record shows that black men and women have been in the forefront of our progress as a Nation. Whatever our history has been; whatever our future brings; the black man has made outstanding contributions toward making this world a better place to live.

This week, February 13 through February 19, is Black History Week—an occasion which has been observed in Los Angeles for a number of years. In view of this observance, I would like to take a few moments to recount just a few of the accomplishments of these Americans whose participation in our Nation's development began in 1619.

Due to the publicity and public adulation received by sports heroes and celebrities, the accomplishments of black athletes, musicians, and singers have often overshadowed the accomplishments of black scientists, inventors, educators, businessmen, and religious leaders.

However, throughout the history of the United States, the black American has made his mark and helped determine the outcome of events. Thus, any history of America must include black Americans.

Jean Baptiste Point DuSable, a black pioneer, founded the settlement of Chicago. Another black pioneer, Matthew Henson, was with Adm. Robert E. Perry when he discovered the North Pole in 1907.

Some 5,000 Negroes served in the Continental Army and Navy during the American Revolution. The first American to die in the cause of freedom was Crispus Attucks, a black man shot by the British at the "Boston Massacre" in 1770.

Nearly a quarter of a million black soldiers and sailors served in the Union forces during the Civil War. Twenty of these men were recognized for valor and received the Nation's highest medal for heroism—the Congressional Medal of Honor.

There were more than 5,000 black cowboys in the Old West. A black man, Bill Pickett, invented the art of "bull-dogging." James P. Beckworth was a black frontiersman who excelled in trapping and hunting.

The first black physician in America was James Derham, who established a prosperous medical practice in Philadelphia. The first doctor to perform open heart surgery was black—Dr. Daniel Hale Williams.

Dr. Charles Drew, a black surgeon, invented the blood bank and became the world's greatest authority on blood plasma.

The achievements of Booker T. Washington and George Washington Carver are well known to students, but how many Americans have read the works of Alexander Dumas, the author of "The Count of Monte Cristo," and realized that he was of African descent as was Samuel Coleridge-Taylor, and Alexander Pushkin. Black Americans such as Paul Laurence Dunbar and Charles Waddell Chestnutt have left their mark in the literary annals of America.

Black men have prospered in the field of business. C. C. Spaulding developed an insurance company that had assets worth $33 million when he died. S. B. Fuller set up a firm in Chicago that manufactures toiletries and cosmetics and distributes them by door-to-door salespeople. The Fuller Products Co. is one of the largest black-owned businesses in America.

Leaders in the movement for civil rights have admired such leaders as Frederick Douglass, and, of course, the outstanding leader, the late Martin Luther King, Jr.

The residents of Los Angeles know the fine architecture of Paul Williams, who designed the Beverly Wilshire Hotel, a Saks Fifth Avenue store, office buildings, and mansions. He ranks high among architects of the world.

The list of accomplishments by black men and women in the sports and entertainment field is endless.

The steps that have been taken toward the goals and the quality of life which we all seek have been made by Americans of all races. Let us never forget those giant steps made by black men and women, and let us take pride in the rich heritage which has been left to us and to future generations by the black pioneers.

Congressional Record. Speech given by Hon. Glenn M. Anderson of California in the House of Representatives, February 16, 1972.

SPEECH TO ENTERTAIN

Either describe a stimulating experience of yours (i.e., an exciting event, a memorable trip, an unforgettable performance) which you feel would be interesting to the class, or deliver a speech in which you use humor to entertain your audience. You may, for example, treat a serious subject lightly or a light subject seriously. Contact is very important; speak directly to your audience. The more clearly the audience can visualize what you describe, the more effective will be your speech.

Choose a subject whose effectiveness will be increased by use of a visual aid. Studies indicate that a person learns more readily when he is given the opportunity to see as well as hear what is being explained. Visual aids may consist of charts, diagrams, maps, pictures, photographs, models, film strips, projectors, records, physical gestures — in short, whatever provides an extra audio or visual dimension to the words the audience hears.

Suggestions

1. Use vivid, colorful language to stimulate the senses of the audience.

2. Organize your material clearly.

3. Be friendly and relaxed. Avoid being overresponsive to your own humor.

4. Read such authors as Art Buchwald, Dick Gregory, Al Capp, and Dorothy Parker to get an idea of effective satirical style.

Sample Topics

1. How to wash a bull elephant
2. How to get a fair share of the government "giveaway"
3. A moment I'll always remember
4. Camping can be fun, for bears
5. My first and last day on the job

Model

Love is a wonderful thing, but, like anything worthwhile, it often has its ups and downs. For about six years prior to our meeting, my husband had been sequestered in the religious life. I knew very soon in our friendship that I was stimulating his interest in women but I could also tell he wasn't very versed in the art of courting and when it came to kissing—YUK!!! Forget it!

His kisses started out as quick stolen little pecks on the cheek and progressed to quick stolen little pecks on the lips. As his kisses increased in length, I saw that some things had to change. First there was the pucker—Now, puckers are fine for babies and grandmothers, but for me—No Sir! Well the pucker soon changed to the tight-lipped method—That was just as bad as the pucker. Another thing was his approach. He wasn't quite sure of whether to jump right in and grab or to slowly sidle up and nonchalantly start kissing. What he didn't realize then was that you don't just attack with a passionate kiss, but that you work up to the really big one with tender little loving kisses.

One particular evening we were standing at the kitchen counter, just talking and drinking iced tea. I figured there was no particular limitation as to time or place, and after all practice makes perfect, so I made the approach this time. Well right in the middle of this fit of passion, just as I was marveling to myself of his improvement, I heard a strange noise, the sound of an iced tea glass being slid—klunk klunk—across the tiled counter. So I opened one eye—and curled one lip from the full press—and quietly said "Did you want a drink of iced tea?" As you can imagine it completely broke the two of us up. It seems I caught him off guard and he was just trying to put the glass back so he could get a better grip. That was the icebreaker, because from that time on it was clear sailing for my Romeo.

Used with permission of the speaker, Pat Kiley.

SPEECH TO INFORM USING A VISUAL AID

Choose a subject whose effectiveness will be increased by use of a visual aid. Studies indicate that a person learns more readily when he is given the opportunity to see as well as hear what is being explained. Visual aids may consist of charts, diagrams, maps, pictures, photographs, models, film strips, projectors, records, physical gestures—in short, whatever provides an extra audio or visual dimension to the words the audience hears.

Delivery: This speech should be delivered extemporaneously. The speaker must be free to move to his map, chart, or diagram, or to use both hands in demonstrating a technique.

Suggestions

1. *Keep visual aids out of sight when not in use.* Don't display your aid until you are ready to use it, and remove it as soon as you are through with it.
2. *Visual aids should be easily seen.* Be sure that the aid is large enough to be seen by all. Stand to the side of an aid so that you can speak directly to the audience.
3. *Visual aids should be clear and relevant.* Unless an aid is easy to understand and related to the subject, it can confuse rather than clarify. Don't use a visual aid just for the sake of appearances.
4. *Practice using your visual aid.* When you practice your speech, have your visual aids ready and use them. If possible, practice using your aid in the room in which you will be speaking. Make sure that the necessary equipment is available. Stand at the back of the room to insure that your aid can be clearly seen or heard.

Sample Topics

1. Mark Twain, America's great wit
2. The laser beam
3. The art of tree dwarfing
4. How to beat the stock market
5. Automobile lubrication

PERSUASION TO CONVINCE

Deliver a 3–5 minute speech or write a 300–500 word essay supporting one point of view in regard to a controversial subject. Analyze the audience beforehand to determine their attitude toward your point of view. Man takes great pride in the fact that he is a rational creature. He has a high regard for intelligence and problem-solving ability. Appeal to your reader or listener's desire to know the truth in order to modify his existing attitudes. Rely chiefly on logical materials to obtain mental agreement from your audience.

Suggestions

1. Don't attempt to do too much in this assignment. You will be successful if you change, even if only the slightest degree, the attitudes and opinions of your audience.
2. Present your material objectively. An audience will react negatively to a reader or speaker who is overly biased.
3. Show that there is need for a change.
4. Show that your proposal is practical.
5. End with a statement of support for your proposal.

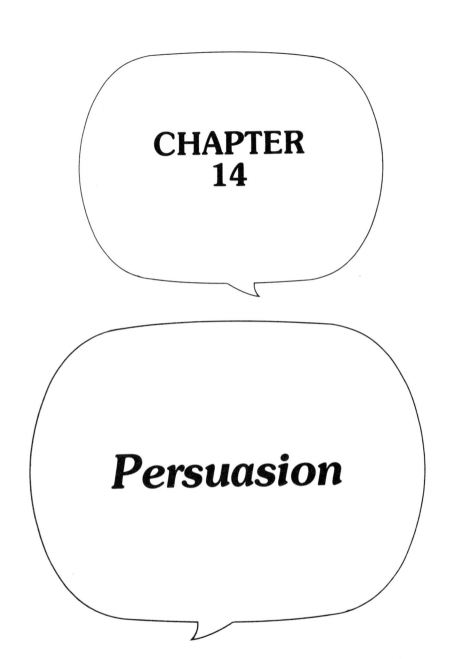

CHAPTER 14

Persuasion

OBJECTIVES

After studying this chapter, you should be able to:

1. Define persuasion.
2. Explain the three characteristics of personal proof.
3. Identify nine specific suggestions you can use to enhance your image as a person of competence, integrity, and goodwill.
4. Explain the relationship between good or bad self-image and credibility.
5. Explain the relationship between good or bad self-image and personality development.

Never before in our society has the technique of persuasion been so important or profitable. Advertising ranks among our nation's billion-dollar enterprises. Political candidates pay staggering amounts to public relations firms to insure election. Motivational researchers make millions telling manufacturers how to sell their product. Few in our society are paid more than the effective salesman. As a result of this, we are constantly bombarded with appeals to "get with it," to "come alive," to enjoy a new "taste sensation." We are the unceasing target for those who would persuade us to buy their product, to accept their viewpoint, or to support their cause. It is obvious, therefore, that because of the intensity of this competition for our money, our time, or our support, we must have an understanding of persuasion if we are to choose wisely.

A WORKING DEFINITION

Persuasion is *the conscious attempt to influence the thought or behavior of others through the use of personal, logical, and psychological appeals.*

The emphasis on persuasion as a "conscious" attempt to influence is important. The more aware you are of exactly what you want done, the more likely you are to be successful. Persuasion must be intentional. A good informative speech or paper may also persuade, but if its primary aim is to inform, then the persuasion is accidental. The persuader must deliberately attempt to influence.

However, you don't have to sell your product immediately to be successful. You don't have to change someone's mind on the spot. Per-

272

suasion can be a long-range process which modifies thought or behavior a little at a time. In some cases it might take a series of speeches, editorials, and meetings to change an existing policy or law.

Suppose that shortly after getting a driver's license you want to use the family car. If your father says, "No, you're not ready yet," you must convince him that you are. Although you might point to your success in passing the driver's test, or an "A" in a Driver's Education course in school, convincing your father that you are ready to take on this new responsibility will probably involve your driving the car a number of times while he is with you. Since you know that each time you do a good job you are influencing him to respond in the way you desire, you are careful to do your best when he is your audience. In this case, as you can see, it will take a series of these demonstrations of your ability to persuade your father to see things your way.

In most cases you will be more successful in persuading your parents or friends than you will be in persuading others. This is because you have a better understanding of those you know; since you are sensitive to their likes and dislikes, you know how to handle them.

Now go back to the example above. You have convinced your father that you should be allowed to use the family car for occasional dates, but you want it on a night when he was considering using it. Getting the car will be difficult. The first thing you must do is approach him when he is in a good mood. This might be after you have given him his pipe and slippers and turned on his favorite TV program. If Mom has more influence with Dad than you have, you make your appeal to her. In any case, you are sensitive to the situation and attitudes of the person or persons to whom you are making the appeal. You are in effect a salesman trying to sell yourself or your ideas. The cash register rings when the response is favorable. If you fail to make a sale, you learn from the experience and try a new approach the next time. As indicated in our definition, there are three appeals or types of proof you can use in selling your product more effectively: personal, logical, and psychological.

PERSONAL PROOF

Perhaps nothing is more important to a salesman's success than the power of his personality. Over two thousand years ago the Greek philosopher, Aristotle, proclaimed that a communicator's character was the most powerful of all his means of persuasion. This same concept relates directly to your credibility as a speaker or writer. No factor is more important to your ability to persuade than the perception a listener or reader has of you as a person. This can involve two factors: (1) the impression the audience has of you prior to the communication, and (2) any change in your audience's perception of you, either favorable or unfavorable, during or following the communication. Ideally, you want your audience to see you as a competent person with integrity and goodwill.

Competence

Everyone admires the person who appears to know what he is talking about, the person who, because of education or experience, can get the job done. To be an effective persuader you must show your reader or listener that you have thought the problem over carefully, considered all the evidence, and decided on the best course of action. A

"Daddy, could your $750 exemption have the car?"

Hesse in the St. Louis Globe Democrat

well-organized, fluent presentation is the mark of a competent communicator.

Your audience also judges your competence by the language you use. The effective persuader chooses words that will convey his meaning accurately, grammatically, and forcefully. He chooses words to communicate, not to display his vocabulary.

Integrity

Even though you are skilled in presenting your ideas, your audience must feel that you are worthy of their trust and respect. In today's society, with its credibility gaps and hypocrisy, the honesty of a writer or speaker is of major concern to his audience. Careful preparation and documentation will help to indicate your sincerity and honesty. Remember, you are judged by what you do and say. Be sure that your audience finds your comments and behavior desirable.

Goodwill

It is important that you indicate goodwill for your audience. When communicating to a reader or listener always be tactful, courteous, and respectful. A feeling of friendliness can often be projected with a good sense of humor. Whenever you can establish a common ground or interest with your audience, do so. Greet them with enthusiasm. Give them credit for having intelligence and ability.

In a March 23, 1775, speech to the House of Burgesses, Patrick Henry faced the difficult task of supporting a resolution of war against strong opposition by rich planters who feared an uprising even more than they feared oppression from the crown. Note how tactfully he compliments those with whom he disagrees.

MR. PRESIDENT:

No man thinks more highly than I do of the patriotism, as well as abilities, of the very worthy gentlemen who have just addressed the house. But different men often see the same subject in different lights; and therefore, I hope it will not be thought disrespectful to those gentlemen, if, entertaining as I do opinions of a character very opposite to theirs, I shall speak forth my sentiments freely and without reserve. This is no time for ceremony. The question before the house is one of awful moment to this country. For my own part, I consider it as nothing less than a question of freedom or slavery. And in proportion to the magnitude of the subject ought to be the freedom of the debate. It is only in this way that we can hope to arrive at truth and fulfill the great responsibility which we hold to God and our country. Should I keep back my opinions at such a time, through fear of giving offense, I should consider myself as guilty of treason toward my country, and of an act of disloyalty toward the Majesty of Heaven, which I revere above all earthly kings.

The Image

Public relations men, advertisers, and motivational researchers are constantly involved in image building. They are acutely aware of the image of their product held by potential customers. They have come to realize that to a great extent it is this image which sells the product. In order for the speaker or writer to gain acceptance of his ideas, he must project an image of himself that will be favorably received by his audience. The manner in which this image is projected is shown in the diagram on page 277.

Note that a person projects his image to others by what he says, what others say about him, and what he does. (He has to back up his words with actions.)

Listed below are some specific suggestions you can use to enhance your image as a person of competence, integrity, and goodwill:

Competence
1. *Indicate your qualifications.* If you have special knowledge, education, and experience which qualify you to deal with your chosen subject, mention these at the beginning of your communication.
2. *Use correct grammar.* A reader or listener is apt to question the validity of your ideas if they are incorrectly written or spoken.
3. *Speak with confidence.* Whether you are speaking in front of a group, in an interview, or in group discussion, be positive in your approach.
4. *Organize clearly.* A reader or listener will react more favorably to your ideas if your material is logically developed.
5. *Be up to date.* Being current and well informed is the mark of a competent person.
6. *Be fluent.* Expressing yourself fluently in writing or speech can best be achieved by allowing ample time for writing and rewriting or for practicing the speech.

Integrity
1. *Be fair minded.* By showing your audience that you can see both sides of an issue, you will avoid giving the impression that you are biased or subjective.

2. *Establish a common bond.* A reader or listener will respond more positively to a communicator whom he sees as having similar problems, goals, values, and experiences.

3. *Dress appropriately.* The communicator whose grooming and dress conform to the expectations of his audience is much more likely to achieve a desired response.

4. *Indicate your motives.* If your audience feels that you are motivated to communicate with them unselfishly, your credibility will be enhanced.

5. *Be sincere.* Using a tone appropriate to what you are saying in either writing or speech is a must for establishing integrity. Even if he does not agree with you, a reader or listener will admire your conviction.

6. *Be prompt.* Whether you are turning in a report, delivering a speech, sending a letter, or arriving for an interview, being on time is the mark of a person with integrity.

Goodwill

1. *Show understanding.* Put yourself in the shoes of your reader or lis-

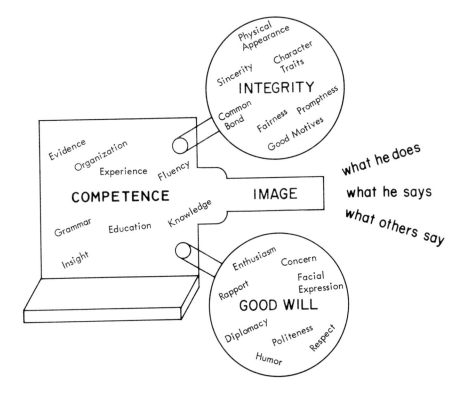

tener, so that you can communicate to him that you are aware and appreciative of his viewpoint.

2. *Be respectful.* Treating your audience with respect is a must in establishing goodwill. Give them credit for being worthy and intelligent.

3. *Be diplomatic.* Whatever the communication situation, use courtesy and tact. If you do, the chances will be much better that you will succeed in your purpose.

4. *Use humor.* When used appropriately, humor is an excellent means of establishing goodwill with an audience. (This is especially true of humor directed at yourself.)

5. *Show enthusiasm.* Showing enthusiasm is an especially effective means of establishing goodwill with an audience, particularly in the speaking situation. Approaching your audience with enthusiastic movement and facial expression will show them that you're happy to be with them.

6. *Establish rapport.* Rapport is a French word for harmony or agreement. Whenever you can, make references to those in your audience. If you are on a first-name basis, by all means make use of this excellent way of showing goodwill.

The Political Image   Probably no group is more concerned with the image they project than politicians. Experts agree that in most cases the image the voters have of a politician determines their reaction to what is said. Jimmy Carter was virtually unknown outside Georgia when he started his campaign. His success is a striking example of the power of personal proof.

One of the reasons Mr. Carter won the election as thirty-ninth president of the United States was the image he projected. He won because a vast number of voters perceived him as a man they could identify with. They saw him as a man of competence, integrity, and goodwill who had a common touch with the people. The accompanying *Milwaukee Journal* editorial comments on this "folksy, down-to-earth," common touch. (Note the caption of the editorial, "Just Plain Jimmy Meets The Folks.")

Some felt that President Carter was overly preoccupied with how others perceived him. The implication of Sanders' editorial cartoon is that image projection was the major concern of the radio call-in. Certainly, President Carter was as aware as anyone of the relationship of image to credibility, but by and large persuasion must work within the limits of facts. The basic personality of the individual determines the image that is projected. All the image-maker or the individual himself can do is to emphasize the positive aspects of personality and minimize the negative ones.

'If you think the radio show was good, listen to this grabber for television—get Billy Graham as co-moderator and schedule it to follow the Waltons!'

Cartoon by Sanders © Used with permission of The Milwaukee Journal.

Just Plain Jimmy Meets the Folks

Because it was radio you couldn't tell whether he was wearing a cardigan, but Jimmy Carter came over the airwaves Saturday about as folksy, down-to-earth and chatty as he could be. He might have been sitting in a courthouse square whittling and gossiping with cronies.

The two-hour call-in show deservedly won high marks. In a way, it was an extension of Carter's two-year campaign for the White House. He always talked to anyone who would listen. And Saturday millions wanted to listen, and millions tried to call.

It turned out—and this would surprise few able politicians—that citizens were mainly concerned with bread and butter issues, with things that affect their daily lives. And Carter sympathized as a good neighbor might.

Even when he talked about international issues Carter was just "Jimmy." It just so happened that he had discussed the problem of the Concorde plane with good ol' President Giscard of France a few days ago. And our allies, especially West Germany, had been helpful in handling that nasty problem with Uganda's Idi Amin. It was refreshing to hear such matters discussed as if over the back fence, without all the highfalutin doubletalk and mystery that has marked orations on foreign affairs in recent years.

And it was reassuring to have the president simply say on occasion: "I don't know." Presidents seldom talk that way.

Some critics may now worry about Carter exploiting folksiness. Could this attractive, unadorned style—combined with ready access to the mass media—be used increasingly to mislead rather than communicate? Then, too, there's some concern about a prestigious anchorman like Walter Cronkite being cast in the cozy role of program moderator. Does that erode the line between press and government?

These are not trivial questions. However, all in all, Carter's call-in show was worth doing. It wasn't a new thing for him. He used to do the same thing when he was governor of Georgia. But it was a big step in the transition from the imperial presidency to the approachable presidency.

The Milwaukee Journal, March 8, 1977. Reprinted by permission.

Credibility

The better a person's image, the more likely we are to believe what he says. The term *credibility* refers to the extent to which we believe what someone tells us. A person who has a good image also has high credibility. Conversely, a person with a poor image has low credibility.

As you can see from the chart on page 277, image projection is a complex process. People form judgments about others on the basis of a variety of factors. Furthermore, these judgments can be made by evaluating what a person does, what he says, and what others say about him. Because of this complexity, the image that a person projects may or may not be an accurate representation of what he actually is.

The society in which we live can often have a decided effect on the image that we develop. A person usually tries to develop an image of which others will approve, and the advertisers try to set the standards. We are told that "blondes have more fun," that a "thinking man" smokes a particular brand of cigarette, and that we should "grab as much out of life as we can," because we only go around once. And we respond. In 1978, the cosmetic industry in this country grossed over 3 billion dollars. Countless more billions are spent each year by Americans to keep in step with the latest fashion or style. It is "in" to belong to a certain group, and this group often determines a person's outward appearance, his speech, his code of ethics, and his conduct. He tries to be what the group wants him to be, and yet, in some cases, what he appears to be is not what he is at all.

Some psychologists feel that this projection of a false image has much to do with our high divorce rate. Two people are often attracted to each other because they believe they see traits that they admire. Then, when they get married, what they saw isn't actually there. The husband, who seemed considerate and charming, was actually selfish and dull. The wife, who appeared self-assured and insightful, was, in fact, withdrawn and insensitive. After the first few months of marriage, when their physical attraction no longer overshadows their daily routine, they find that the one they thought they married does not really exist.

As we have seen, a person often tends to evaluate what someone says in the light of his projected image. If the impression is good, his credibility is high; if it is bad, his credibility is low. The following cases indicate how credibility is related to this received impression.

Tom's Father

Tom's father, the owner of a small factory, is a highly respected member of his community. He goes to church regularly, contributes generously to charity, and belongs to several civic and fraternal organizations. He is considered by many people to be a man of intelligence, integrity, and goodwill, and consequently he enjoys a high degree of credibility with them. Tom, however, has a different image of his father. He has heard his father say that it was "good for business" to be seen at church on Sunday or to give to charity. He has heard his father brag about the "tax loopholes" and "payoffs" that he enjoys, and he strongly suspects him of infidelity on business trips. For this reason, Tom's father possesses little credibility in Tom's eyes, particularly in dealing with issues regarding morality.

John and Harry

John and Harry both attend a small, Midwestern junior college. They share a small two-bedroom apartment and get along very well together although their style of dress and appearance are entirely different. John has shoulder length hair, rimless glasses, a full beard, and wears beads, levis, and an old army jacket. Harry, on the other hand, has a crewcut, black framed glasses, is clean shaven, and usually wears neatly pressed slacks and a sports coat. When rapping with fellow students who are little influenced by their manner of dress, their credibility is about equal. However, this changes markedly when speaking to their landlord, a middle-class businessman. Harry enjoys rather high credibility, while John's credibility is quite low. The landlord generally listens to Harry's opinions thoughtfully, while almost always dismissing John's as radical. He allows Harry to put up his "sister" over the weekend but threatens to call the police when John brings his girl home for a midnight snack.

Relationship of Image to Credibility

We have seen that what your audience thinks of you has a definite effect on their reaction to your persuasion. Tom's judgment of his father is based on knowledge that others do not possess. Because the landlord has a preconceived picture in his mind of both John and Harry, he is unable to react to them objectively. Although John had apparently done nothing to warrant it, the landlord responded negatively to him. He formed an image of John on the basis of outward appearance. The image *he perceives* of John is poor; therefore John's credibility is low.

This relationship of image to credibility can be seen clearly in advertising. The job of the advertiser, simply stated, is to convince the consumer that his product is better than that of his competitor. As one advertiser put it, "What makes one product different from another is how people feel about it." Therefore, the advertiser must make the customer feel kindly disposed toward his product. In a marketplace jammed with competitive goods, this poses a problem. How, for instance, do you outsell your competition in an area as overcrowded as cosmetics, liquor, or cigarettes? The answer is to create an image of the product that will appeal to the public. Joseph Seldin analyzes the relationship between cigarette advertising and image building.

As the advertising pages were converted into an image-building Donnybrook, the cigarette companies entered with some of the most virile-looking males ever to squint at the consuming public. First came the Marlboro Man with a crew haircut, squared-off jaw and provocative hand tattoo who was supposed to erase from the public mind that the Marlboro cigarette was a tainted female brand. The Marlboro Man soon had rugged company in the Viceroy Man who thought for himself, the L&M Man who lived modern, the Chesterfield Man who liked his pleasure big, and the Lucky Strike Man who knew a real smoke. It became almost a physiognomical impossibility to tell what brand the craggy character was smoking on TV until he announced his allegiance after a satisfying puff at the cigarette. But he undoubtedly entranced millions of desk-bound white-collar males and females with the immense benefits of the great outdoors.

Among the farmers, truck drivers, cabbies, steelworkers, divers, jet pilots, loggers, construction workers, ski patrolmen, Coast Guardsmen, firemen, and cowboys who puffed satisfyingly on one brand or another, the cowboys seemed to emerge for the tobacco companies as the epitome of American manhood. Indeed the cowboys seemed destined to become the leading authorities on whiskeys, automobiles, and many other products, as they became the hired hands of an increasing number of advertisers. A staff columnist on *Advertising Age,* who patently took advantage of his anonymity to criticize the rugged cowboys, objected to their aggrandizement in U.S. life. The particular cowhands he had met, the columnist said, had excited him chiefly for their resemblance, intellectually, to the animals they husbanded. They were no doubt an outstanding symbol of masculinity—at its worst and lowest form. Considering their exaggerated pleasure in personal ornamentation, drinking, brawling, and regarding females largely in the herd, the columnist wondered how "civilized" admen could parade them before America as individuals "whose habits are worthy of copying."

From Joseph J. Seldin, *The Golden Fleece* (New York: The Macmillan Company, 1963). Reprinted with permission.

You project an image to others by what you say and do, and by what you say about you. You have seen how important this image can be, how it, in effect, sells the product. Improve your image and you will sell yourself and your ideas more effectively. The first step toward improving your projected image is to improve your self-image. This can be accomplished by getting to know yourself better.

Personality Development

We develop our personalities largely as a result of our relationships with others. We learn to communicate by imitating those around us. Our views on life are shaped by those with whom we come in contact. We often mirror the attitudes and sentiments of our parents and friends. Our speaking habits are usually similar to the habits of those closest to us as we grow up. Problems like mispronunciation and unclear diction can usually be traced to parents or friends with the same difficulties.

The reaction of others to us as we are growing up also has an effect on our personalities. People tell us by their responses whether we are important or unimportant, good or bad, smart or dumb, and we develop a picture of ourselves accordingly. Furthermore, we tend to act like the person we conceive ourselves to be. Thus, a child who developed the self-concept of being unimportant because of his parents would probably respond by being withdrawn and unfriendly. The child who was thought of by his classmates as being dull and a troublemaker would probably live up to this label.

The first step to personality improvement is careful self-appraisal. Obviously, the more accurate a picture a person has of himself, the more clearly he can see how to improve himself, how to develop his strengths and eliminate his weaknesses. If, for example, John is strongly attracted to Jane but sees himself as being inferior to her in terms of personality and attractiveness, he is apt to communicate this attitude to her in uneasy, superficial, and, therefore, nonproductive conversation. On the other hand, if John can see his own strengths and weaknesses in their proper perspective and recognize his own self-worth, he will be more likely to communicate his interest to Jane.

The key to John's success with Jane is self-worth. Before anyone else can like you, you first have to like yourself. Communicate this attitude of self-worth to others by the careful preparation and practice of your speeches and the critical proofreading and rewriting of your papers and you will project a more effective image.

Good writers and speakers are not born; they are developed as the result of commitment and hard work. Before you can become proficient at either skill, you have to want to work at it. It took John Steinbeck six years to complete his novel *East of Eden*. Ernest Hemingway once said, "The first four times I write a paragraph it reads like any one else's writing. It's the fifth time that it becomes Ernest Hemingway." "Getting by" wasn't enough for them. If you want to project a good image, it can't be enough for you either.

EXERCISES

I. The advertisement on page 285 is designed to project an image of Equitable Company to the reader. Indicate in a speech or essay how the advertiser tends to humanize the company for the audience. How, for example, is the reader shown that the company possesses a strong sense of social responsibility or contributes to the common good?

1. What character traits are possessed by the boy feeding the baby? Explain.
2. Why weren't adults included in the picture?
3. What is the reason for using white and black models? Are they friends? What attitude does the boy watching the feeding have?
4. Does this picture say something about Equitable's attitude toward equal opportunity? What?
5. Is there any special reason for specifically mentioning Birmingham?
6. How does this ad tend to humanize the Equitable Life Assurance Society in the public mind?

Who cares if these boys have good homes to grow up in?

Equitable cares. For countless children, home is cracked plaster, broken plumbing, dingy rooms. Equitable thinks children deserve better. We're trying hard to make sure they get it. From Seattle to Birmingham, we've invested over $95,000,-000 to build better housing for those who need it most.

As a company deeply involved with helping people build a better life, we feel it's our responsibility to do what we can to rebuild our cities.

We're glad so many of our agents feel the same way. By getting involved with urban renewal projects in their own communities, they're helping make life better for all of us.

THE EQUITABLE

© The Equitable Life Assurance Society of the United States,
New York, N.Y. 1969.
An Equal Opportunity Employer, M/F

Courtesy of the Equitable Life Assurance Society.

II. In a eulogy at his brother Robert's funeral, Edward Kennedy projects an image of his dead brother by telling his audience what his brother said and did, and what others thought about him. Read the speech carefully and make a list of character traits that the speech indicates Robert Kennedy possessed.

A TRIBUTE TO HIS BROTHER

Your Eminences, your excellencies, Mr. President. In behalf of Mrs. Kennedy, her children, the parents and sisters of Robert Kennedy, I want to express what we feel to those who mourn with us today in this cathedral and around the world.

We loved him as a brother and as a father and as a son. From his parents and from his older brothers and sisters, Joe and Kathleen and Jack, he received an inspiration which he passed on to all of us.

He gave us strength in time of trouble, wisdom in time of uncertainty and sharing in time of happiness. He will always be by our side.

Love is not an easy feeling to put into words. Nor is loyalty or trust or joy. But he was all of these. He loved life completely and he lived it intensely.

A few years back Robert Kennedy wrote some words about his own father which expresses the way we in his family felt about him. He said of what his father meant to him, and I quote:

"What it really all adds up to is love. Not love as it is described with such facility in popular magazines, but the kind of love that is affection and respect, order and encouragement and support.

"Our awareness of this was an incalculable source of strength. And because real love is something unselfish and involves sacrifice and giving, we could not help but profit from it."

And he continued:

"Beneath it all he has tried to engender a social conscience. There were wrongs which needed attention, there were people who were poor and needed help, and we have a responsibility to them and this country.

"Through no virtues and accomplishments of our own, we have been fortunate enough to be born in the United States under the most comfortable conditions. We therefore have a responsibility to others who are less well off."

That is what Robert Kennedy was given.

What he leaves to us is what he said, what he did and what he stood for.

A speech he made for the young people of South Africa on their day of affirmation in 1966 sums it up the best, and I would like to read it now.

"There is discrimination in this world and slavery and slaughter and starvation. Governments repress their people. Millions are trapped in poverty, while the nation grows rich and wealth is lavished on armaments everywhere.

"These are differing evils, but they are the common words of man. They reflect the imperfection of human justice, the inadequacy of human compassion, our lack of sensibility towards the suffering of our fellows.

"But we can perhaps remember, even if only for a time, that those who live with us are our brothers, that they share with us the same short moment of life, that they seek as we do nothing but the chance to live out their lives in purpose and happiness, winning what satisfaction and fulfillment they can.

"Surely this bond of common faith, this bond of common goals, can begin to teach us something. Surely we can learn at least to look at those around us as fellow men. And surely we can begin to work a little harder to bind up the wounds among us and to become in our own hearts brothers and countrymen once again.

"The answer is to rely on youth, not a time of life but a state of mind, a temper of the will, a quality of imagination, a predominance of courage over timidity, of the appetite for adventure over the love of ease. The cruelties and obstacles of this swiftly changing planet will not yield to the obsolete dogmas and outworn slogans; they cannot be moved by those who cling to a present that is already dying, who prefer the illusion of security to the excitement and danger that come with even the most peaceful progress.

"It is a revolutionary world which we live in, and this generation at home and around the world has had thrust upon it a greater burden of responsibility than any generation that has ever lived. Some believe there is nothing one man or one woman can do against the enormous array of the world's ills. Yet many of the world's great movements of thought and action have flowed from the work of a single man.

"A young monk began the Protestant Reformation. A young general extended an empire from Macedonia to the borders of the earth. A young woman reclaimed the territory of France, and it was a young Italian explorer who discovered the New World, and the 32-year-old Thomas Jefferson who explained that all men are created equal.

"These men moved the world, and so can we all. Few will have the greatness to bend history itself, but each of us can work to change a small portion of events, and in the total of all those acts will be written the history of this generation.

"Each time a man stands for an ideal, or acts to improve the lot of others, or strikes out against injustice, he sends forth a tiny ripple of hope.

"And crossing each other from a million different centers of energy and daring, those ripples build a current that can sweep down the mightiest walls of oppression and resistance. Few are willing to brave the disapproval of their fellows, the censure of their colleagues, the wrath of their society. Moral courage is a rarer commodity than bravery in battle or great intelligence. Yet it is the one essential vital quality for those who seek to change a world that yields most painfully to change.

"And I believe that in this generation those with the courage to enter the moral conflict will find themselves with companions in every corner of the globe.

"For the fortunate among us there is the temptation to follow the easy and familiar paths of personal ambition and financial success so grandly spread before those who enjoy the privilege of education. But that is not the road history has marked out for us.

"Like it or not, we live in times of danger and uncertainty. But they are also more open to the creative energy of men than any other time in history. All of us will ultimately be judged and as the years pass, we will surely judge ourselves, on the effort we have contributed to building a new world society and the extent to which our ideals and goals have shaped that event.

"Our future may lie beyond our vision, but it is not completely beyond our control. It is the shaping impulse of America that neither faith nor nature nor the irresistible tides of history but the work of our own hands matched to reason and principle that will determine our destiny."

There is pride in that, even arrogance, but there is also experience and truth, and in any event it is the only way we can live. That is the way he lived. That is what he leaves us.

My brother need not be idealized or enlarged in death beyond what he was in life. He should be remembered simply as a good and decent man who saw wrong and tried to right it, saw suffering and tried to heal it, saw war and tried to stop it.

Those of us who loved him and who take him to his rest today pray that what he was to us, and what he wished for others, will some day come to pass for all the world.

As he said many times, in many parts of this nation, to those he touched and who sought to touch him:

"Some men see things as they are and say why. I dream things that never were and say, why not."

Vital Speeches XXXIV:18 (July 1, 1968), pp. 546–47.

STEREOTYPES: FORM A

Below are descriptions of three different people. Based on the information given, what is your best guess about their personalities? Place a checkmark somewhere on the rating scale. For example, if you think Jane is probably very friendly, put a checkmark at or near the 1 point on the scale. If you think she is probably very unfriendly, then place the checkmark at or near the 5 point on the scale. If you have absolutely no opinion, place the checkmark at the 3 point on the scale. Remember that there are no right or wrong answers; this is not a test, merely a survey of your opinion.

1. Jane is 18 years old and a freshman college student. She is five feet, two inches tall and has red hair. She makes average grades, and dates about once a week. She probably is:

FRIENDLY	1	2	3	4	5	UNFRIENDLY
INTELLIGENT	1	2	3	4	5	STUPID
EASYGOING	1	2	3	4	5	HOT TEMPERED
CONCEITED	1	2	3	4	5	MODEST
ATTRACTIVE	1	2	3	4	5	UNATTRACTIVE

2. James Winthrop is 48 years old, is a college professor, is married, and has four children. He probably is:

FRIENDLY	1	2	3	4	5	UNFRIENDLY
INTELLIGENT	1	2	3	4	5	STUPID
ALERT	1	2	3	4	5	ABSENT MINDED
FAIR	1	2	3	4	5	UNFAIR
LAZY	1	2	3	4	5	AMBITIOUS

3. George Smith is 30 years old, a black, married, a high school graduate, and works at a gas station. He probably is:

FRIENDLY	1	2	3	4	5	UNFRIENDLY
INTELLIGENT	1	2	3	4	5	STUPID
SUPERSTITIOUS	1	2	3	4	5	UNSUPERSTITIOUS
LAZY	1	2	3	4	5	AMBITIOUS
SERIOUS	1	2	3	4	5	HAPPY-GO-LUCKY

Reprinted by permission of Terrence Adams.

FORM B

Below are descriptions of three different people. Based on the information given, what is your best guess about their personalities? Place a checkmark somewhere on the rating scale. For example, if you think Jane is probably very friendly, put a checkmark at or near the 1 point on the scale. If you think she is probably very unfriendly, then place the checkmark at or near the 5 point on the scale. If you have absolutely no opinion, place the checkmark at the 3 point on the scale. Remember that there are no right or wrong answers; this is not a test, merely a survey of your opinion.

1. Jane is 18 years old and a freshman college student. She is five feet two inches tall and has dark hair. She makes average grades, and dates about once a week. She probably is:

FRIENDLY	1	2	3	4	5	UNFRIENDLY
INTELLIGENT	1	2	3	4	5	STUPID
EASYGOING	1	2	3	4	5	HOT TEMPERED
CONCEITED	1	2	3	4	5	MODEST
ATTRACTIVE	1	2	3	4	5	UNATTRACTIVE

2. James Winthrop is 48 years old, is a TV repairman, is married, and has four children. He probably is:

FRIENDLY	1	2	3	4	5	UNFRIENDLY
INTELLIGENT	1	2	3	4	5	STUPID
ALERT	1	2	3	4	5	ABSENT MINDED
FAIR	1	2	3	4	5	UNFAIR
LAZY	1	2	3	4	5	AMBITIOUS

3. George Smith is 30 years old, married, a high school graduate, and works at a gas station. He probably is:

FRIENDLY	1	2	3	4	5	UNFRIENDLY
INTELLIGENT	1	2	3	4	5	STUPID
SUPERSTITIOUS	1	2	3	4	5	UNSUPERSTITIOUS
LAZY	1	2	3	4	5	AMBITIOUS
SERIOUS	1	2	3	4	5	HAPPY-GO-LUCKY

Reprinted by permission of Terrence Adams.

Exercise: **Choose a political candidate you support, and in a short speech or essay indicate those character traits that he or she has demonstrated which provide personal proof to that candidacy.**

Exercise: **Compile a list of character traits in order of importance, that you think would be desirable for a member of the opposite sex. Compile a similar list for your own sex.**

CHAPTER 15

Logical Proof

We humans are rational creatures who take a great deal of pride in the fact that we have the ability to reason, to analyze, to think things out for ourselves. We are appreciative of intelligence and the ability to solve problems, and being adept at problem-solving is important to us. Throughout our lives we use reasoning to decide what to buy, what to wear, what school to attend, or what to contribute in terms of time and money to our church or charity. In order to protect our self-image we must be able to justify our beliefs to others. We must rationalize our behavior to ourselves and defend it to our loved ones and friends. Therefore, an understanding of logical reasoning is imperative.

ARGUMENTATION

Reasoning is the process of drawing conclusions from evidence. When the relationship between the evidence and the conclusion is communicated to others in an attempt to influence belief, it is called argumentation.

In its simplest form argumentation consists of two statements, a premise and a conclusion drawn from that premise. The statements below are arguments in which the italicized conclusion is drawn from the premise.

1. John has been sent to the office three times this week for causing disturbances in class. Therefore, *he is a troublemaker.*
2. John is a member of the SDS. Therefore, *he is a troublemaker.*

Both of these arguments involve a premise-conclusion relationship. In the first example the conclusion was drawn from an examination of three individual situations: "John has been in the office three times. Therefore, he is a troublemaker."

292

When we examine individual cases and draw a conclusion, we are using *inductive reasoning*. The following situations involve the inductive process:

1. A poll predicting the winner in an upcoming election.
2. Tests conducted on a group of people to determine the effectiveness of a new vaccine.
3. The decision to put a traffic light on a street corner after a series of accidents.
4. A student deciding to become a college business major on the basis of previous interest and high school performance.

In each instance, the reasoning proceeds from specific cases to a general conclusion. In the first example, pollsters take a random sampling from a cross section of the voting population. On the basis of the results of this survey they conclude that the voting preference of the cross section will be typical of the vote of the entire group involved. The second example is similar: If the vaccine is effective for 95 per cent of the test group, it will probably be effective for 95 per cent of the total population. The third example—the decision to install the traffic light—also demonstrates movement from specific instances to a general conclusion. In the fourth case, the student considers experiences in his background before reaching a conclusion about his future. The movement in all of these cases has been from specific, individual experiences to a general conclusion.

Now let us return to the second of the two arguments concerning John: "John is a member of the SDS. Therefore, he is a troublemaker." It has been concluded that John is a troublemaker, not because he has been seen in individual situations in which he has caused trouble, but because membership in a certain group carries with it that label. You have come to some previous conclusion about members of the SDS being troublemakers. Since John is a member of that group, he, according to your stereotype, is a troublemaker. Reasoning in this manner, from a general rule to an individual (specific) case, is called deductive reasoning.

As you have seen, reasoning can take two forms—inductive and deductive. To test your understanding, indicate whether the following are examples of inductive or deductive reasoning.

1. I wouldn't eat that meat. It's been out of the refrigerator for days.
2. He couldn't be the burglar. He's a policeman.
3. I'll never learn to drive; I backed into the pool again.
4. I'm never playing cards again. I lost a bundle last night.
5. Don't trust him. He's a former CIA agent.

6. I'm through with women. I got taken to the cleaners by one again.

7. I'm never using that kind of fertilizer again. It burned out all my grass.

8. Don't go around with those Jones boys, son. Their father is an ex-con.

THE PROCESS OF INDUCTION

As a result of an examination of specific cases, the writer or teacher comes to a general conclusion on the basis of his observations. The three principal forms of induction are those of generalization, causal relation, and analogy.

Generalization

We generalize when we examine examples from a class and then draw conclusions about the whole class. We conclude that characteristics true of the cases examined are also true of similar cases not examined. For example, if we have had good service from three Buicks, we might come to the conclusion that a Buick is a good car to own. If we have done poorly in English throughout high school, we might conclude that English courses are not our "cup of tea."

As you can see, generalization is an often-used form of reasoning in our daily lives. Testing the reliability of generalization may be summed up in these questions.

1. Are the instances examined sufficiently large to warrant the generalization? The number of instances examined depends upon the proposition. For example, you might be justified, on the basis of only one or two observations, in concluding that overly fat women should avoid wearing slacks. Coming to a conclusion in this way is called an *inductive leap,* and in some instances it is warranted. However, if you were investigating the protective qualities of a new vaccine, you might have to examine thousands of people before you could justify a conclusion. If in doubt, a good rule of thumb is the more cases examined, the more reliable the generalization.

2. Are the instances examined typical? The examples in a generalization must be representative of those in the class which are not examined. For example, an adverse conclusion about teenagers based on a few newspaper stories would probably be slanted, since many newspapers generally deal with the

sensational rather than the commonplace. All possible care should be taken to insure that the examples used are typical. The best method of doing this is to choose examples at random. A random sample is one selected entirely by chance, as in choosing the first and last name on every page in the phone book.

3. Is the information used true? We do not limit examples used in generalization to those we examine personally, but also include instances we hear or read about. In a court of law, hearsay evidence is usually inadmissible as testimony. It is important that the evidence used be accurate.

4. Are there any negative instances which invalidate the conclusion? A negative instance will not invalidate a generalization if it can be shown to be an exception to the rule. Suppose you conclude that people on welfare are living in extreme deprivation. Someone points out that a man receiving welfare payments was also working full time. If you can show that documented statistics indicate that less than 1 percent of welfare cases involve fraud, you will explain why the above case is an exception to the rule.

Causal Relation

Reasoning from causal relation is based on the principle that every cause has an effect. Causal reasoning may move from effect to cause or cause to effect. In either event, we reason from a known to an unknown. For example, in effect-to-cause reasoning, we see an increase in illegitimacy, and we infer an increase in promiscuity. We read of the high drop-out rate for students at a particular university, and we infer that the school has rigid academic standards. We begin with a known effect and attribute it to a probable cause. In cause-to-effect reasoning, we read about a tax increase on beer and infer a rise in beer prices. We observe a new school being built in our district and anticipate an increase in next year's taxes.

Cause-and-effect relationships can be most clearly shown in a carefully controlled scientific experiment in which a control group is used to determine whether there are other causes operating in such a way as to contribute to the alleged effect. For example, suppose that researchers are interested in developing a vaccine for prevention of a new variety of Asian flu. They would use the control group method. Ideally, the control group should be composed of subjects matched in every pertinent way with those in the experimental group, except that the experimental group receives the vaccine while the control group does not. If the two groups are alike in every respect other than the isolated variable (the vaccine), we can conclude with some confidence that any effect in regard to immunity to this strain of flu is due to the vaccine.

When using cause-and-effect, be careful to include the important links in the chain of causation, or else your reasoning may be unclear. Notice how a series of events which develops a logical cause-and-effect relationship can be made unclear because of poor communication.

> A student was late for his first hour class because he shut his alarm clock off and fell asleep.
> When he finally re-awoke, he glanced in horror at the time, hurriedly dressed, and ran to his car.
> In his rush to get to school, he exceeded the speed limit considerably.
> He noticed a truck at an approaching crossroad too late to avoid a collision.
> When questioned by the police as to why the accident had occurred, he replied, "Because I shut the alarm off and went back to bed."

Had the student explained the series of events as outlined above, his reply would have constituted a logical causal relationship. Instead, his brief reply, omitting essential links in the chain of causation, probably caused the policeman to wonder whether his reasoning had been affected by the accident.

Cause-and-effect relationships are more difficult to establish where strict controls cannot be implemented. This is especially true in the area of social problems, where causes may be so many that causal relation is almost impossible to define.

Analogical Reasoning

Use of analogy is a popular and colorful way of supporting a point. It assumes that if things are alike in known respects, they will also be alike in unknown respects. We conclude that a son who has been trustworthy when he was home will also be trustworthy when he is away at school. We reason that if there is discontent among ghetto area residents of one city, there will be discontent in the ghetto area of another city of similar size, population, job opportunity, and city management. For analogical reasoning to be persuasive, the points of similarity must clearly outweigh the points of difference.

It is important to examine carefully the essential comparative features in the analogy. Remember, the strength of the similarity is more important than the number of similarities found. As was true in regard to cause-and-effect relationships, it is difficult to make valid comparisons between people and between groups of people, because of the complexity of the problem. For example, in the analogy that a student will be unsuccessful in college because he got lower than average grades in high school, suppose that the student spends a number of years working before he enters college, and is thus highly motivated to succeed. This significant difference might outweigh the similarities and render the analogy invalid.

EXERCISE

Indicate whether the inductive reasoning used is generalization, cause-and-effect, or analogy.

1. I forgot to put gas in the car. I'll bet we won't make it home. C
2. George was late for class. I'll bet he overslept. C
3. I'll never learn to dance, Mother. I stepped on Emma's foot again. G
4. I'm not letting you drive the car. You can't even ride a bike safely. A
5. I'll never play cards with you again, Sam. That's the third time I caught you cheating. C
6. I'll never learn to bowl, Carl. I forgot to let go of the ball again. G
7. If you can't get the money from your own dad, how can you expect to get it from a friend? A
8. You had better take an umbrella along. Look at those black clouds. G
9. I'll never be at ease with a girl. Every time I talk to one alone I get "all clutched up." G
10. Sure I flunked English, Dad. Mr. McCarthy only likes the girl students. G
11. I don't think Myron is going to do well in college. He got lost again this morning trying to find the school. G
12. I didn't go to church yesterday. Watch me lose at cards. A

THE PROCESS OF DEDUCTION

Deduction is that form of reasoning which proceeds from a general truth to a particular conclusion. It is typically expressed in a three-step pattern known as the *syllogism*. The three statements are so arranged that the last can be inferred from the first two. They are known as the major premise, minor premise, and conclusion. The three most common types of syllogism are the conditional, the alternative, and categorical.

The conditional syllogism is based on an if-then relationship, such as "If I don't study, I won't pass the test." When stated formally, the conditional syllogism appears as follows:

Major Premise: If I don't study, I won't pass the test.
Minor Premise: I have to pass the test.
Conclusion: Therefore, I must study.

The alternative syllogism limits the number of choices in the argument to two. To come to a conclusion you must make one choice or another. The three statements are arranged this way:

Major Premise: Either he's not studying or he's stupid.
Minor Premise: He's not stupid.
Conclusion: Therefore, he's not studying.

The most often-used syllogism is the categorical syllogism. It gets its name from the fact that the major premise states a general proposition about a category of "things" (animals, people, religions, political parties, and so on). A typical categorical syllogism would be:

Major Premise   All cows eat grass.
(general proposition
about a category)

Minor Premise   Bessy is a cow.
(falls within the
category)

Conclusion   Therefore, Bessy eats grass.
(what is true of the
category is true of
all parts of the category)

As can be seen, the conclusion is simply a statement of what is clearly implied in the major and minor premises. If we know that all cows eat grass and that Bessy is a cow, we know that Bessy eats grass because eating grass is a characteristic of a cow.

There are two tests used to determine validity in deduction. The first applies to the major premise, which is a statement about a category and must be stated in a universal sense; that is, "all" or "every" or "none" of the things in the category have a particular characteristic. If there are exceptions which cannot be explained, you begin with an inaccurate assumption which invalidates the conclusion.

> Some cows eat grass.
> Bessy is a cow.
> Therefore, she might/or might not eat grass.

Second, if the subject of the minor premise does not belong to the category referred to in the major premise, the conclusion will be invalid.

> All cows eat grass.
> My cat eats grass.
> Therefore, my cat is a cow.

For some experience in recognizing validity in categorical syllogisms, examine the following premises in order to see what conclusions can be drawn from them. Keep in mind the tests discussed above.

> **M.P.** Some college instructors are bald.
> **m.p.** My English teacher is a college instructor.

No conclusion can be drawn from these premises since the term used is "some," not "all." Remember, the distribution in the category must be universal, or, if there are exceptions, they must be satisfactorily explained.

> **M.P.** All college instructors are bald.
> **m.p.** My English instructor has long flowing hair.

The conclusion is that my English teacher is not a college instructor. If he is not bald, he does not qualify, according to the major premise.

> **M.P.** No college professor is bald.
> **m.p.** My English instructor is bald.

The conclusion is that my English teacher is not a college instructor. His baldness rules him out of the category, according to the major premise.

> **M.P.** All college instructors are bald.
> **m.p.** My mother-in-law is bald.

No conclusion can be drawn from these premises. The major premise does not say that all people who are bald are college professors; it says only that all college professors are bald. Remember, a deduction can draw only those conclusions implied in the premises.

EXERCISE

Read the following syllogisms. Indicate which are valid and which are invalid. When a syllogism is not valid, briefly explain why.

1. All good citizens vote. President Carter voted. Therefore, President Carter is a good citizen.
2. No tigers have wings. This creature has wings. Therefore, this creature is not a tiger.
3. All athletes eat Wheaties for breakfast. Jerry is an athlete. Jerry eats Wheaties for breakfast.
4. Men of distinction drink Coors beer. I drink Coors beer. I am a man of distinction.
5. Some guys like girls. George is a guy. Therefore George likes girls.
6. Any golfer who makes a hole-in-one is lucky. Jack Nicklaus made a hole-in-one. Jack Nicklaus was lucky.
7. No nice person uses vulgar language in public. He uses vulgar language in public. He is not a nice person.
8. Anyone who reads Karl Marx is a communist. Mr. Schwartz reads Karl Marx. Mr. Schwartz is a communist.
9. All communists read Karl Marx. Mr. Schwartz reads Karl Marx. Mr. Schwartz is a communist.

How do these ideas relate to the persuader? The idea is to get your audience to agree with your premises. If they accept the premises as true, and if the premises are set up properly, then they must logically accept the conclusion. Some of the premises above, from which a conclusion could be drawn, were not acceptable, e.g., "All college instructors are bald." This premise is false (fallacious). A syllogism may be fallacious and still valid, since validity refers to the structure of the syllogism.

Faulty deduction often occurs when people accept generalizations about classes of people as being general truths. Such generalizations are called stereotypes and are generally wrong when used as the major premise in a categorical syllogism. We develop stereotypes of the "conservative," "liberal," "communist," "Catholic," "Protestant," "stockbroker," "Jew," "black," "college instructor," and so on. The following stereotypes are stated as general rules from which people have reasoned incorrectly:

All Negroes are shiftless.
All politicians are dishonest.
All effeminate males are homosexuals.
All college professors are intellectual.
All members of SDS are troublemakers.
All teenagers are rebellious.

Although these statements are all incorrect, you can find those who use them as general truths from which to reason. Take the first, "All Negroes are shiftless." A racist employer might reason this way and never hire a black person. The syllogism is valid, since it is structurally sound, but fallacious because the major premise is untrue. In order to be reliable, deduction must start from true premises.

EXERCISE

Some of the syllogisms below are valid and others are not. If the syllogism is invalid, briefly explain why. If you think that a valid syllogism is fallacious, briefly explain why.

1. All hippies have long hair. He has long hair. He is a hippy.
2. Jewish people may not eat pork. He is Jewish. He may not eat pork.
3. No full-blooded Indian can grow a beard. He has a beard. He is not a full-blooded Indian.
4. All welfare recipients who are physically able to work and do not are lazy. She is physically able to work. She is lazy.
5. Anyone who goes to church regularly is charitable. He goes to church regularly. He is charitable.
6. Anyone who believes in premarital sex relations is promiscuous. She believes in premarital sex relations. She is promiscuous.
7. All policemen are oppressive. He is a policeman. He is oppressive.
8. Anyone who is promiscuous believes in premarital sex relations. She believes in premarital sex relations. She is promiscuous.
9. All Scotsmen are tight-fisted. He is a Scotsman. He is tight-fisted.
10. All college professors are well-qualified in the subjects they teach. He is a college professor. He is well-qualified in the subject he teaches.

FALLACIES

Fallacious reasoning can be the result of faulty induction or deduction, or the acceptance of misleading argumentation. Some of these fallacies occur so often that they have been isolated and labeled. The most common of these are treated below.

Unwarranted or Hasty Generalization

A generalization is fallacious when it is based on insufficient or unfair evidence, or when it is not warranted by the facts available. For example, "All hippies are dirty," "All welfare recipients are lazy," and so on.

Errors in Causal Induction

Fallacy in causal induction occurs when there is no logical relationship between a cause and an effect. Two most common cause-and-effect fallacies are *post hoc* (after this, therefore, because of this) and *non sequitur* (it does not follow).

Post Hoc   *Post hoc* is the fallacy of thinking that an event which follows another is necessarily caused by the other. Thus, you might conclude that the Democratic Party promotes war, that television viewing increases juvenile delinquency, and that an easing of censorship causes an increase in immorality.

The error in post hoc reasoning occurs because the reasoner ignores other factors which may have contributed to the effect. A survey of former college debaters revealed, for example, that they were considerably more successful in their chosen field of work than their nondebating counterparts. To assume from this that their experience as debaters was the cause of their success would be fallacious. Other factors must be considered: Students who become debaters usually possess superior verbal ability, have keen analytical minds, and are highly motivated by competition. No doubt these factors, which led them into debate, also contributed to their success.

Non Sequitur   In this fallacy the conclusion reached does not necessarily follow from the facts argued. The argument that because a man is kind to animals he will make a good husband ignores the possibilities that the man may make a bad husband, drink excessively, cheat, or beat his wife.

Begging the Question

An argument begs the question when it assumes something as true when it actually needs to be proven. For instance, the declaration that "these corrupt laws must be changed" asserts the corruption but does not prove it, and consequently the conclusion is not justified.

Begging the question also occurs when we make a charge and then insist that someone else disprove it. For example, to answer the question, "How do you know that the administration is honest?" would put the respondent in the position of trying to disprove a conclusion which was never proven in the first place. Remember, whoever makes an assertion has the burden of proof.

Ignoring the Question

Ignoring the question occurs when the argument shifts from the original subject to a different one, or when the argument appeals to some emotional attitude which has nothing to do with the logic of the case. An example of the first would be a man replying, "Haven't you ever done anything dishonest? when accused of cheating on his wife. He ignores the question of his infidelity by shifting to a different argument.

An argument that appeals to the emotional attitudes of the reader or listener would be the statement, "No good American would approve of this communistic proposal."

False Analogy

To argue by analogy is to compare two things which are alike in germane known respects and to suggest that they will also be alike in unknown respects. This method is accurate if the things being compared are genuinely similar: "George will do well in graduate school; he had an excellent academic record as an undergraduate." It is likely to be fallacious when they are dissimilar: "There's nothing to handling a snowmobile; it's just like riding a bicycle."

Analogies are more difficult to prove when the comparison is figurative rather than literal. In a political campaign, the incumbent might admonish the voter "not to change horses in the middle of the stream," while the opponent replies that "a new broom sweeps clean."

Either/or Fallacy

The either/or fallacy is reasoning that concludes there are only two choices to an argument when there are other possible alternatives. A tragic example would be the reasoning that escalated the Vietnam war. The argument was: either we fight and win in Vietnam or all of South East Asia will fall to the communists. Of course, we didn't win and all of South East Asia didn't fall to the communists.

Ad Hominem

In this fallacy the argument shifts from the proposition to the character of the opponent. Unfortunately, this abuse often occurs in politics, and the voters who fall for it wind up casting their votes against a candidate rather than for one. "I wouldn't trust him. His best friend is a homosexual," or "You're not going to believe a former convict?" are examples of this fallacy.

Red Herring

The red herring is similar to the ad hominem fallacy but does not attack the opponent's character. It gets its name from the superstition that if you drag a red herring across your path it will throw any wild animals following you off the track. Information is introduced which is not relevant to the question at hand in the hope that it will divert attention from the real issue. In politics an opposing candidate is pictured as being overly religious, ultrarich, or divorced. If the trait has nothing to do with the way he will perform in office, the argument is a red herring.

Ad Populum

The ad populum argument appeals to the theory that whatever the masses believe is true. Make no mistake; popularity is not always an accurate determiner of truth. Consider the landslide victory of Richard Nixon in 1972. A typical ad populum fallacy is: "Unconditional amnesty is wrong, because most people are against it."

EXERCISE

Identify the following fallacies by employing these identifications: hasty generalization, inadequate causal relation, false analogy, begging the question, ignoring the question, red herring, ad hominem, ad populum, either/or.

1. My English grades were always good in high school. The fact that I got a

Non sequiter

D in English proves that there is something wrong with this English course.

2. Because he doesn't smoke, drink, or swear, he'll make some woman a wonderful husband. *non sequitur*

3. There's no sense in not spanking your children. The neighbors on each side of me are opposed to physical punishment and their kids are monsters. *false analogy or ad hominew*

4. We wouldn't have all this crime and immorality if people would return to the church. *ignoring the question*

5. Would you listen to a man who spent a year behind bars?

6. Giving to charity is like throwing your money down a sewer. ·

7. Premarital sex is right on. Everyone is doing it.

8. I understand my opponent visited a psychiatrist for some months. I hope he's cured.

9. John flunked the test because he didn't study. Or else the teacher didn't like him.

10. It's no skin off my nose but everyone knows my opponent is living with his secretary.

11. Before I tell you if I've quit smoking or not, let me ask you this. Have you?

12. The theaters are full of nothing but movies about sex. In last night's paper, for instance, there were six X-rated movies advertised.

13. This unfair law should be abolished.

14. This proposal would be unacceptable to any real American.

15. You're gonna have to steal to get the money unless you want to beg your dad for it.

16. What's wrong with cheating? Everyone does.

17. He's a Ph.D., isn't he? He must know what he's talking about.

18. Me, vote for a divorced man for governor? If he couldn't keep his marriage together, how can he run our state government?

19. I didn't go to church Sunday; watch me lose my shirt.

20. He'll make a fine senator; he's a good Christian.

EXERCISES

I. Give an example other than those mentioned in this chapter of the following fallacies: (1)hasty generalization, (2) error in causal relationship, (3) begging the question, (4) ignoring the question, (5) false analogy, (6) either/or, (7) ad hominem, (8) red herring, (9) ad populum.

II. Select an editorial or short essay which supports or criticizes an organization, program, or policy. Comment on its effectiveness as persuasion. Indicate whether the reasoning used is inductive or deductive.

III. Deliver a two-to-three minute speech or write a 200–300 word essay in which you support or refute a stand taken on a controversial campus issue. Develop your communication inductively or deductively.

CHAPTER 16

Psychological Proof

Logical proof appeals to the reason of the audience. Psychological proof, on the other hand, makes its appeal to the audience's attitudes and motives. People do things as a result of two factors, motive and desire. We are predisposed to act in certain ways because of goals, attitudes, sentiments, and motives which we have developed as part of our personality. When the desire to satisfy this "inner drive" becomes strong enough, we act.

ATTITUDES

Through learning and experience we build up reaction tendencies, which cause us to respond in predisposed ways to situations, people, values, and events. These reaction tendencies are called *attitudes*. Our attitudes are developed from our own experiences and from information handed down to us by parents, teachers, and friends. Thus, we form attitudes toward religion, LSD, mothers-in-law, blacks, sex, liquor, and so on. These attitudes give direction to our behavior, causing us to react in positive or negative ways. Keep in mind the fact that attitudes direct behavior—motives stimulate it. The following example should help you to see the difference between attitudes and motives:

A young girl is attacked by a man wielding a knife. She is stabbed repeatedly while a number of people watch. When the knife-wielder leaves, one or two run forward to aid the dying girl. The others hang their heads, ashamed that they stood by while this horror occurred. All of the people who watched had attitudes which were in sympathy with the victim. Why didn't they help? Probably because they were held back by motives related to their own safety which were stronger than those motives which would have caused them to act.

MOTIVES

As you have just seen, *motive* is the inner drive or impulse that stimulates behavior. If we look at attitude as the directive force of behavior, we can call motive the driving force. All of us have certain physical and social desires and wants. The inner force which moves us to satisfy these wants is called a motivating force. Motive is defined, therefore, as an impulse or drive which causes a person to act in a certain way. There are two basic types of motives: (1) physical motives — hunger, thirst, self-preservation, shelter, and sex; and (2) social motives — security, approval, popularity, success.

Physical Motives

All of us have essentially the same basic physical wants. We try to eat when hungry, rest when tired, and protect ourselves when threatened. The more money we have, the more we spend to achieve the greatest possible comfort. We put money aside to escape heat in the summer and cold in the winter. We buy heated swimming pools, air-conditioned cars, and remote-controlled appliances to insure the comfort and protection of our most priceless possession, ourselves. We are, to a considerable degree, creatures of the body. Few could imagine how many business deals or sales have been made to clients who have been put into the right mood with a steak dinner and all the trimmings.

Hunger and Thirst   Although one and a half billion people in the world exist on a starvation diet, few Americans know what it is to go hungry. Therefore, advertisers do not attempt to satisfy the hunger or thirst of an audience, but to create desire which will cause them to want to eat or drink. In short, the persuader attempts to stimulate the appetite of his audience in order to sell the product. We read of a product's "delicious goodness," "enticing aroma," "frosty freshness," or "tantalizing taste," and if we are sufficiently motivated, we buy.

A typical ad shows a group of men working in the heat of the summer sun. Near them, on a table in the shade, is a tray with four ice-cold schooners of beer.

The caption reads:

It's hot and sticky and you've been working hard. You need a little lift and you know nothing will cool you off the way the refreshing taste of _____ beer does. So get with it. Grab a taste of gusto and cool off.

Self-Preservation   No drive is stronger in man than the drive for survival. Any account of the unbelievable horror and pain that men have endured in prison camps, in hospitals, or on the battlefield in an effort to stay alive testifies to the strength of this drive. The persuader who appeals to this basic want tries to create a need on the part of the reader or listener. Slogans like "Drive carefully; the life you save may be your own," and "Stop smoking; it's a matter of life and breath," direct themselves to establishing this need. Note how the accompanying Christian Children's Fund ad points out that the person willing to become a sponsor will save the life of the child.

Sex   No appeal is used more widely in advertising than the appeal to the sex drive. Our society is supersaturated with sex in advertising to sell everything from spark plugs to corporate image. The degree of subtlety employed in advertising based on sex appeal depends upon the specific audience the ad is intended to reach. The General Cigar Company designed the ad on page 312 to sell its product to the readers of *Playboy* Magazine.

A typical TV commercial shows a skinny, bespectacled young lad approaching a football stadium in his new car. He is met by a campus beauty walking arm in arm with a football player, a magnificent physical specimen who appears to be the hero of the game. When the girl sees the car, she pushes the hero aside and hops into the front seat with love in her eyes. Moral: When you buy Mustang, you buy sex appeal.

Shelter   While some in our society live under deplorable conditions of poverty, most of us live in relative comfort. For this reason, advertisers make their appeal to man's drive for shelter in terms of the "desire for comfort" which is evident among most Americans. An air conditioned restaurant on a sweltering July day might be more inviting than a sign promising excellent cuisine. The additional cost of building a fireplace in a new home is offset by the thought of sitting in front of its warm blaze on a chilly evening.

There are, however, times when the persuader must make an appeal on behalf of those who are in such desperate circumstances that the audience, having little experience of hardship themselves, would lack a basis for grasping fully the seriousness of the problem. It is then up to the persuader to make the situation as real as possible for

Little Maria had been hungry all her life.

Maria lives in a slum in Brazil and has suffered from malnutrition all her young life. When she was accepted into our CCF-assisted nutrition program, she was about five and a half years old but was unable to walk. She weighed only sixteen pounds—less than half her estimated normal weight for a child her age.

Little Maria's home is a four room shack made of poles, mud and partially covered with tiles, flattened tin cans and pieces of scrap lumber. Holes in the walls are patched with cardboard. She shares this home with her mother and father, five sisters, five brothers and a nephew.

While Maria's father works hard, he is totally unskilled and can only get work as a porter, carrying immense loads on top of his head. His income is so meager he cannot possibly provide for his family. Maria's mother does not have a job and stays home to care for the children.

Now Maria has a chance for a better life with help from her CCF sponsor. After she was enrolled in the nutrition project, she showed rapid signs of improvement. She became able to crawl around the recovery room. She could smile and talk. She could even draw and our report shows that her physical state was improving normally. Hopefully she will make a good recovery and the marks of malnutrition will disappear.

But there are many other youngsters like Maria who suffer from severe malnutrition and who must wait for the assistance they so urgently need. You can help such a child by becoming a CCF sponsor. The cost is only $15 a month (tax deductible) and you will have the privilege of developing a person-to-person relationship with the child you assi

You will receive the child's photograph, name and mailing address so that you can exchange letters and cards. Most important, you will have the satisfaction that comes from sharing your love with someone who needs you. And boys and girls like Maria urgently need your help. Malnutrition can cause many permanent defects even if it does not immediately lead to disease and death.

Won't you help? Please fill out the coupon at the bottom of the page indicating the sex and country of the child you'd like to sponsor. In about two weeks you will receive your personal sponsor folder on the child who has been placed with you.

Sponsors urgently needed in Brazil, India and Indonesia.

We will be glad to send you a Statement of Income and Expense upon request.

Write today: Dr. Verent J. Mills

CHRISTIAN CHILDREN'S FUND, Inc.
Box 26511, Richmond, Va. 23261

I want to sponsor a ☐ boy ☐ girl in
(Country)_____
☐ Choose any child who needs my help. I will pay $15 a month. I enclose first payment of $_____. Please send me child's name, mailing address and photograph.
☐ I can't sponsor a child now but I do want to give $_____.
☐ Please send me more information.

Name_____
Address_____
City_____
State_____ Zip_____
Member of International Union for Child Welfare, Geneva. Gifts are tax deductible. Canadians: Write 1407 Yonge, Toronto 7.   LL33 00

With permission of the Christian Children's Fund, Inc.

Should a gentleman offer a Tiparillo to a dental hygienist?

"The doctor is a little late, sir. Will you have a seat?"

She's the best thing to hit dentistry since novocaine. "Hey Dummy," your mind says to you, "why didn't you have this toothache sooner?"

Maybe if...well, you could offer her a Tiparillo.® Or a Tiparillo M with menthol. An elegant, tipped cigar. Slim. And your offer would be cleverly psychological. (If she's a bit of a kook, she'll take it. If not, she'll be flattered that you *thought* she was a bit of a kook.) And who knows? Your next visit might be a house call.

the audience. The picture and story of little Maria is designed to make the reader feel what it must be like to go without adequate food or care.

Putting one's self in another person's place is called empathy. When we cry or are saddened because of another person's grief, or when we are happy because another person is happy, we are responding empathically to that person. In order to get your reader or listener to respond in a desirable way, you must make your description real enough to produce empathic response.

Social Motives

The physical drives we have talked about thus far are called basic drives and are common to all higher forms of animal life. However, while animals conform only to the law of the jungle, man is a social being and must live within the framework of the group. Even in the most primitive society, man has values, mores, and customs to which he must adhere in order to avoid the condemnation of his fellows. If he would live in harmony within his society, man must satisfy his physical drives in socially acceptable ways.

Early in life you learned to conform to certain rules if you wanted to maintain the approval of those around you. As you grew older and

"Bastards!"

Reprinted from True Magazine. Copyright © 1969, Fawcett Publications, Inc.

came in contact with more people, you found that this "code of conduct" became more complex. In order to achieve satisfaction and still conform to the rules, you developed a set of secondary, social motives. We list these motives as security, approval, popularity, and success. They seldom operate singly, but frequently combine to effect behavioral response.

Different groups within the society have different codes of expectations. Therefore, in discussing values and customs we will be talking about those common to most Americans. It is our belief that, in order to survive, every free society must have a common set of values to which most of its members ascribe.

Security   Foremost among man's social motives are those that provide for his survival. These include desire for money, property, health care, provision for loved ones.

The force of this drive for security is clearly evident in today's world. The effect that it has on us and our loved ones shapes our consideration of the war and the draft. Our appraisal of birth control is made in terms of our own sentiments, our religious attitude, and the health factor. The specter of pollution is a threat to our very existence. We attend college to assure ourselves a better future; we "go steady" to insure a dependable date; we buy insurance to provide for health care or income protection. In this world of violence and uncertainty, no generation of Americans has been as security-minded as this one. Countless ads like the one for Pirelli tires shown here emphasize security as their major appeal.

Approval   Some of you are probably attending college now because you want to maintain the approval of your parents, friends, or employer. You might even dress in a style which is not particularly becoming to you because it is the in thing to do. Any store that promises the latest styles is selling approval along with its product. The drive for approval is particularly forceful. A person might spend months building a recreation room or weaving a fancy tapestry for the reward of being able to say, "I made this myself." The young hoodlum might risk a prison sentence to impress his fellow gang members with a particular daring crime. Approval is achieved by living up to or exceeding the expectations of others. It can be gained for a desirable personality trait or for some skill or ability. Most people admire such character traits as honesty, dignity, integrity, courage, and morality, and those who demonstrate these traits to others generally win their approval.

Popularity   Close to our desire for approval is the drive for popu-

A WAGON BUILT TO CARRY CARGO MORE PRECIOUS THAN GROCERIES.

Any station wagon can take a load of stuff from one place to another.

The Volvo wagon, on the other hand, was designed to take a load off your mind as a parent.

Volvo realizes, for example, that it's impossible to keep both eyes on the road if you have to keep one eye on the back seat.

So to keep the kids in place, we provide you with things like child-proof door locks on *all* the rear doors. Including the back one.

And to virtually guarantee that you can focus your attention on the road at all times, we give you defrosters for the front side windows, and the rear window comes with its own wiper, washer, and defroster.

On the road, the first thing you'll notice is how quickly our overhead cam engine can put trouble behind you. Should trouble appear ahead, you'll appreciate the way our rack and pinion steering can help you steer clear of it. And our four-wheel power disc.

In spite of all these precautions, accidents do happen. So we've planned for the unplanned.

Where many wagons may feature a front end designed to impress the neighbors, the Volvo wagon features a front end designed to help absorb the impact of a collision.

Our passenger compartment is surrounded by a protective steel cage.

Our doors have steel tubes running through their insides for added protection, instead of imitation wood running down their outsides for frivolous decoration.

There's also a padded dashboard. A collapsible steering wheel. A gas tank designed not to rupture in a rear end collision.

Look at it this way.

There's finally a wagon that shows as much concern for your children as you do.

VOLVO
The car for people who think.

ROOF RACK OPTIONAL. © 1977 VOLVO OF AMERICA CORPORATION. LEASING AVAILABLE.

larity. If approval means to be "liked," popularity means to be "well-liked." It is strongest among young people, where being in the right group, learning the latest dance step, having a lot of dates, getting many yearbook signatures, and being well-liked are major goals.

The success of dance studios, charm courses, and books on personality development attest to the large number of older people who also have this need. This motive is closely linked to the sex motive. The American public is assured popularity if they buy the right deodorant, go to the right school, drive the right auto, and wear the right undergarments.

Success The desire for success can be called the great American dream. The man who starts out on a shoestring and amasses a fortune, the beauty who becomes a star overnight, and the local rock group that wins national acclaim with a hit record are all forms of this dream.

For some, the drive for success can be so strong that it overshadows all others. Men have lied, cheated, stolen, and even killed for the sake of personal ambition. Some have endured years of hard work and deprivation in an attempt to develop an artistic or musical talent. Others have sought success by keeping up with the Joneses or living in the right neighborhood. Advertisers use the success appeal to sell products ranging from razor blades to real estate. Ads promising sartorial splendor, palatial elegance, and prestigious luxury appeal to this motive.

One major toothpaste commercial shows a young boy, Tommy, who repeatedly finishes second best to his friend George. Tommy sits on the bench while George quarterbacks the team to victory. George's ninth inning homer wins the ballgame after Tommy's error permitted the opposition to tie the game in the eighth. George presses his lips to those of the campus queen in the back seat of the car while Tommy presses his nose to the windshield, straining to see out into the storm.

But finally the tables are turned. George, a member of the control group in an experiment conducted by _____ toothpaste, has a mouthful of cavities. Tommy, our new hero, is a member of the experimental group that has conquered tooth decay. Moral: Buy the right toothpaste and be a success.

It should be pointed out that because they are abstract, the four social motives discussed above can mean different things to different people. To some, success might mean achieving wealth, power, or prestige. To others, success could be gaining membership in an "in" group, experiencing self-actualization, or doing something to be proud of, like raising a well-adjusted family.

Perhaps you see achieving wealth as a matter of security, attaining prestige as a reason for approval, and gaining membership in the group as an indication of popularity. In any event, be assured that whatever you see security, approval, popularity, and success as being, they motivate people's lives.

EXERCISE

Below is a list of social motives common to the field of psychology. These are variously titled human wants, human motivations, or motive appeals. Indicate which of these could be considered security, approval, popularity, or success motives. Be prepared to defend your choice.

Social acceptance
Creativity
Long life
Status
Companionship
Prestige
Education
Power
Pleasure
Knowledge
Self-actualization
Possession
Welfare for others

Good health
Getting along well
Status
Group belonging
Fame
Membership
Acquisition of property
Self-esteem
Altruism
Being accepted
Imitation
Invention

ETHICS IN PERSUASION

The question of ethics is complicated. What some might feel is an appeal to undesirable motives might be perfectly acceptable to others. What might appear to be a subjective use of information to some, might be defended by others as necessary to obtain the desired response. For this reason, we offer one principle: Persuasion is unethical when it is used intentionally to mislead an audience.

Unfortunately, there are those in our society who operate with the attitude of getting away with whatever they can. Too many persuaders justify their intentional trickery with the slogan, "caveat emptor," let the buyer beware. With the vast influence wielded by professional persuaders in shaping opinion in our country, it is critical that we become more conscious of what is ethical in persuasion.

The list of nine propaganda techniques below should be helpful to you in analyzing persuasion. Avoid using them yourself and learn to recognize them when others use them.

1. **Name calling.** This technique of giving an idea a bad label is used to cause a person to reject an idea before examining all the evidence. Words like *communist, chauvinist, radical,* and *racist* are common examples of name calling.

2. **Glittering generalities.** This technique is the opposite of name calling. It associates something with a virtuous label, hoping to make a person approve it without examining the evidence. The name "Students for a Democratic Society" drew many idealistic students into the SDS until they found out how radical and destructive the group was.

3. **Transfer.** Transfer carries the qualities of something desirable and respected over to some other category in order to make it acceptable; or it carries the qualities of disapproval to cause a person to reject something.

4. **Testimonial.** A testimonial is an endorsement of an idea, program, or product by some person of prominence. Endorsements by an athlete or movie star of an aftershave or a political candidate are typical examples of testimonials.

5. **Plain folks.** This is a technique by which the persuader tries to convince his audience that he is just like them so they will feel he has their best interests at heart.

6. **Card stacking.** Card stacking involves the unfair selection and use of statistics or the use of misleading statements in order to give the best or worse possible case for an idea, program, or product.

7. **Bandwagon.** In this technique the propagandist tries to convince us that just about everyone is buying or participating or believing in his proposal and that we must follow the crowd and jump on the bandwagon.

8. **Flag waving.** This propaganda technique employs an unfair or undeserved appeal to patriotism. A classic example was the response, "America—love it or leave it," to the critics of the Vietnam war.

9. **Doublespeak.** Doublespeak is the intentional use of words to deceive—saying one thing and meaning another. In 1975 the doublespeak award was given to Palestine Liberation Organization leader Yasser Arafat for his answer to a charge that his organization wanted to destroy Israel. He said, "They are wrong. We do not want to destroy any people. It is precisely because we have been advocating coexistence that we have shed so much blood."

EXERCISES

I. Arrange the following words in some reasonable order and defend that order orally or in writing as your instructor directs.

Fame   Ability
Integrity   Honesty
Charity   Affluence
Courage   Wisdom
Intelligence

II. Write an appeal similar to the one on page 311 to seek a response to the plight of the child in the accompanying photograph.

III. Indicate the physical and social motives to which the Navy ad on page 321 appeals.

PERSUASION TO REINFORCE

Deliver a 3–4 minute speech or write a 300–500 word essay to reinforce. Persuasion to reinforce seeks to increase an audience's concern with a problem or course of action. The persuader should rely chiefly on pyschological proof. He will appeal to the audience's emotions, motives, attitudes, and sentiments. The persuader must determine which appeals he can use to gain the desired response from his audience, so careful audience analysis is a necessity.

Delivery: This speech should be delivered extemporaneously. The speech to reinforce attempts to arouse the enthusiasm of the audience. The listener must feel that the speaker is sincere. Spontaneity and directness are fundamental qualities of such a speech.

Sample Topics

1. Seatbelts save lives.

2. Be honest with yourself.

3. Be proud of your school.

4. We *are* our brother's keeper.

No one has to take a Navy Nurse by the hand

But some people do.

As an officer in the Navy Nurse Corps you're not only looked up to—you're looked at. It's a nice feminine kind of feeling.

And since most females get their way, so will you. Go where you want (here and abroad). Live like you want. And do what you want—in fields that range from coronary care nursing to operating-room management; from pediatrics to research and anesthesia.

Learn, advance, and have the time of your life doing life-giving work.

Mail the coupon below—you'll be in good hands.

The Navy If you're going to be something, why not be something special?

> If you need a spare hand in the Navy Nurse Corps, I'm interested. Please tell me more.
>
> Name_____Date of Birth_____
>
> Address_____
>
> City_____State_____Zip____
>
> ___I am a registered professional nurse.
> ___I am enrolled in an accredited school of nursing and would be interested in your Candidate Program. 4.9-0014N

MAIL TO: Bureau of Medicine and Surgery Code 321, Navy Department, Washington, D.C. 20390

Reprinted by permission of the United States Navy Department.

CHAPTER 17

Group Communication

Hardly a day goes by without your participating in a number of small group discussions. Most of them are informal talks with others about matters of mutual interest. Others occur more formally in organized committees and action groups.

Discussions have also been a vital part of your formal education. Most of us got our first taste of class discussion in kindergarten or first grade. Probably a majority of the courses you are now taking are lecture-discussion. Yet, in spite of your considerable experience with group communication, many of the discussions that you engage in fail to produce fruitful results.

There are a number of reasons why discussions fail. Sometimes the participants do not have the necessary information and the discussion becomes a "pooling of ignorance." At other times the discussion lacks a spirit of cooperation and ends in aimless argument. Lack of communication, lack of understanding, and a tendency to stray from the subject may also lessen the possibility of agreement or understanding. How many discussions between parents and children have ended with the participants stalking off because of any or all of the above obstacles?

The advantages of becoming a more effective discussion member are obvious. A study of the forms and principles of group discussion, together with guided practice, will help you to become more effective in both formal and informal discussion situations.

PARTICIPATING IN DISCUSSION

There are those who take part in discussion but contribute little or nothing to the outcome. Some think they have all the answers and reject any view contrary to their own. Others are so poorly prepared that they have nothing to offer in solving the problem. Still others lack an understanding of the nature of discussion. They would be glad to participate, but just don't know the rules of the game. The quality of participation may mean the difference between success and failure of the discussion. The duties of the discussant may be characterized as follows.

Be Prepared

There is a tendency among participants to let someone else do it when preparing for a group discussion. If the topic for discussion can be investigated ahead of time, do so. When you locate evidence important to the discussion, put it down on note cards, being sure to document it carefully. In a symposium, have your speech well enough prepared for an effective extemporaneous delivery with good eye contact.

Be Cooperative

Effective group thinking can only take place when members of the discussion put the common good of the group above personal interests. The purpose of the problem-solving discussion is to arrive at a solution acceptable to the entire group. This means that the members must be willing to compromise their viewpoints in order to resolve the conflict.

Be Friendly

Effective discussion is only possible when an attitude of goodwill prevails. When you find yourself disagreeing with others in the group, be sure to do so in a pleasant, friendly way. Remember, group thinking depends on teamwork. Personality clashes or any form of hostility in discussion inhibits participation. The free expression of ideas occurs only in an open, friendly atmosphere. To promote friendliness, discussion members should be encouraged to call each other by their first names.

Keep An Open Mind

To be an effective participant in a discussion, you should learn to appreciate the views of others. When you listen to another's opinion, try to put yourself in his place, remembering that no two people see things alike. That doesn't mean that you should accept everything he says, but rather that your mind should be open to new avenues of thought. While it is important to value your own opinion, you must be willing to admit that other opinions may also be reasonable. Be aware that your opinion might be wrong and be willing to alter it. Only a fool never changes his mind.

Share the Spotlight

While you should take a full and active part in attempting to solve the problem, don't monopolize the discussion to the extent that others cannot be heard. In fact, when you notice that one of the discussants is not contributing, try to draw him out; find out how he is reacting to the ideas being presented. Group thinking is, necessarily, thinking out loud. Unless every person in the group makes his thoughts known to others, the full value of their knowledge and experience will not be brought to bear upon the problem.

Listen Carefully

Listening critically is indispensable to effective group thinking. Pay careful attention in an attempt to understand fully what the other fellow means. Too many discussion members comment on what they "thought" someone meant without first making sure their understanding was correct. If you are in doubt, ask. Furthermore, it is each member's responsibility to test the thinking of others as it is expressed in the discussion. If you think someone is unclear in his thinking or on the wrong track, say so before the discussion continues.

Participate Freely and Enthusiastically

Each member of the group has a responsibility to participate. If you have a comment that you think is appropriate, make it. Avoid long speeches. Submit your contribution in one or two short sentences, or perhaps in the form of a question. The right question may prove to be just what the group needs to move forward in settling a problem. Furthermore, a question has a tendency to promote cooperation, whereas a critical comment might evoke hostility. Use your own background and experience to appraise and evaluate the contributions of others.

Stick to the Point

If you are like most discussion members, you probably have opinions or ideas that you would like to present to the group at the outset. You will greatly aid the progress of the discussion if you will withhold these remarks until they are pertinent. When you speak, speak to the point. This is especially important while evaluating and analyzing the problem. Follow the suggested pattern of the discussion and deal with the issues at hand. If you can deal with each aspect of the problem completely, you will avoid delay caused by backtracking to an issue that should already have been resolved.

MODERATING THE DISCUSSION

Although each member of the group must share the responsibilities of leadership, it is often wise to choose a moderator to guide the discussion. The specific duties of the moderator are to:

1. Open by briefly introducing the topic and the group members to the audience.
2. Guide the discussion, using a flexible outline.
3. Resolve tension by using tact and humor.
4. Stimulate all members to participate.
5. Provide transitions and summaries to help members see what has been accomplished and what remains to be done.
6. Be aware of the time to insure that all points are discussed.
7. Encourage informal, spontaneous participation.
8. Summarize the progress made at the close of the discussion and indicate the differences that remain unresolved.
9. Take charge of the forum period.

As indicated above, some specific duties of the moderator are to keep the discussion moving, to resolve tension, and to stimulate participation. Five problem situations that can block effective discussion are shown in the accompanying table, together with suggestions as to how they might be handled.

TYPE OF PROBLEM	HOW TO HANDLE IT

WON'T TALK

SUGGESTION: YOU HAVE TO FIND SOME WAY OF DRAWING HIM OUT WITHOUT EM-BARASSING HIM.

SAY — " _____ , how do you feel about . . . ?"

"May we hear from anyone else?"

"Has everyone had a chance to have their say?"

TALKS TOO MUCH

SUGGESTION: BE DIPLOMATIC. HE MAY JUST BE EAGER TO HAVE A SUCCESSFUL DISCUS-SION.

SAY — " _____ , could you summarize your remarks, so we can get to some other opinions?"

"Good point _____ ! Can we hear what some others think?"

UNCLEAR

SUGGESTION: TRY TO FIND HIS MAIN POINT AND THEN RESTATE IT SO THAT IT MAKES SENSE.

SAY — "If I understand you correctly, you feel . . . ."

"Now let's see if I've gotten this straight. You . . ."

ARGUMENTATIVE

SUGGESTION: KEEP YOUR COOL. A FRIENDLY RESPONSE WILL HELP TO CHECK HIS AN-GER. FIND SOMETHING YOU CAN AGREE WITH.

SAY — "I see your point _____ ! Now let's look at a different side."

"That's one way of looking at it. How about anyone else?"

INATTENTIVE

SUGGESTION: BE FRIENDLY. THE PERSON MIGHT HAVE A PERSONAL PROBLEM THAT IS DISTRACTING HIM.

SAY — " _____ , we've kind of left you out of the discussion. What do you think?"

"Sally seems to feel . . . . What is your opinion _____ ?"

WORDING THE DISCUSSION PROBLEM

It is important that the discussion topic be carefully worded. A well-written problem will increase the likelihood that the group will come to a satisfactory conclusion within the time limit. When phrasing a discussion problem, keep in mind the following suggestions:

1. The problem should be worded as a question. Discussion is a process of inquiry. The members of the group are searching for an answer.

2. State the problem clearly. The group will save considerable time if the discussion question is phrased as clearly as possible. Discussion problems are usually unclear for one of two reasons: They are too complex, or they are too general. Use familiar words that can easily be understood. Be as specific as possible.

3. Phrase the problem-question objectively. Avoid writing a question that suggests a bias for a particular point of view. The question, "Should the alarming violence on television be regulated?" suggests a fixed attitude before the discussion even begins.

4. Make the problem-question multisided. A multisided problem is one that allows for more than one or two answers. The question, "Should marijuana be legalized?" can be answered either yes or no. This could be done by simply polling the group. Why have a discussion? The question would be made more multisided if it read: "What changes should be made in the marijuana laws?"

5. The problem-question should be open-ended. A discussion question must consider all possible answers. In our example, "What changes should be made in the marijuana laws?" we are ignoring the question, "Should the laws be changed at all?" To make the discussion problem open-ended, add the phrase "if any." Thus your open-ended question would read, "What changes, if any, should be made in the marijuana laws?"

TYPES OF DISCUSSION

The eight basic types of discussion are the panel, the symposium, the round table, the lecture-forum, the film-forum, the dialogue, the interview, and role-playing.

The Panel

A panel discussion usually involves from three to eight members, including a moderator. They sit in front of an audience in a circle or semicircle so that they can see and react to each other. Ideally, the members of a panel have varied backgrounds and viewpoints which make for an active exchange of ideas and experiences. The language of panel discussion is usually informal, with each member expressing his opinion in a normal, conversational way.

Many panels are followed by an open forum, an audience participation period. After the moderator has summarized the discussion, he invites the audience to ask questions of or make statements to individual members or the panel as a whole. It is the moderator's job to field the questions, repeating or rephrasing them when necessary.

The Symposium

While the panel discussion is essentially informal, give-and-take conversation, the symposium consists of a series of prepared speeches. The subject or problem is divided into parts, and each speaker develops the part assigned to him. The available speaking time is divided

From Parade Publication, Inc. Cartoon by Boltinoff. Reprinted with permission.

equally among the speakers, who talk directly to the audience rather than to each other. A moderator opens the discussion and introduces each speaker and his topic. After each speaker has come to the lectern and addressed the audience, either the moderator or the speakers themselves summarize the discussion. Following the summary, the moderator may turn the symposium into a panel or move to a forum period.

The Round Table

As its name implies, this form of discussion generally takes place around a round table or in a circle. The reason for the round table is to provide those involved members with a feeling of equality. The circle has traditionally been a symbol of unity; when seated in a circle, everyone is in a position equal to that of his neighbor. Like the panel, the round table discussion is a kind of magnified conversation, since the participants look at each other. The difference is that in this form of discussion everyone is involved; there is no audience. Committee meetings and conferences are usually conducted as round table discussions. This form is especially appropriate for classroom discussion, where a stimulating topic handled well can result in a lively give and take among all members of the class.

The Lecture-Forum

In the lecture-forum, a single speaker delivers a prepared speech on a subject. After he has covered his topic thoroughly (lecture), he answers questons from his audience (forum). Variations of the lecture-discussion technique are frequently used by classroom instructors and political candidates. A challenging speaker can stimulate an enthusiastic reaction from his audience. The lecture-forum can be an effective discussion form in the classroom if the student speaker has the necessary expertise to give a subject the extended treatment necessary.

The Film-Forum

Sometimes students show a lack of enthusiasm for an issue because they know little about it. One discussion technique designed to deal with this type of situation is the film-forum. The success of this form of discussion is dependent to a great extent on the quality of the film used. Since the purpose of the film is to give information rather than to persuade, the film-forum is most effective when the film being used is objective rather than slanted. When used in the classroom, films should not exceed 15 minutes in length to allow time for adequate discussion.

The Dialogue

Perhaps you have taken a college-credit course on television that used the dialogue approach. The dialogue is a form of discussion involving two persons. It is highly effective when the participants know their subject well and engage in an articulate and meaningful exchange of ideas. Dialogue is a useful form of discussion in the classroom, since it provides the students with the opportunity to do team research. Students choose their own partner, because rapport between dialogue participants is vital.

The Interview

In the dialogue, both participants share responsibility for the presentation of material. In the interview, the person being interviewed is the source of information. The interviewer's job is to keep the discussion moving and on the right track. A good interviewer can get a wealth of information from a knowledgeable guest.

The interview is an excellent means of revealing information. For the best results, an interview should be carefully planned. A line of questioning should be blocked out in advance so that both participants know where the discussion is heading.

Role-Playing

An excellent way to introduce a discussion problem is through the technique of role-playing. In role-playing the players take part in a brief drama built on a "real-life" problem. The actors in the drama each take the part of a specific character in the problem. They then act out the situation, expressing the views they feel the character they are playing would have. The drama is unrehearsed, and the problem is usually given to the participants on the day the role-playing is to take place.

Role-playing can be an effective way of pretesting a situation. Skill in handling oneself in an interview could make the difference between a student's getting a job or missing it. A series of mock interviews with students playing the roles of personnel director and interviewee provides excellent practice. Students will derive a greater feeling of confidence toward the interview situation and an increased understanding of management's position as well.

Role-playing is particularly useful in clarifying a situation. Often, after seeing the roles played, a group can more fully understand the problem. Role-playing, for example, can be used to facilitate the case-problem approach to discussion. In discussing case-problem 1 on page 340, a group may decide that to solve the problem the superintendent should call the doctor and tell him to give Mary a tetanus shot. At this point, the instructor might step in and say, "All right, class, let's see how well that solution will work. Joan would you play the role of the doctor? And Fred, how about you being the superintendent who is going to make the call?"

Selecting a Role-Playing Problem   The problems below, which we have used for our classes, have been prepared with today's college student in mind. Additional problems may be developed by members of a group in a discussion situation, or by individual students as part of a class assignment.

One final note. After engaging in role-playing these problems, allow time for those in the audience to give their views and reactions to the drama.

1. A student who is of legal age is asked by his friends to buy the liquor for a weekend beach party. He knows he can get charged with contributing to the delinquency of minors if he

PEANUTS ®   By Charles M. Schulz

©1956 United Features Syndicate, Inc.

is caught. He also wants to keep the status he has among his friends. What should the student do?

2. A new employee in a plant has a mother who must have open-heart surgery. She lives in another state, and the employee would like to take a four-day leave of absence to be with her. The plant is behind in filling orders and everyone is working a seven-day week. How should the employee handle the situation?

3. The students in an English class feel that the instructor assigns an excessive amount of homework each day. The instructor is teaching the course for the first time. How should the students handle the situation?

4. A student who will graduate in three weeks is offered a job that will start on the morning of his last exam. His instructor has indicated that he will give no early or make-up exams. What should the student do?

5. A secretary has recently begun a new job for an insurance company. The fringe benefits are excellent, the pay is good, but she runs into a problem. Her immediate supervisor is constantly making advances toward her that she resents. How should she handle the situation?

6. A first-year bank employee has been late for work an average of two or three times a week for the last month. His wife, who is in the hospital, will remain there for at least another week. The reason he has been late is that he has to feed, dress, and drive his three school-age children to school each day. His supervisor has called him in to talk about his tardiness. How should the bank employee handle the situation?

Additional Suggestions for Role-Playing

1. You have just graduated and are being interviewed for your first job.
2. A persistent salesman refuses to leave when you tell him to.
3. A policeman is about to ticket your car as you arrive on the scene.
4. A clerk who waited on you 15 minutes ago now refuses to accept a return because you misplaced the receipt.
5. A teacher wrongfully accuses you of cheating.
6. A friend denies that he owes you $20.

THE FUNCTIONS OF DISCUSSION

In general, discussion has two functions: educative (information-seeking) and problem-solving.

Educative Discussion

Many of the discussions in which you participate do not seek agreement or action. Some are strictly social gatherings whose purpose is recreation or enjoyment. And yet, many times you get more than enjoyment from these discussions. They benefit you by adding to your background and experience. Their function is to make you better informed about the topic discussed. You often talk with others about dating, drugs, politics, or any matter of genuine interest in an attempt to increase your understanding. If you are lucky, and the information you get is accurate, you might become better equipped to make up your own mind on the question. Discussions of this type are called informative or educative discussions. Perhaps the most familiar example is classroom discussion, one of the important purposes of which is to stimulate thinking. This makes it especially appropriate for a course in communication skills. A lively classroom discussion of a controversial speech or essay can stimulate a speaker's or writer's thinking and motivate him to communicate to what has now become a more "real" audience. The informal exchange of ideas about a book or movie can often provide feedback as to the views of other members of the class. An all-class discussion during the first few weeks of the course can clear up many students' misconceptions about a communications course and indicate which attitudes need to be developed during the coming semester.

Problem-Solving Discussion

Life is a succession of personal problems and decision-making. Questions arise which require answers. Should I experiment with drugs? What kind of car should I buy? What should I major in? How far should I go with sex? What should we name the baby? Although these problems can be solved by the individual himself, chances are that a group solution will be more soundly conceived. Properly guided, group thinking offers a number of advantages over independent problem-solving.

First, the more people working on a problem, the more information is available to solve it. One individual's background and experience can seldom match those of a group. In order to be effective, there should be enough members in the discussion to provide for adequate contributions. Too few members limit the flow of ideas; too many create confusion. The preferred number of participants in a problem-solving discussion should range from three to eight, although a good classroom discussion of a provocative problem can be held with as many as 25.

Second, group thinking provides greater opportunities for problem-solving. The more people you have looking at a problem, the more likely you are to solve it correctly. In a group, an error by one individual is likely to be spotted by someone else.

A Pattern for
Problem-Solving Discussion

The process of group thinking can be organized into a series of steps roughly paralleling John Dewey's steps to reflective thinking. The sequence of steps can be used as an outline or pattern for discussion. The discussion usually begins with identification of the problem and proceeds step by step to implementation of the solution. The steps in the process are as follows.

Identifying the Problem Many discussions fail to get off the ground because the problem is not clearly understood by the participants. The first step in discussion, therefore, is to have the members pinpoint the discussion problem. Good teamwork in thinking can only begin when each member has a clear understanding of the problem at hand. Problems for discussion should always be stated as questions.

If the group is careful in phrasing the question as clearly as possible, they will avoid confusion later. For example, the question, "How can we halt pollution?" is unclear. Whom do we mean by "we"? Do we mean the group, the government, the people of the world? What type of pollution are we talking about? Do we mean air pollution, water pollution, noise pollution, or every type of pollution there is? The question, "What steps should the U.S. government take to curb industrial pollution of air and water?" avoids needless quibbling over definition of terms.

Analyzing the Problem Once the members have demonstrated a common understanding and agreement as to the issues, the causes and nature of the problem should be explored. There are times when a solution becomes obvious after the causes of a difficulty are identified. Once the causes are listed and agreed upon, an exploration of the problem can begin. The group should consider such questions as these: "Who is affected by the problem?" "How serious is it?" "Under what conditions must it be solved?"

A thorough investigation of the present situation will give members of the discussion a clear picture of the conditions that need correcting.

Finding the Best Solution   This step involves proposing possible solutions and then measuring them by the guidelines established above. It is usually a good idea to list all of the solutions before evaluating them. Such questions as these are asked: "How long will it take to carry out the solution?" "How much will it cost?" "Is the solution practical?" An important part of this step is for the group to determine that the solution will not cause some new problem.

Actuating the Solution   Whenever you deal with people, it is wise to consider just how a solution is going to be fulfilled. It might be useful to have members of the group role-play the parts of those people involved in carrying out the solution. When considering how people may react to a course of action, the group may discover that they cannot put their solution into operation.

The following example illustrates how a group of junior college students handled a problem, using the pattern discussed above:

Identifying the Problem   Consider the following situation:

> Your job is production foreman in an automotive parts fabricating plant. Company policy is to reward the first person who turns in a useful suggestion in written form. John has developed an idea concerning a manufacturing problem, but George, a second employee, learns of the idea and submits it as his own. These facts are known to you.
> What should you do?
>
> Adapted with permission of the author from William E. Utterback, *Group Thinking and Conference Leadership* (New York: Holt, Rinehart and Winston, Inc., 1964).

Analyzing the Problem   In dealing with this situation, the group agreed that the foreman was faced with a dilemma; he should reward one of the employees, but which one? To reward John would violate company policy, which states that an idea must be submitted in written form. To reward George for stealing John's idea brought up the question of ethics. Either alternative was bound to cause repercussions. In order to determine the best way to handle the situation, the group began a search for the causes of the problem.

Their search revealed three contributing causes:

1. Although John developed the idea, he did not submit it in written form.
2. John revealed his idea to others before submitting it.
3. George submitted the idea as his own.

It can be assumed that both George and John have friends among their fellow workers who will have some reaction to whatever decision is reached.

Finding the Best Solution   The group next began to consider guidelines for selecting a solution to the problem. In the light of the factors discussed above, they arrived at the following guidelines:

1. The solution should be acceptable to the other workers.
2. The solution should be implemented as soon as possible.
3. The solution should be acceptable to John.

In establishing guidelines, the group concluded that plant harmony was an important consideration: The solution should be acceptable to the other workers and implemented as soon as possible. They further reasoned that whatever would be acceptable to both John and George would also be acceptable to the other workers. Therefore, they agreed on the following solution:

As soon as possible, have John and George work out an agreement among themselves as to a division of the money.

Actuating the Solution   After evaluating possible ways that the foreman could handle the situation, the group came up with the following suggestions:

Step 1. The foreman should call George and John into the office and explain to them that he is aware of the facts in the case, and that, in the interest of plant harmony, the two of them should settle the matter themselves.

Step 2. If George and John cannot reach an agreement, the foreman should call George into the office and in a very candid and forceful manner indicate his attitude toward the importance of honesty. If George still refuses to cooperate, as a final resort the foreman should tell him that he will do whatever he can to prove it was John's idea.

Step 3. Have the foreman submit a recommendation to his superior that John be rewarded instead of George.

It should be pointed out that a group need not always think through a problem or arrive at a decision in the order we have indicated. Some of the steps may be eliminated because they are obvious. For example, an understanding of the problem might be perfectly apparent to the group, and they can start with the second step. At times the order may be varied. While establishing guidelines, for example, it might be necessary to consider how a solution is going to be carried out. Nevertheless, discussion groups will be more effective in problem-solving when they think their way through to a decision in the manner described above.

USING CASE PROBLEMS

Ability in group discussion is best developed through guided practice. The writers have found that the use of case problems as discussion questions is an effective way of stimulating this practice. Students respond to the challenge of coping with real issues geared to their level of interest and understanding.

Another advantage to dealing with problems in human relations is that they aid in developing those characteristics which contribute to the development of effective citizens—an understanding of and flexible attitude toward the beliefs and opinions of others, the recognition of a variety of points of view, a realization of the effectiveness of group problem-solving, and a greater belief in the worth of one's own opinion.

These case problems are brief scenes from everyday life and show only the incident, not its outcome. They are the kinds of situations that the student has encountered or is likely to encounter at home, at work, or at school. They are designed to encourage the student to think carefully, analytically, and understandingly about the situations they describe.

There is no "right" or "wrong" answer to these case problems. The solution chosen will be a reflection of the attitudes and sentiments of the group. The group members should make every effort to reach agreement on a solution for each problem. If they cannot come to unanimous agreement, the solution should be chosen by majority opinion. A suggested format is the following:

1. Moderator introduces panelists.
2. Moderator identifies the problem.
3. Panelists, under the moderator's direction, analyze the problem, suggesting possible solutions.
4. Moderator opens the discussion to the entire group. Questions

and comments may be addressed to the group or to individual panelists.

5. Moderator summarizes the conclusion of the panel.

EXERCISE

CASE PROBLEMS

1. Mary F., who works at a sewing factory, ran a sewing machine needle through her finger. As superintendent of the factory you sent her to the company doctor. He declared it was a clean wound and sent her back to work without giving her a tetanus shot as a precaution against lockjaw. The company is responsible for payment of all expenses incurred by a worker in connection with a job-connected injury.
What should you do?

2. Mr. Smith and Mr. Jones both worked at the same plant and have been good friends for several years. Smith, being more aggressive, was promoted and is now Jones's boss. Smith is getting along very well with all of his men except Jones, who has been causing a lot of trouble because he is jealous of Smith.
What should Smith do about the situation?

3. Fred and John, close personal friends, work together part-time stocking shelves at a local supermarket. Fred has been working to buy himself a new car while John has taken the second job to help support his widowed mother and nine brothers and sisters. One night after closing time, Fred notices John carrying a case of powdered milk out to his car.
What should Fred do?

4. You have two close friends, Bob and Jim. Jim has just been arrested for possession of heroin. The police found the heroin in Jim's car but Jim claims that he doesn't know how it got there. You know that Bob hid it there for safekeeping. Bob refuses to reveal this.
What should you do?

5. John, a white student at a small out-of-state technical college, has fallen in love with Cindy, a black student at the same school. He plans to take her home for Christmas, but he doesn't plan to tell his parents beforehand that she is black. He argues that his parents have always insisted that they are unprejudiced, and now he will be able to judge by their reaction if they are honest. Cindy does not agree.
How should the situation be handled?

6. Joan and Donna have been friends since childhood. Both are eighteen. Lately, Donna has been seeing a lot of an older married man. Joan ad-

vises Donna to break this off, but Donna is convinced that the man plans to get a divorce and marry her. Donna has told her parents that she will be visiting Joan for the weekend so that she and the man can go off together.

What should Joan do?

7. Upon your college roommate's return from summer vacation, he tells you that he is engaged. When he shows you his fiancee's picture, you recognize her as a former classmate who has a reputation for being promiscuous. You like your roommate very much.

What should you do?

8. You have been assigned a term paper by your history instructor which will count for one third of your total final grade. After you have worked it out carefully, you find out from a reliable source, that over one half of those in the class have bought term papers from an underground operation near your campus.

What should you do?

9. Paul found what he believed were LSD tablets in his sister's room. When he questioned her about it, she insisted they were antibiotics for a cold. He has noticed that she has seemed unusually withdrawn lately. He has revealed all this to his parents who have told him not to let his imagination run away with him.

What should he do?

10. Don and Alice are required by law to take a blood test before marriage. During the examination it is discovered that Don has had a venereal disease. When Alice questions him about it, he refuses to answer her.

What should Alice do?

11. When visiting his friend Ralph for the weekend, Carl sees him take $10 from his mother's purse. On the following day Carl is present as the mother accuses Ralph's brother Tim of stealing the money. She punishes Tim by taking away his use of the car for one month.

What should Carl do?

12. While you are riding home with Ed, a good friend, he backs into a parked car, causing considerable damage. Although he has liability insurance, he declines to leave his name, explaining that he has already had two accidents this year, and that another will result in his insurance policy's being canceled. Ed drives you to and from work every day.

What should you do?

13. Harry and Tom are hometown neighbors and dormitory roommates in college. Tom is concerned because Harry has been experimenting with hard drugs which have seriously affected his school work and his personality. Tom feels that something must be done before Harry becomes hopelessly addicted.

What should Tom do?

14. Paul writes very poorly in class. His essays indicate a lack of understanding of the simplest rules of grammar. The term paper that he hands in at the end of the semester is very well written and without error. The instructor suspects outside help but cannot prove it.
What should the instructor do?

15. Julia is engaged to be married to Fred. The wedding is less than two months away and Fred suggests that they begin their sexual relationship so that they will be sure that there are no physical or psychological barriers to a happy marriage. Julia believes very strongly that she should remain chaste before the marriage. Fred insists.
What should Julia do?

16. In 1950 John Graff was sentenced to life imprisonment for the murder of his business partner, Harry Fosdick. During his trial and imprisonment, John had protested his innocence. After being released in April, 1970, having served the full twenty years at Joliet Prison in Illinois, he returned to Chicago, his hometown. Two days later he ran across Harry Fosdick, the man he had been convicted of murdering. At this meeting, Fosdick, in the presence of witnesses, admitted that he had intentionally framed Graff. The following day Fosdick was found murdered. When arrested for the murder, Graff admitted his guilt but claimed that he was temporarily insane at the time.
What punishment, if any, should Graff get?

17. Betty and Ralph have been married for nine months. They live in a small apartment decorated and furnished with second-hand items. Lately, Betty's parents have been buying her expensive clothes. They have also insisted that she go shopping with them to pick out some new furniture that they will pay for. Ralph resents this.
How should this situation be handled?

18. Henry, a rookie police officer, has been assigned to the vice squad temporarily to do undercover work. His job, for which he has grown a full beard, is to uncover prostitution. During his first night on the job, he is propositioned by a woman he recognizes as the wife of a fellow police officer. Because of the beard, she does not recognize him.
What should he do?

19. Penny Smith, a white coed, worked as a volunteer staff person for the political campaign of Wanda Jones, a young, idealistic black woman. Wanda ran against George Alport, a member of the American Nazi Party. Wanda won a narrow victory which Penny, through involvement in the election, can prove was the result of voter fraud.
What should Penny do?

20. Barbara is a student at a two-year junior college. The school homecoming dance is one week away and she is hoping to be asked by Eric, the most popular male on campus. That night George, a plain but nice guy, asks her to the dance and she accepts. Two days later Eric asks her. He explains he had intended to ask her earlier but the death of a close relative had shaken him so much he forgot.

What should Barbara do?

Problems 1 and 2 are taken with permission of the author from William E. Utterback, *Group Thinking and Conference Leadership* (New York: Holt, Rinehart and Winston, Inc., 1964).

DISCUSSION RATING FORM

The accompanying discussion rating form is designed for both student and instructor evaluation. It lists the characteristics to be considered when evaluating a discussion.

DISCUSSION RATING FORM

Scale / 1 / 2 / 3 / 4 /
superior   above ave.   average   poor

	Names	(John M.)	(Mary S.)	(Robert R.)	(George S.)
PARTICIPATION—Listened carefully; was prepared; was spontaneous; used pertinent information; tested the thinking of others.					
ATTITUDE—Was friendly; tactful; cooperative; flexible; objective.					
THOUGHT PROGRESSION—Spoke to the point; stayed on the subject; used time wisely.					
COMMUNICATIVE SKILLS—Used adequate volume; was clear, was conversational; observed the rules of grammar.					

OVERALL RATING FOR GROUP _____

COMMENTS:

DISCUSSION FLOW CHART

The purpose of a flow chart is to record the number and direction of contributions made by each participant. When a group member contributes, an arrow is drawn from his name to the name of the person to whom he is speaking. If the remark is made to the entire group, the arrow is drawn with broken lines and stops in the center of the circle.

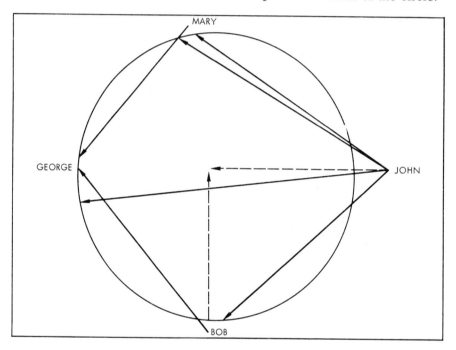

EXERCISES

1. Prepare a list of topics suitable for class discussion.
2. Write an original case problem that would be suitable for class discussion.
3. a. The instructor will divide the class into groups of four to six each. Each group will have a planning meeting to elect a chairman and choose a discussion topic.
   b. The group should decide upon an outline listing points in the order in which they will be discussed. A time limit should be established for the discussion.
   c. After the planning session, each member should research the topic in order to support his opinion with factual evidence and testimony.

CHAPTER 18

Mass Communication

WHAT IS MEANT BY MASS COMMUNICATION?

One way to define mass communication is to distinguish it from the kind of communication in which people are involved most of the time—*interpersonal communication*.

Interpersonal communication usually takes place face to face between two people or among a few people in a small group. One of the specific characteristics of interpersonal communication is that it is "two-way": there is a continual give and take between the two persons in the communication situation. The sender usually can frame the message with a specific receiver in mind and then modify subsequent messages depending on how they are apparently being received. The receiver usually has an opportunity to respond to the communication, to ask for clarification, or to react in other ways.

Political candidates frequently like to meet with potential voters in small intimate groups, to discuss issues and seek help, contributions, and votes. In the course of discussing the issues, if the candidate happens to make an apparently unpopular statement, the listeners in the room will be able to respond with groans, grimaces, or questions. The candidate, if sufficiently aware and clever, should be able to clarify the statement and reassure the audience. In the future he will probably have to rethink his position on that particular issue and either *change* the position or at least try to express his ideas in a more diplomatic way.

This chapter was written by Laurance J. Riley.

346

Mass communication is characteristically devoid of any face-to-face contact between sender and receiver. The message is "mediated," that is, processed through a medium. Further, the message is framed and delivered without the "benefit" of immediate reaction by the receiver. The response is usually delayed by a matter of hours or days. Mass communication is generally one-way communication. The intended audience is almost always a group of people.

All political candidates seek as much media exposure as possible. Generally they want television time, because they can be seen and heard by large numbers of people. However, they must compose their messages to be acceptable to the largest number of voters possible. They won't know how they came across in a particular television appearance until they read the newspaper "reviews" the following day or look at their mail several days later. By that time it may be too late to correct a misinterpretation of their position or to make any strategic retreats. The absence of immediate feedback frequently creates a difficult situation for political candidates trying to get their positions publicized.

Interpersonal communication is the process of transmitting information, ideas, and attitudes from one person to another, who in turn gives feedback in the form of reactions and responses. Interpersonal communication is directed to a specific person with individual quirks and idiosyncracies, or to a small group of persons whose likes and dislikes are rather specifically known by the sender. Intimacy is frequently gained and enhanced.

Again, the political candidate in a friend's living room can look at his audience and, after some questions and answers, he should be able to determine how liberal or conservative his audience is, what their occupations and income levels are, and how they might tend to respond to his positions on various issues. He can address parts of his remarks to individuals in the room, relate to questions asked earlier, mention individuals by name, and look them squarely in the eye.

The interpersonal communication message, generally, is the product of an individual sender.

Everything the candidate says will be of his own choosing. How he presents himself will largely be dependent upon his own personal communication skills.

Mass communication is directed to as large an audience as possible. Group characteristics rather than individual idiosyncrasies are addressed. The audience is really "anonymous" to the sender. Further, the sender is often anonymous to the audience. Intimacy in the message is lost. The *message* in mass communication is much like a "To whom it may concern" letter.

> The political candidate, while making a public speech on television, must try to frame a message which does not exclude many potential viewer-voters. The message tries to appeal to men and women of all racial, social, economic, religious, and ethnic groups. That's a pretty difficult goal to achieve and may account, at least in part, for the bland impression that many political candidates leave with viewers.

The ultimate mass communication message is generally the work of many minds and hands.

> Often political speeches represent the combined efforts of a number of persons on the candidate's staff. Various individual staff members might research certain issues and write reports. Another person might be responsible for pulling all that material together, editing, and revising it. Even after the candidate has approved the trial copy, the television crew affects the message. The camera angles and shots may produce a distorting effect. An extreme close-up, for example, of the candidate's drooping eyelids could produce the impression that the candidate had been relaxing with a couple of martinis before the speech! That impression, created by the media, would be outside of the candidate's control.

Our discussion of interpersonal communication and mass communication may have helped to show what mass communication isn't. Let's try to define it more positively.

In a larger sense, mass communication refers to a series of complicated processes involved in the communication-interactions among large numbers of people. It encompasses people and everything they do while they originate, send, and receive messages. It encompasses the mass media—the channels through which those messages are sent. "Mass communication" refers to the processes involved in this communication transaction. "Mass media" refers to the technologies we employ in the process. A way of further defining the term is to say that the mass media are those electronic and print devices that permit the sender of a message to have rather fast and immediate access to large, anonymous audiences.

We generally divide the mass media into print and electronic media. Print media are those channels in which messages are encoded into words and pictures to be read by the public audience. In this category are books, newspapers, magazines, newsletters, leaflets, brochures, billboards, public signs, and any other written form of message composed for large anonymous audiences. Electronic or broadcast media include television, radio, motion pictures, phonographs, and tape recorders.

THE MEDIUM

Let's look more closely at what we mean by *medium*. The medium is the channel through which the sender sends the message. The sender may elect to send the message through a variety of mediums. For example, (1) the sender might quietly whisper to a person standing nearby that a building is on fire, or (2) the sender may choose to *shout* the message, "There's a fire on the top floor of the building at 6th and State Street!" (3) The sender might make a telephone call and transmit the same information. (4) The sender might quickly scrawl the words on a large poster board for passersby to read, or (5) the sender, using nonverbal communication, might gesture and point and jump up and down until someone got the idea. (6) If a mobile "on-the spot" television camera crew happened to be on the scene, the sender might be able to broadcast the message to thousands of viewers instantly. In each case the message is affected by the medium the sender happens to choose. While the actual words of the message might remain the same in each case, "A building is on fire . . . ," you can see that the impact will differ, depending upon the medium chosen. There is a great difference between whispering, "There's a fire on the top floor of a building on 6th and State Street," on the one hand, and showing thousands of viewers live television pictures of the event.

The electronic media (radio, television, film) and print media (newspapers, magazines, books, pamphlets) extend the range of our senses, especially sight, and bring directly to us various image-messages that originated, in many instances, a great distance from us. Any message that a receiver gets from a newspaper, magazine, radio, television, or film is "mediated." A television reporter is sent out to investigate an event. The television viewer watches and hears about the event on the six-o'clock news. The "mediating" takes place between these two occurrences. Generally, it happens as follows: The reporter witnesses an event and directs the camera crew to film it; then the reporter writes a report and presents it to the news editor, who accepts or rejects it. If the story is accepted, it undergoes revision. The story is then passed through the hands of those who decide whether it is to be included on that day's news program, when it will appear in the news, how much time will be given to it, how much film will accompany it, and how much promotion that item will receive. Since different technologies are involved, different kinds of experts and technicians work with the story before it gets to the home viewer. They make whatever decisions are necessary so that that story can be carried and transmitted electronically. This is the mediation of the message. Newspaper articles, magazine articles, films, radio news, and the others go through a similar process.

The specific characteristics of the mediational system depend on the particular medium used to transmit the message. A televised message goes through different changes than does a message in a magazine. The technologies differ, and therefore the ways in which the message is symbolized differ. The televised message is put into voice and moving pictures. The magazine message is put into written words and still pictures. Furthermore, the various kinds of people who affect the message differ from one medium to the other. The television message is affected by writers, editors, producers, directors, set designers, actors, audiovisual technicians, and others. The newspaper item passes from the reporter to the editor, layout designers, typesetters, and printers, and finally into the hands of the newspaper carrier.

THE GATEKEEPER

A term sometimes used to refer to some of these "mediators" is *gatekeeper*. A gatekeeper is a person who is in a position to accept, modify, or reject media content. The gatekeeper exists in one way or another in every mass medium. The role of the "gatekeeper" is fairly easily seen when we trace the sequence from an initial event all the way to the account of that event that appears in a newspaper.

We can see the beginning of gatekeeping when we look at the role of the reporter. A reporter travels to the scene of an event to get the facts and information for his story. We can't really expect him to be completely objective. Since he can't tell every single aspect of the event he is covering, he will tend to select those elements that he understands, that he thinks are interesting, and that he feels will interest his reader. No reporter is able to capture the event completely. Consequently, the process of selection and of gatekeeping begins. The reporter looks at life and events through his own background, training, biases, and prejudices.

A photographer may appear on the scene to take pictures of the news event. The photographer also presents his view of the event. He freezes time for us for a moment. Conceivably this picture could give

a distorted interpretation of what actually happened. Newspaper readers generally believe that pictures that accompany news articles reflect accuracy and honesty. However, the photographer looks at the
situation through his own biases, prejudices, and experience.

The reporter then feeds his story and the accompanying photographs to the editor or a team of editors. Editors find mistakes, attempt
to discover whether facts were left out, and try, perhaps, to improve
the writing. Often the editor is forced to cut the length of the article
because of space limitations. Sometimes he has to make a decision
about omitting the article entirely. The editor is acting as a gatekeeper. He can let through the gate those articles or parts of articles
that he thinks are important or that will help to sell more newspapers.
The editor, like the reporter and the photographer, will tend to emphasize aspects of the article that support his personal views and the
views and policies of the newspaper. And so, the process of selection
that began with the reporter and continued with the photographer
comes to a peak on the desk of the editor. What the editor decides
will go in, is what we finally receive as the news. The final article
may or may not bear a close resemblance to events that actually occurred.

The process of *selectivity* continues after the mass message is received by individuals within the mass audience. We all pay attention
to and actually *receive* only those messages which we *choose* to receive. As members of a mass audience, we are selective about what
we see, hear, and read. While thousands of people may have the same
TV news broadcast on, it is unlikely that they are receiving the same
messages from it. One viewer may pay close attention to the sports report, another to the weather. One person may attend to a report of a
national disaster and "tune out" a human interest story. The same
"message" is being broadcast into each viewer's home, but it is the
viewer who decides whether to watch and listen intently or to leave
the room to get a snack from the refrigerator. Further, for those who
actually pay attention, the message may have various *meanings*. The
person who receives the message gives *meaning* to it in terms of his
or her particular background, education, or interests.

By way of brief summary, then, two characteristics of the mass
media are (1) the presence of gatekeepers and (2) a high degree of audience selectivity.

The gatekeepers largely determine what messages can be received.
The selectivity of the audience determines which of those messages
are actually received and *how* they are received.

FLOW OF INFORMATION

What effect do these mass media messages have on the various mass audiences? What use do audiences make of them?

Two theories regarding the *flow of information* might help to explain how the mass media affect their audiences. One theory states that people make decisions, form significant opinions, and solidify their beliefs and values on the basis of information they receive from what are called opinion leaders. In deciding on whom to vote for in an election, most people tend to be influenced more by friends, neighbors, spouses, and union leaders than by newspapers or television. A minority of people, the opinion leaders, are directly influenced by the mass media, and they in turn influence the majority of people. This process is known as the *two-step flow of information.*

The two-step flow of information theory, proposed by Paul Lazarsfield in the early 1940s, is probably an oversimplification. Since then, a more complex explanation has come into the study of mass media to describe how information is transmitted to the masses through various media.

Some people, according to the more recent theory, will use the mass media as a direct source of information on various topics, such as movie reviews, education, home decorating, etc. Other people will rely on the mass media for information on other subjects, such as current fashions, health care, and automobile purchases. Those people, called "opinion leaders," who have a definite interest in a particular subject communicate among themselves after exposure to the mass media, solidifying their views and impressions and beliefs. They then communicate their *solidified* attitudes to other people, second-level opinion leaders, who tend to use the mass media less to develop attitudes and opinions on various subjects. These "second-level opinion leaders" combine both the impressions they have received from the mass media and the impressions they have received from the "first-level opinion leaders" and communicate this combined impression to others who may not have gotten any information at all on this subject from the mass media. This process is referred to as the *multistep flow of information.*

Let's examine the way this multistep flow of information would work in an actual situation:

Jean Smith and Oscar Jones are deeply interested in films and the film industry. They generally pay special attention to movie reviews on television given, for example, by Rona Barrett or Gene Shallit. They usually read the movie reviews in daily newspapers and in magazines before they read other sections in these periodicals. Invariably, they discuss movies and movie reviews when they take a coffee break at work. Sally Ames and Randolph Lewis often join Jean and Oscar for coffee and listen, with interest, to these discussions of movies. Sometimes Sally and Randolph listen to a TV review or read a newspaper review, but this is relatively rare. When Sally and Randolph go to their homes, they often influence their families' decisions about movie selection. Mr. Ames and Mrs. Lewis pay *no* attention to movie reviews, so they are willing to base their decisions on information provided by Sally and Randolph. Mr. Ames and Mrs. Lewis also will pass information to others regarding the film reviews. Sally and Randolph, you'll remember, derived much of their information from Jean and Oscar, not directly from the mass media. It was Jean and Oscar who derived their information directly from the mass media.

This example should show you, generally, how information passes from the mass media through several layers of "opinion leaders" to the mass audiences.

Continuing the example of Jean and Oscar and Sally and Randolph, you can imagine that Sally, for example, might tend to draw much information on a subject of interest to her *directly* from the mass media. She may be involved in political matters, read much about political events, watch television reports concerning politics, and listen to in-depth radio discussions of politics. The same process will go into effect regarding politics that we saw in the case of movie reviews. Sally will communicate her impressions of the world of politics (impressions gained largely and directly from the mass media) to Randolph, Jean, and Oscar, who pay somewhat less attention to mass media treatments of politics. Randolph, Jean, and Oscar, second-level opinion leaders, pass information on to their families. Their families pass information on to still others.

This multistep flow of information, then, is a filtering process. The point is that, *generally*, most people do not derive their information on most subjects directly from the mass media; instead, the information is passed along by various levels of opinion leaders.

We have looked at some of the general characteristics of all the mass media and some of the theories and principles that underlie each medium. Now let's discuss, in some detail, two of the print media: newspapers and magazines; and two of the electronic media: radio and television. We'll look briefly at the historical development of each and point out some problems and issues connected with it.

NEWSPAPERS

The first press was set up in New England in the year 1638. Originally all of the thirteen colonial governments had presses, which were used to print and publish almanacs and legal forms. They also published the laws of the colonies and posted them for the people to read. These early presses were vehicles of the government and printed only noncontroversial material.

About fifty years after the first press came to New England, the first newspaper was started. Benjamin Harris developed a monthly paper entitled *Public Occurrences, Both Foreign and Domestic.* He ran into trouble with the Massachusetts authorities when he included some gossip about the King of France. Apparently, the government of Massachusetts was worried that the gossip in the paper would endanger the delicate diplomacy that existed between the colonies and France.

In 1721 James Franklin, the brother of Benjamin Franklin, started a newspaper called *The New England Courant.* His newspaper specialized in witty criticism of people in power and especially of Puritan religious leaders. James Franklin eventually was put in jail and was forbidden to continue in the publishing business. It was then that he named his younger brother, Benjamin, as publisher. The newspaper continued, but without the daring that it had when James was actively involved in it.

Through the years newspapers developed in the colonies, but until the Revolution they were generally free to publish only material that was not critical of the government.

One of the most famous cases in the history of the press was the trial of John Peter Zenger, which occurred in New York around the year 1733. John Peter Zenger, a printer, published a newspaper called the *New York Weekly Journal.* Zenger was critical of the Governor of New York, and his newspaper openly carried criticisms and attacks upon him.

Zenger was charged with seditious libel and with attempting to harm the reputation of the governor and other officials. During the trial his attorney, Andrew Hamilton, convinced the jury that Zenger could be found guilty only if the stories he had printed were not true. In other words, he could not be accused of libel if the stories he had written were accurate. The jury found John Peter Zenger not guilty on the grounds that the stories that he had printed were true. This important case marked a step toward freedom for the American colonies. It meant that citizens could openly protest against the government. It meant that ordinary citizens would have the right to decide upon a verdict. And it established the very important idea that criticism of the government or criticism of government officials was not a crime if the criticism were true.

The modern newspaper had its origin in the early 1830s when Benjamin H. Day instituted the *New York Sun* and sold it for one cent a copy. While other newspapers had existed before the *Sun*, their circulation tended to be low because of their high price. The content and style of these other papers also tended to place them outside the range of interest of most "ordinary" readers. They appealed to a fairly elite readership. Benjamin Day's *Sun* appealed to the average "person on the street." The idea of the low-cost, widely circulated newspaper caught on throughout the nation. By the beginning of the twentieth century, seventy years after Day's *Sun* was published, some newspapers had achieved circulations of over one million.

By 1910 the number of newspapers in America reached the astounding number of 2200 dailies and 11,800 weeklies. In 1977 there were about 1790 dailies and 8500 weeklies; *The Wall Street Journal* and *The Los Angeles Times* led all other newspapers with circulations of 1,463,641 and 1,024,040, respectively. For many years it appeared that the newspaper as an institution was dying. Many major newspapers went under, but many survived. Newspapers survive on advertising revenue, which in 1977 was estimated at about seven million dollars annually. While readership of newspapers may be increasing, it is disappointing to note the steady decrease in the number of newspapers available. Publishing and circulation costs have made it impossible for most American cities to support more than one daily newspaper, eliminating healthy competition. Furthermore, because in many well-populated cities the newspaper, radio, and television stations are owned by the same large corporation, the question of media control arises.

EXERCISES

Following are some suggestions on the subject of newspapers, which you can use as springboards for writing either a single paragraph or a complete theme, for delivering a speech, or for stimulating a class discussion. It may be necessary, in order to intelligently discuss these topics, to do some research in the library, or to contact a newspaper representative to help you.

1. Examine several major newspapers of the same date. Look carefully at the front page. Compare the content, placement, and length of articles. Read articles in various papers on the same subject. Can you make any tentative observations about the tendency of one paper to lead the reader to a particular opinion through emotionally charged words, examples, or headlines? Does one newspaper give more adequate coverage to a topic

than another paper? Does one paper place various points of view side by side to give the reader a better overview of the situation? Repeat this process a number of times over a period of weeks to confirm or correct your initial impression.

2. Look at the sports pages of several newspapers. Notice the style of the writing, especially the use of emotionally charged verbs. Do you find the writing more or less objective than straight news reporting? Is the home team generally favored in the reporting, regardless of whether it wins or loses? How much detail is given to opposing teams? Is there a standardized, formula approach to reporting games and scores?

3. Choose an issue on which you would like to be heard. Explore as many avenues of public communication as you can. Keep careful records. Describe the success or lack of success you have had in being heard. Discuss such questions as: (a) What vehicles of expression are accessible or closed to a citizen? (b) Why do some people turn to demonstration or violence as a means of expressing themselves on various issues? (c) Should access to the means of public communication be made easier and more convenient for citizens?

4. Witness a newsworthy event first hand (e.g., trial, school board meeting, demonstration, etc.). Read as much about it as you can in the local press. Clip all related articles. From your vantage point, do you think the coverage of the event was accurate and complete? Misleading? Was the interpretation of the event fair or slanted? Was the coverage of the event impartial? Was it helpful to the community at large? Was it helpful to the particular group involved in the original event? Record your reactions and analysis.

MAGAZINES

Magazines emerged as a mass medium in the early 1830s in response to a popular need for a supplement to the newspaper. Increased education and literacy in the United States coupled with decreased printing and production costs made the magazine an attractive product.

One of the most famous and widely read magazines in America was the *Saturday Evening Post*, first published in 1821. It lasted for almost 150 years, was discontinued, and recently has been revived. Other magazines, such as the *Atlantic Monthly* and *The New Yorker*, brought to public attention many well-known American literary figures, including Longfellow, Irving, Emerson, Thoreau, Twain, Hawthorne, and Poe.

After the Civil War several magazines for women appeared. By the end of the 1800s such magazines as *McCall's, Vogue, Women's Home Companion, Good Housekeeping*, and *Ladies Home Journal* were popular; *Ladies Home Journal* had achieved a per-issue circulation of around 1,000,000.

Several different kinds of magazines remain popular today:

1. News magazines, such as *Time, Newsweek,* and *U.S. News & World Report.*
2. Current affairs magazines, including *The New Republic, Nation, Ramparts,* and the *National Review.*
3. Humor magazines, such as *Mad* and the *National Lampoon.*
4. General-interest magazines, such as *Reader's Digest, Esquire,* and *The New Yorker.*
5. Special-interest magazines, including *T.V. Guide, American Legion Magazine, Sports Illustrated,* and *Outdoor Life,* to name just a few.
6. Sex-oriented magazines, such as *Playboy, Playgirl,* and *Penthouse.*

Like newspapers, the number of magazines has tended to decline. Many general-interest magazines, such as *Saturday Evening Post, Look,* and *Life* became defunct even though circulation was high; at the time of its "death" the *Saturday Evening Post* had about 4 million regular subscribers. Publication costs had become so high that the advertisers could no longer bear them—and without advertisers, a magazine cannot survive.

Currently special-interest magazines seem to be thriving. Thousands of business and social organizations nationwide publish periodicals for their own membership. Specialty magazines devoted to specific subjects such as stereo and hi-fi, racing, sports cars, and teenage fashions seem to have taken the place of the general-interest magazines. However, one general-interest magazine, the *Reader's Digest,* has flourished since its inception in 1922, growing to a readership that exceeds 80 million. This magazine, high in advertising content, clearly is on the side of middle American standards and values. It opposes "big government," increased taxes, and welfare. The content of the magazine is obviously intended *not* to offend its advertisers. Interspersed among articles on these politically safe topics are inspirational verses, one-line jokes, and inoffensive anecdotes.

While the *Reader's Digest* reprints articles that have appeared in other magazines, it has been said that some of its articles have orginally been commissioned by the editors, published in other magazines, and then reprinted in the *Digest.* "One current estimate is that as much as 70 percent of its articles are either staff-written for the *Digest* or planned and planted by the *Digest* in other publications, especially for reprint."[1]

---

[1] Peter Jaeger, *Mass Media: Our Moving Fingers,* p. 21.

EXERCISES

Following are some statements and suggestions dealing with the subject of magazines. Use them as springboards for writing a paragraph or a complete theme, for delivering a speech, or for stimulating a class discussion.

1. Women's magazines constitute a large part of specialized publications. Compare issues of *Ms., Ladies' Home Journal,* and *Women's Day.*
   a. Make a list of the general categories of articles in each magazine (e.g., fashion, cooking, legal problems of women, etc.). Do you see much duplication of content among the magazines?
   b. Record a list of the differences in types of stories, articles, advertising, and staff listings (for example, are the staff persons mostly male or female?) Can you see any particular differences in the images of modern women these magazines reflect?

2. Clip several magazine ads to look for some of the key "attention-getter" words. Look also for phrases or words that are deceptive or perhaps even meaningless but that lead people to believe the product is something special. For example, look at how many products advertise themselves as "new and improved." How new are they? In what substantial ways have they been improved? Some ads give the *impression* of making a statement about the product, but really don't. "New Eve 120's: Finally a 120 that tastes as good as it looks." Does this cigarette *really* look any better than any other cigarette? Some ads draw upon entertainment personalities for endorsement. *Sanka* coffee shows Robert Young, former star of Marcus Welby, M.D., saying "It's the coffee you can feel good about." What does that mean? Does a reader believe the ad because Robert Young, an actor, says Sanka is good, or because Marcus Welby, M.D., says so? Find other magazine ads and analyze their impact. Discuss which ads appeal to you and which turn you off; discuss why you believe this happens.

3. Compare copies of *Time, Newsweek,* and *U.S. News & World Report* of the same date. Set up columns listing major topics (politics, economy, labor, art, medicine, etc.) Are these three magazines similar (identical?) in the topics they cover? Compare the headlines each uses for an article on the same subject. Does one magazine use more emotionally charged words in headlines than the others? Is the reporting in each magazine strictly factual, or is an attempt made to influence the readers' opinions and judgments? In attempting to analyze the magazines' styles, compare their use of verbs, adjectives, and adverbs to determine their contribution to the articles' readability and credibility. Do some magazines rely heavily on the "pop-fizz" kinds of verbs? Compare such items as sentence length and word difficulty.

4. Compare the treatment of the same major news story as it originally appeared in the newspaper and as it appeared in a weekly and in a monthly magazine. Does the perspective of time change the interpretation? Does public opinion (as you may remember it) affect the treatment in the maga-

zines? Discuss the differences between newspaper and magazine coverage of the same event.

RADIO

Radio was introduced commercially during the 1920s. Because it could transmit messages to all parts of the country instantly, a feat no other medium had performed, radio was regarded as something of a miracle. The thirties and forties witnessed radio's greatest growth. Well-known figures in the world of entertainment became even greater through their exposure to mass audiences on radio. Comedians such as Bob Hope, Jack Benny, Fred Allen, George Burns, and Gracie Allen delighted the country. Lowell Thomas, H. V. Kaltenborn, and Edward R. Murrow, well-known commentators, kept Americans glued to their radio sets with news of the progress of World War II in Europe. The nation followed the lives of "Pepper Young," "Stella Dallas," "Young Doctor Malone," and "One Man's Family." Spines tingled at the lines: "Who knows what evil lurks in the hearts of men? The Shadow knows!" Fibber McGee and Molly were regular visitors to most American homes.

Radio reached the height of its popularity in the 1940s. Until television became accessible late in that decade, roughly 17 million people spent their evenings around the radio. But television changed that. The once loyal listeners and advertisers quickly switched from radio to television, and the after-dinner listening audience dwindled quickly; the 17 million listeners became 3 million. Radio was clearly in mortal danger.

Radio struggled to adapt to its new situation. Because much of the network programming disappeared along with the advertisers, local radio stations attempted to fill the time with their own programming. Instead of big-star entertainment, local broadcasters gave listeners frequent news headlines, music of all kinds, sports coverage, and "help-your-neighbor" shows. The disc jockey became a new kind of celebrity—faceless, but with a well-known voice and personality.

Technology came to the rescue in the 1950s with portable transistor radios that grew popular and inexpensive; in the late fifties and early sixties car radios became practically a necessity. Although radio today provides a rather meager fare of music, sports, and news, compared with the grand-scale entertainment of the 1940s, radio sales are soaring. It is estimated that today there are more radios than people in America. More people listen to radio today than at any time in its history. Radio certainly has not died.

EXERCISE

Following are some suggestions for possible individual or class assignments on the subject of radio which you can use as springboards for writing a paragraph or a complete theme, for delivering a speech, or for stimulating a class discussion. It may be necessary, in order to intelligently discuss these topics, to do some research in the library or to interview a radio personality or a representative of the management of a radio station.

1. Have various members of your class check different radio stations to determine the amount of time given over to commercials during morning or afternoon "rush hours." What are the products advertised? Are the commercials acceptably done, or do you find them offensive for any reason? Is the volume of sound increased during the commercials? Who do you think is the intended audience of the commercials? Is the same product advertised in different ways on various radio stations? As a result of your activities, what conclusions do you come to about radio advertising?

2. If you have never toured a radio station, make arrangements to do so. Record the image you have of a radio station *before* you go; compare that record with your image *after* you have gone.

3. Interview a radio news personality. Is the news person trained in reporting? What is his or her source of news (such as wire service, listener call-in, eyewitness reporting)? Discuss with the newsperson his/her feelings about the amount of time devoted to any particular news item on the radio. Does he/she believe more *should* be said?

4. Give a report to the class regarding the duties of a disc jockey. Spend a couple of hours watching him at work; record his activities.

5. Some radio stations occasionally feature radio dramas. Listen to one of these dramas. Discuss your reaction to it after years of becoming accustomed to television performances.

6. Survey the students in your class or in your school to determine the radio stations and programs they most frequently listen to. Set up a panel discussion to probe the appeal of those stations and programs.

TELEVISION

Television had its experimental beginnings in the 1930s. It developed slowly during World War II and emerged as a popular entertainment medium in the late 1940s.

In the 1950s, when it became economically feasible for most Americans to own television sets, the networks began to offer programming that altered the American life style. During the day now there are quiz programs, game shows, and soap operas. Variety shows, dramas, and news appear on night time TV.

The new medium at first simply transplanted the old radio programs and added pictures. Instead of just listening to "The Lone Ranger" or "The Eddie Cantor Show," the television audience could now watch as well as listen. The old radio networks quickly became the new television networks, using many of the same stars, the same programs, and almost the same formats.

Gradually, with television's increased popularity, all this changed. Sponsors attracted by the unlimited possibilities of television bid higher and higher for new and better shows. Leaders saw that it was a medium with the capability to create an American society in which the citizens were informed and culturally aware. It was evident that this medium, more than the other media, could bring great minds, artists, entertainers, and teachers into the living room; the great events of the day could be instantly seen and heard by the great majority of Americans. The primary ingredient of democratic society, a well-informed public, could now be realized as never before. But has that dream been realized—or is television really a vehicle for pandering shoddy goods and distorted values, as some critics have suggested?

Whatever we may consider to be its worth, television is universal; more than 95 percent of America's homes are TV households, and viewing television is the dominant leisure-time activity in our society. For many men, the weekend means spectator sports. They can watch skiing in Innsbruck, cliff-diving in Acapulco, and race-car driving in Indianapolis, all in the space of twenty minutes. But the variety of sports coverage actually extends over a period of days.

Television is currently dominated by the three major networks. Their goal is to provide general programming for massive audiences, rather than special content for limited, easily defined special-interest groups. Recall that the primary role of the magazine is specialization. Television's primary role is just the opposite: It aims for mass production and mass audiences. It transmits mass-produced messages for the largest possible audience. It can be turned on and tuned into for approximately 20 hours a day (24 hours in some large cities), 365 days a year. Thus, like no other mass medium, it has the potential of reaching and affecting, negatively or positively, almost all of the people, almost all of the time!

While it may be open to criticism for its excesses and failures, it is the only medium capable of instantly providing us with a front-row seat to an Apollo moon landing, a Presidential inauguration, or the Watergate hearings.

As cable television becomes more of a reality, television's power for good and for evil grows. Cable television would, for most large city areas, make it possible for a viewer to tune into 50 or 60 channels. Some of those channels would provide individuals and groups a forum for communicating their own particular views and values to a large audience.

As miraculous as television may seem to us now, we are really seeing it in its childhood. It will grow and develop in ways we haven't yet thought of.

EXERCISE

Following are some statements and suggestions on the subject of television. React to these suggestions. Use them as springboards for writing a paragraph or a complete theme, for delivering a speech, or for stimulating a class discussion. It may be necessary, in order to intelligently discuss these topics, to do some research in the library or to tour a television station and speak with a station representative.

1. Many critics view children's television programming as excessively violent, overburdened with hard-sell advertising, and generally lacking in educational value. Evaluate several children's programs. Try to cover the range of children's shows. Discuss the potential effect (good or bad) that a particular show might have on its viewers. Compare your personal views on violence in children's television programs with the views of authors of books and magazine articles on the same subject.

2. One of the first steps in improving the quality of your local television station is to seriously question how it is abiding by the rules that regulate broadcasting. Although it will be time-consuming, it might be very interesting to do the following:

   a. Write to the FCC (Federal Communications Commission, Washington, D.C.) requesting a copy of the regulations that apply to local broadcasters as well as a statement of citizens' right to inspect the public records of the television station.

   b. Read the regulations and watch your local television station carefully to look for examples of adherence to or departure from the regulations.

   c. Take a trip to the station and ask, politely, to view their public records.

   d. Make note of the station's willingness or lack of willingness to accommodate you. (Present your copy of the FCC Public Notice, which outlines your rights.)

   e. If you do not receive satisfaction, or if you are denied access to these records, write to:

      Chief of Complaints and Compliance
      Division of the FCC
      1919 M Street N.W.
      Washington, D.C. 20554

   f. Make a report to the entire class regarding your experiences.

3. In order for a television station to retain its license, it must show that it is serving the public interest. The Federal Communications Commission (FCC) has indicated 14 categories that fulfill the requirement for serving

the public interest. Make a chart for each local television station, listing each of the 14 categories. Consult the weekly television programming schedule and fill in the names of programs that fulfill the requirements, the length of those programs, the time and the day they appear. What conclusions do you come to about each local station? Is one more community-minded than another? What generalizations can you make about the times these kinds of programs are offered?

PUBLIC INTEREST PROGRAMMING – TV STATION _____

Category	Program Title(s)	Program Length(s)	Weekly Time
Opportunity for local expression			
Development and use of local talent			
Programs for children			
Religious programs			
Educational programs			

PUBLIC INTEREST PROGRAMMING — TV STATION *(continued)*

Category	Program Title(s)	Program Length(s)	Weekly Time
Public affairs programs			
Editorialization by licensees			
Political broadcasts			
Agricultural programs			
News programs			
Weather and market reports			
Sports programs			

Category	Program Title(s)	Program Length(s)	Weekly Time
Service to minority groups			
Entertainment programs			

4. Make a list of general categories that cover most TV programs (detective/private eye shows, comedies, children's programs, movies, etc.); then fit into the categories each program aired in your area during the primetime hours (7:30 p.m. to 11:00 p.m.) for one week. Evaluate the chart in terms of how effectively TV is functioning as a public service medium. What does competition among the networks do to the viewer's choice of programming?

Index

DATE DUE